Mastering R for Quantitative Finance

Use R to optimize your trading strategy and
build up your own risk management system

**Edina Berlinger, Ferenc Illés, Milán Badics, Ádám Banai,
Gergely Daróczi, Barbara Dömötör, Gergely Gabler,
Dániel Havran, Péter Juhász, István Margitai, Balázs Márkus,
Péter Medvegyev, Julia Molnár, Balázs Árpád Szűcs, Ágnes Tuza,
Tamás Vadász, Kata Váradi, Ágnes Vidovics-Dancs**

PUBLISHING

BIRMINGHAM - MUMBAI

Mastering R for Quantitative Finance

First published: March 2015

Production reference: 1030315

Published by Packt Publishing Ltd.
Livery Place
35 Livery Street
Birmingham B3 2PB, UK.

ISBN 978-1-78355-207-8

www.packtpub.com

Credits

About the Authors

Edina Berlinger has a PhD in economics from the Corvinus University of Budapest. She is an associate professor, teaching corporate finance, investments, and financial risk management. She is the head of the Finance department of the university, and is also the chair of the finance subcommittee of the Hungarian Academy of Sciences. Her expertise covers loan systems, risk management, and more recently, network analysis. She has led several research projects in student loan design, liquidity management, heterogeneous agent models, and systemic risk.

This work has been supported by the Hungarian Academy of Sciences, Momentum Programme (LP-004/2010).

Ferenc Illés has an MSc degree in mathematics from Eötvös Loránd University. A few years after graduation, he started studying actuarial and financial mathematics, and he is about to pursue his PhD from Corvinus University of Budapest. In recent years, he has worked in the banking industry. Currently, he is developing statistical models with R. His interest lies in large networks and computational complexity.

Milán Badics has a master's degree in finance from the Corvinus University of Budapest. Now, he is a PhD student and a member of the PADS PhD scholarship program. He teaches financial econometrics, and his main research topics are time series forecasting with data-mining methods, financial signal processing, and numerical sensitivity analysis on interest rate models. He won the competition of the X. Kochmeister-prize organized by the Hungarian Stock Exchange in May 2014.

Ádám Banai has received his MSc degree in investment analysis and risk management from Corvinus University of Budapest. He joined the Financial Stability department of the Magyar Nemzeti Bank (MNB, the central bank of Hungary) in 2008. Since 2013, he is the head of the Applied Research and Stress Testing department at the Financial System Analysis Directorate (MNB). He is also a PhD student at the Corvinus University of Budapest since 2011. His main research fields are solvency stress-testing, funding liquidity risk, and systemic risk.

Gergely Daróczi is an enthusiast R package developer and founder/CTO of an R-based web application at Rapporter. He is also a PhD candidate in sociology and is currently working as the lead R developer at CARD.com in Los Angeles. Besides teaching statistics and doing data analysis projects for several years, he has around 10 years of experience with the R programming environment. Gergely is the coauthor of *Introduction to R for Quantitative Finance*, and is currently working on another Packt book, *Mastering Data Analysis with R*, apart from a number of journal articles on social science and reporting topics. He contributed to the book by reviewing and formatting the R source code.

Barbara Dömötör is an assistant professor of the department of Finance at Corvinus University of Budapest. Before starting her PhD studies in 2008, she worked for several multinational banks. She wrote her doctoral thesis about corporate hedging. She lectures on corporate finance, financial risk management, and investment analysis. Her main research areas are financial markets, financial risk management, and corporate hedging.

Gergely Gabler is the head of the Business Model Analysis department at the banking supervisory division of National Bank of Hungary (MNB) since 2014. Before this, he used to lead the Macroeconomic Research department at Erste Bank Hungary after being an equity analyst since 2008. He graduated from the Corvinus University of Budapest in 2009 with an MSc degree in financial mathematics. He has been a guest lecturer at Corvinus University of Budapest since 2010, and he also gives lectures in MCC College for advanced studies. He is about to finish the CFA program in 2015 to become a charterholder.

Dániel Havran is a postdoctoral research fellow at Institute of Economics, Centre for Economic and Regional Studies, Hungarian Academy of Sciences. He also holds a part-time assistant professor position at the Corvinus University of Budapest, where he teaches corporate finance (BA, PhD) and credit risk management (MSc). He obtained his PhD in economics at Corvinus University of Budapest in 2011.

I would like to thank the postdoctoral fellowship programme of the Hungarian Academy of Sciences for their support.

Péter Juhász holds a PhD degree in business administration from the Corvinus University of Budapest and is also a CFA charterholder. As an associate professor, he teaches corporate finance, business valuation, VBA programming in Excel, and communication skills. His research field covers the valuation of intangible assets, business performance analysis and modeling, and financial issues in public procurement and sports management. He is the author of several articles, chapters, and books mainly on the financial performance of Hungarian firms. Besides, he also regularly acts as a consultant for SMEs and is a senior trainer for EY Business Academy in the EMEA region.

István Margitai is an analyst in the ALM team of a major banking group in the CEE region. He mainly deals with methodological issues, product modeling, and internal transfer pricing topics. He started his career with asset-liability management in Hungary in 2009. He gained experience in strategic liquidity management and liquidity planning. He majored in investments and risk management at Corvinus University of Budapest. His research interest is the microeconomics of banking, market microstructure, and the liquidity of order-driven markets.

Balázs Márkus has been working with financial derivatives for over 10 years. He has been trading many different kinds of derivatives, from carbon swaps to options on T-bond futures. He was the head of the Foreign Exchange Derivative Desk at Raiffesien Bank in Budapest. He is a member of the advisory board at Pallas Athéné Domus Scientiae Foundation, and is a part-time analyst at the National Bank of Hungary and the managing director of Nitokris Ltd, a small proprietary trading and consulting company. He is currently working on his PhD about the role of dynamic hedging at the Corvinus University of Budapest, where he is affiliated as a teaching assistant.

Péter Medvegyev has an MSc degree in economics from the Marx Károly University Budapest. After completing his graduation in 1977, he started working as a consultant in the Hungarian Management Development Center. He got his PhD in Economics in 1985. He has been working for the Mathematics department of the Corvinus University Budapest since 1993. His teaching experience at Corvinus University includes stochastic processes, mathematical finance, and several other subjects in mathematics.

Julia Molnár is a PhD candidate at the Department of Finance, Corvinus University of Budapest. Her main research interests include financial network, systemic risk, and financial technology innovations in retail banking. She has been working at McKinsey & Company since 2011, where she is involved in several digital and innovation studies in the area of banking.

Balázs Árpád Szűcs is a PhD candidate in finance at the Corvinus University of Budapest. He works as a research assistant at the Department of Finance at the same university. He holds a master's degree in investment analysis and risk management. His research interests include optimal execution, market microstructure, and forecasting intraday volume.

Ágnes Tuza holds an applied economics degree from Corvinus University of Budapest and is an incoming student of HEC Paris in International Finance. Her work experience covers structured products' valuation for Morgan Stanley as well as management consulting for The Boston Consulting Group. She is an active forex trader and shoots a monthly spot for Gazdaság TV on an investment idea where she frequently uses technical analysis, a theme she has been interested in since the age of 15. She has been working as a teaching assistant at Corvinus in various finance-related subjects.

Tamás Vadász has an MSc degree in economics from the Corvinus University of Budapest. After graduation, he was working as a consultant in the financial services industry. Currently, he is pursuing his PhD in finance, and his main research interests are financial economics and risk management in banking. His teaching experience at Corvinus University includes financial econometrics, investments, and corporate finance.

Kata Váradi is an assistant professor at the Department of Finance, Corvinus University of Budapest since 2013. Kata graduated in finance in 2009 from Corvinus University of Budapest and was awarded a PhD degree in 2012 for her thesis on the analysis of the market liquidity risk on the Hungarian stock market. Her research areas are market liquidity, fixed income securities, and networks in healthcare systems. Besides doing research, she is active in teaching as well. She mainly teaches corporate finance, investments, valuation, and multinational financial management.

Ágnes Vidovics-Dancs is a PhD candidate and an assistant professor at the Department of Finance, Corvinus University of Budapest. Previously, she worked as a junior risk manager in the Hungarian Government Debt Management Agency. Her main research areas are government debt management (in general) and sovereign crises and defaults (in particular). She is a CEFA and CIIA diploma holder.

About the Reviewers

Matthew Gilbert works as a quantitative analyst in a Global Macro group at CPPIB based out of Toronto, Canada. He has a master's degree in quantitative finance from Waterloo University and a bachelor's degree in applied mathematics and mechanical engineering from Queen's University.

Dr. Hari Shanker Gupta is a senior quantitative research analyst working in the area of algorithmic trading system development. Prior to this, he was a postdoctoral fellow at Indian Institute of Science (IISc), Bangalore, India. He has obtained his PhD in applied mathematics and scientific computation at IISc. He completed his MSc in mathematics from Banaras Hindu University (BHU), Varanasi, India. During his MSc, he was awarded four gold medals for his outstanding performance in BHU, Varanasi.

Hari has published five research papers in reputed journals in the field of mathematics and scientific computation. He has experience of working in the areas of mathematics, statistics, and computation. These include the topics: numerical methods, partial differential equations, mathematical finance, stochastic calculus, data analysis, time series analysis, finite difference, and finite element methods. He is very comfortable with the mathematics software Matlab, the statistics programming language R, Python, and the programming language C.

He has reviewed the books *Introduction to R for Quantitative Finance* and *Learning Python Data Analysis* for Packt Publishing.

Ratan Mahanta holds an MSc degree in computational finance. He is currently working at GPSK investment group as a senior quantitative analyst. He has 3.5 years of experience in quantitative trading and developments for sell side and risk consulting firms. He has coded algorithms on Github's open source platform for "Quantitative trading" areas. He is self-motivated, intellectually curious, and hard-working, and loves solving difficult problems that lie at the intersection of market, technology, research, and design. Currently, he is developing high-frequency trading strategies and quantitative trading strategies. He has expertise in the following areas:

Quantitative Trading: FX, Equities, Futures and Options, and Engineering on Derivatives.

Algorithms: Partial differential equations, Stochastic differential equations, Finite Difference Method, Monte-Carlo, and Machine Learning.

Code: R Programming, Shiny by RStudio, C++, Matlab, HPC, and Scientific Computing.

Data Analysis: Big-Data-Analytic [EOD to TBT], Bloomberg, Quandl, and Quantopian.

Strategies: Vol-Arbitrage, Vanilla and Exotic Options Modeling, trend following, Mean reversion, Cointegration, Monte-Carlo Simulations, Value at Risk, Stress Testing, Buy side trading strategies with high Sharpe ratio, Credit Risk Modeling, and Credit Rating.

He has also reviewed the book *Mastering Scientific Computing with R, Packt Publishing*, and currently, he is reviewing the book *Machine Learning with R cookbook, Packt Publishing*.

www.PacktPub.com

Support files, eBooks, discount offers, and more

For support files and downloads related to your book, please visit www.PacktPub.com.

Did you know that Packt offers eBook versions of every book published, with PDF and ePub files available? You can upgrade to the eBook version at www.PacktPub.com and as a print book customer, you are entitled to a discount on the eBook copy. Get in touch with us at service@packtpub.com for more details.

At www.PacktPub.com, you can also read a collection of free technical articles, sign up for a range of free newsletters and receive exclusive discounts and offers on Packt books and eBooks.

https://www2.packtpub.com/books/subscription/packtlib

Do you need instant solutions to your IT questions? PacktLib is Packt's online digital book library. Here, you can search, access, and read Packt's entire library of books.

Why subscribe?

- Fully searchable across every book published by Packt
- Copy and paste, print, and bookmark content
- On demand and accessible via a web browser

Free access for Packt account holders

If you have an account with Packt at www.PacktPub.com, you can use this to access PacktLib today and view 9 entirely free books. Simply use your login credentials for immediate access.

Table of Contents

Preface

Mastering R for Quantitative Finance is a sequel of our previous volume titled *Introduction to R for Quantitative Finance*, and it is intended for those willing to learn to use R's capabilities for building models in Quantitative Finance at a more advanced level. In this book, we will cover new topics in empirical finance (chapters 1-4), financial engineering (chapters 5-7), optimization of trading strategies (chapters 8-10), and bank management (chapters 11-13).

What this book covers

Chapter 1, Time Series Analysis (Tamás Vadász) discusses some important concepts such as cointegration (structural), vector autoregressive models, impulse-response functions, volatility modeling with asymmetric GARCH models, and news impact curves.

Chapter 2, Factor Models (Barbara Dömötör, Kata Váradi, Ferenc Illés) presents how a multifactor model can be built and implemented. With the help of a principal component analysis, five independent factors that explain asset returns are identified. For illustration, the Fama and French model is also reproduced on a real market dataset.

Chapter 3, Forecasting Volume (Balázs Árpád Szűcs, Ferenc Illés) covers an intraday volume forecasting model and its implementation in R using data from the DJIA index. The model uses turnover instead of volume, separates seasonal components (U shape) from dynamic components, and forecasts these two individually.

Chapter 4, Big Data – Advanced Analytics (Júlia Molnár, Ferenc Illés) applies R to access data from open sources, and performs various analyses on a large dataset. For illustration, K-means clustering and linear regression models are applied to big data.

Chapter 5, FX Derivatives (Péter Medvegyev, Ágnes Vidovics-Dancs, Ferenc Illés) generalizes the Black-Scholes model for derivative pricing. The Margrabe formula, which is an extension of the Black-Scholes model, is programmed to price stock options, currency options, exchange options, and quanto options.

Chapter 6, Interest Rate Derivatives and Models (Péter Medvegyev, Ágnes Vidovics-Dancs, Ferenc Illés) provides an overview of interest rate models and interest rate derivatives. The Black model is used to price caps and caplets; besides this, interest rate models such as the Vasicek and CIR model are also presented.

Chapter 7, Exotic Options (Balázs Márkus, Ferenc Illés) introduces exotic options, explains their linkage to plain vanilla options, and presents the estimation of their Greeks for any derivative pricing function. A particular exotic option, the Double-No-Touch (DNT) binary option, is examined in more details.

Chapter 8, Optimal Hedging (Barbara Dömötör, Kata Váradi, Ferenc Illés) analyzes some practical problems in hedging of derivatives that arise from discrete time rearranging of the portfolio and from transaction costs. In order to find the optimal hedging strategy, different numerical-optimization algorithms are used.

Chapter 9, Fundamental Analysis (Péter Juhász, Ferenc Illés) investigates how to build an investment strategy on fundamental bases. To pick the best yielding shares, on one hand, clusters of firms are created according to their past performance, and on the other hand, over-performers are separated with the help of decision trees. Based on these, stock-selection rules are defined and backtested.

Chapter 10, Technical Analysis, Neural networks, and Logoptimal Portfolios (Ágnes Tuza, Milán Badics, Edina Berlinger, Ferenc Illés) overviews technical analysis and some corresponding strategies, like neural networks and logoptimal portfolios. Problems of forecasting the price of a single asset (bitcoin), optimizing the timing of our trading, and the allocation of the portfolio (NYSE stocks) are also investigated in a dynamic setting.

Chapter 11, Asset and Liability Management (Dániel Havran, István Margitai) demonstrates how R can support the process of asset and liability management in a bank. The focus is on data generation, measuring and reporting on interest rate risks, liquidity risk management, and the modeling of the behavior of non-maturing deposits.

Chapter 12, Capital Adequacy (Gergely Gabler, Ferenc Illés) summarizes the principles of the Basel Accords, and in order to determinate the capital adequacy of a bank, calculates value-at-risk with the help of the historical, delta-normal, and Monte-Carlo simulation methods. Specific issues of credit and operational risk are also covered.

Chapter 13, Systemic Risk (Ádám Banai, Ferenc Illés) shows two methods that can help in identifying systemically important financial institutions based on network theory: a core-periphery model and a contagion model.

Gergely Daróczi has also contributed to most chapters by reviewing the program codes.

What you need for this book

All the codes examples provided in this book should be run in the R console that is to be installed first on your computer. You can download the software for free and find the installation instructions for all major operating systems at http://r-project. org. Although we will not cover advanced topics such as how to use R in Integrated Development Environment, there are awesome plugins for Emacs, Eclipse, vi, or Notepad++ besides other editors, and we also highly recommend that you try RStudio, which is a free and open source IDE dedicated to R.

Apart from a working R installation, we will also use some user-contributed R packages that can be easily installed from the Comprehensive A Archive Network. To install a package, use the install.packages command in the R console, shown as follows:

```
> install.packages('Quantmod')
```

After installation, the package should also be loaded first to the current R session before usage:

```
> library (Quantmod)
```

You can find free introductory articles and manuals on the R home page.

Who this book is for

This book is targeted to readers who are familiar with the basic financial concepts and who have some programming skills. However, even if you know the basics of Quantitative Finance, or you already have some programming experience in R, this book provides you with new revelations. In case you are already an expert in one of the topics, this book will get you up and running quickly in the other. However, if you wish to take up the rhythm of the chapters perfectly, you need to be on an intermediate level in Quantitative Finance, and you also need to have a reasonable knowledge in R. Both of these skills can be attained from the first volume of the sequel: Introduction to R for Quantitative Finance.

Conventions

In this book, you will find a number of text styles that distinguish between different kinds of information. Here are some examples of these styles and an explanation of their meaning.

Any command-line input or output is written as follows:

```
#generate the two time series of length 1000
set.seed(20140623)       #fix the random seed
N <- 1000                #define length of simulation
x <- cumsum(rnorm(N))    #simulate a normal random walk
gamma <- 0.7             #set an initial parameter value
y <- gamma * x + rnorm(N) #simulate the cointegrating series
plot(x, type='l')        #plot the two series
lines(y,col="red")
```

New terms and **important words** are shown in bold. Words that you see on the screen, for example, in menus or dialog boxes, appear in the text like this: "Another useful visualization exercise is to look at the Density on log-scale."

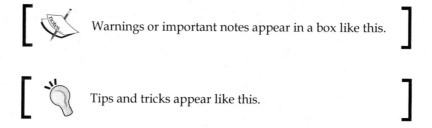

Warnings or important notes appear in a box like this.

Tips and tricks appear like this.

Reader feedback

Feedback from our readers is always welcome. Let us know what you think about this book—what you liked or disliked. Reader feedback is important for us as it helps us develop titles that you will really get the most out of.

To send us general feedback, simply e-mail feedback@packtpub.com, and mention the book's title in the subject of your message.

If there is a topic that you have expertise in and you are interested in either writing or contributing to a book, see our author guide at www.packtpub.com/authors.

Customer support

Now that you are the proud owner of a Packt book, we have a number of things to help you to get the most from your purchase.

Downloading the example code

You can download the example code files from your account at `http://www.packtpub.com` for all the Packt Publishing books you have purchased. If you purchased this book elsewhere, you can visit `http://www.packtpub.com/support` and register to have the files e-mailed directly to you.

Errata

Although we have taken every care to ensure the accuracy of our content, mistakes do happen. If you find a mistake in one of our books—maybe a mistake in the text or the code—we would be grateful if you could report this to us. By doing so, you can save other readers from frustration and help us improve subsequent versions of this book. If you find any errata, please report them by visiting `http://www.packtpub.com/submit-errata`, selecting your book, clicking on the **Errata Submission Form** link, and entering the details of your errata. Once your errata are verified, your submission will be accepted and the errata will be uploaded to our website or added to any list of existing errata under the Errata section of that title.

To view the previously submitted errata, go to `https://www.packtpub.com/books/content/support` and enter the name of the book in the search field. The required information will appear under the **Errata** section.

Piracy

Piracy of copyrighted material on the Internet is an ongoing problem across all media. At Packt, we take the protection of our copyright and licenses very seriously. If you come across any illegal copies of our works in any form on the Internet, please provide us with the location address or website name immediately so that we can pursue a remedy.

Please contact us at `copyright@packtpub.com` with a link to the suspected pirated material.

We appreciate your help in protecting our authors and our ability to bring you valuable content.

Questions

If you have a problem with any aspect of this book, you can contact us at
questions@packtpub.com, and we will do our best to address the problem.

1
Time Series Analysis

In this chapter, we consider some advanced time series methods and their implementation using R. Time series analysis, as a discipline, is broad enough to fill hundreds of books (the most important references, both in theory and R programming, will be listed at the end of this chapter's reading list); hence, the scope of this chapter is necessarily highly selective, and we focus on topics that are inevitably important in empirical finance and quantitative trading. It should be emphasized at the beginning, however, that this chapter only sets the stage for further studies in time series analysis.

Our previous book *Introduction to R for Quantitative Finance, Packt Publishing*, discusses some fundamental topics of time series analysis such as linear, univariate time series modeling, **Autoregressive integrated moving average (ARIMA)**, and volatility modeling **Generalized Autoregressive Conditional Heteroskedasticity (GARCH)**. If you have never worked with R for time series analysis, you might want to consider going through *Chapter 1, Time Series Analysis* of that book as well.

The current edition goes further in all of these topics and you will become familiar with some important concepts such as cointegration, vector autoregressive models, impulse-response functions, volatility modeling with asymmetric GARCH models including exponential GARCH and Threshold GARCH models, and news impact curves. We first introduce the relevant theories, then provide some practical insights to multivariate time series modeling, and describe several useful R packages and functionalities. In addition, using simple and illustrative examples, we give a step-by-step introduction to the usage of R programming language for empirical analysis.

Multivariate time series analysis

The basic issues regarding the movements of financial asset prices, technical analysis, and quantitative trading are usually formulated in a univariate context. Can we predict whether the price of a security will move up or down? Is this particular security in an upward or a downward trend? Should we buy or sell it? These are all important considerations; however, investors usually face a more complex situation and rarely see the market as just a pool of independent instruments and decision problems.

By looking at the instruments individually, they might seem non-autocorrelated and unpredictable in mean, as indicated by the Efficient Market Hypothesis, however, correlation among them is certainly present. This might be exploited by trading activity, either for speculation or for hedging purposes. These considerations justify the use of multivariate time series techniques in quantitative finance. In this chapter, we will discuss two prominent econometric concepts with numerous applications in finance. They are cointegration and vector autoregression models.

Cointegration

From now on, we will consider a vector of time series y_t, which consists of the elements $y_t^{(1)}, y_t^{(2)} \cdots y_t^{(n)}$ each of them individually representing a time series, for instance, the price evolution of different financial products. Let's begin with the formal definition of cointegrating data series.

The $n \times 1$ vector y_t of time series is said to be cointegrated if each of the series are individually integrated in the order d (in particular, in most of the applications the series are integrated of order 1, which means nonstationary unit-root processes, or random walks), while there exists a linear combination of the series $\beta' y_t$, which is integrated in the order $d-1$ (typically, it is of order 0, which is a stationary process).

Intuitively, this definition implies the existence of some underlying forces in the economy that are keeping together the n time series in the long run, even if they all seem to be individually random walks. A simple example for cointegrating time series is the following pair of vectors, taken from *Hamilton (1994)*, which we will use to study cointegration, and at the same time, familiarize ourselves with some basic simulation techniques in R:

$$x_t = x_{t-1} + u_t, \quad u_t \sim N(0,1)$$

$$y_t = \gamma x_t + v_t, \quad v_t \sim N(0,1)$$

The unit root in y_t will be shown formally by standard statistical tests. Unit root tests in R can be performed using either the `tseries` package or the `urca` package; here, we use the second one. The following R code simulates the two series of length `1000`:

```
#generate the two time series of length 1000
```

```
set.seed(20140623)         #fix the random seed
N <- 1000                  #define length of simulation
x <- cumsum(rnorm(N))      #simulate a normal random walk
gamma <- 0.7               #set an initial parameter value
y <- gamma * x + rnorm(N)  #simulate the cointegrating series
plot(x, type='l')          #plot the two series
lines(y,col="red")
```

Downloading the example code

You can download the example code files from your account at `http://www.packtpub.com` for all the Packt Publishing books you have purchased. If you purchased this book elsewhere, you can visit http://www.packtpub.com/support and register to have the files e-mailed directly to you.

The output of the preceding code is as follows:

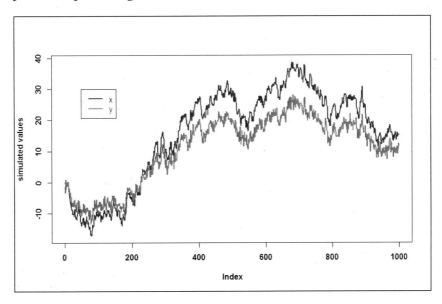

By visual inspection, both series seem to be individually random walks. Stationarity can be tested by the Augmented Dickey Fuller test, using the `urca` package; however, many other tests are also available in R. The null hypothesis states that there is a unit root in the process (outputs omitted); we reject the null if the test statistic is smaller than the critical value:

```
#statistical tests
install.packages('urca');library('urca')
#ADF test for the simulated individual time series
summary(ur.df(x,type="none"))
summary(ur.df(y,type="none"))
```

For both of the simulated series, the test statistic is larger than the critical value at the usual significance levels (1 percent, 5 percent, and 10 percent); therefore, we cannot reject the null hypothesis, and we conclude that both the series are individually unit root processes.

Now, take the following linear combination of the two series and plot the resulted series:

$$z_t = y_t - \gamma x_t$$

```
z = y - gamma*x        #take a linear combination of the series
plot(z,type='l')
```

The output for the preceding code is as follows:

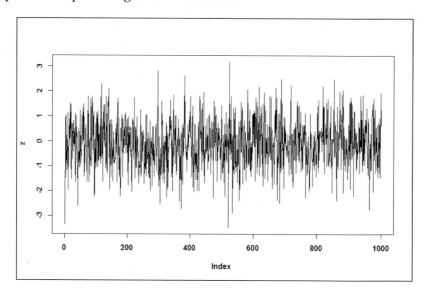

z_t clearly seems to be a white noise process; the rejection of the unit root is confirmed by the results of ADF tests:

```
summary(ur.df(z,type="none"))
```

In a real-world application, obviously we don't know the value of γ; this has to be estimated based on the raw data, by running a linear regression of one series on the other. This is known as the Engle-Granger method of testing cointegration. The following two steps are known as the Engle-Granger method of testing cointegration:

1. Run a linear regression y_t on x_t (a simple OLS estimation).
2. Test the residuals for the presence of a unit root.

> We should note here that in the case of the n series, the number of possible independent cointegrating vectors is $0 < r < n$; therefore, for $n > 2$, the cointegrating relationship might not be unique. We will briefly discuss $r > 1$ later in the chapter.

Simple linear regressions can be fitted by using the `lm` function. The residuals can be obtained from the resulting object as shown in the following example. The ADF test is run in the usual way and confirms the rejection of the null hypothesis at all significant levels. Some caveats, however, will be discussed later in the chapter:

```
#Estimate the cointegrating relationship
coin <- lm(y ~ x -1)          #regression without intercept
coin$resid                    #obtain the residuals
summary(ur.df(coin$resid))    #ADF test of residuals
```

Now, consider how we could turn this theory into a successful trading strategy. At this point, we should invoke the concept of **statistical arbitrage** or pair trading, which, in its simplest and early form, exploits exactly this cointegrating relationship. These approaches primarily aim to set up a trading strategy based on the spread between two time series; if the series are cointegrated, we expect their stationary linear combination to revert to 0. We can make profit simply by selling the relatively expensive one and buying the cheaper one, and just sit and wait for the reversion.

> The term statistical arbitrage, in general, is used for many sophisticated statistical and econometrical techniques, and this aims to exploit relative mispricing of assets in statistical terms, that is, not in comparison to a theoretical equilibrium model.

What is the economic intuition behind this idea? The linear combination of time series that forms the cointegrating relationship is determined by underlying economic forces, which are not explicitly identified in our statistical model, and are sometimes referred to as long-term relationships between the variables in question. For example, similar companies in the same industry are expected to grow similarly, the spot and forward price of a financial product are bound together by the no-arbitrage principle, FX rates of countries that are somehow interlinked are expected to move together, or short-term and long-term interest rates tend to be close to each other. Deviances from this statistically or theoretically expected comovements open the door to various quantitative trading strategies where traders speculate on future corrections.

The concept of cointegration is further discussed in a later chapter, but for that, we need to introduce vector autoregressive models.

Vector autoregressive models

Vector autoregressive models (VAR) can be considered as obvious multivariate extensions of the univariate autoregressive (AR) models. Their popularity in applied econometrics goes back to the seminal paper of *Sims (1980)*. VAR models are the most important multivariate time series models with numerous applications in econometrics and finance. The R package vars provide an excellent framework for R users. For a detailed review of this package, we refer to Pfaff (2013). For econometric theory, consult *Hamilton (1994), Lütkepohl (2007), Tsay (2010),* or *Martin et al. (2013).* In this book, we only provide a concise, intuitive summary of the topic.

In a VAR model, our point of departure is a vector of time series y_t of length n. The VAR model specifies the evolution of each variable as a linear function of the lagged values of all other variables; that is, a VAR model of the order p is the following:

$$y_t = A_1 y_{t-1} + \cdots + A_p y_{t-p} + u_t$$

Here, A_i are $n \times n$ the coefficient matrices for all $i = 1 \cdots p$, and u_t is a vector white noise process with a positive definite covariance matrix. The terminology of vector white noise assumes lack of autocorrelation, but allows contemporaneous correlation between the components; that is, u_t has a non-diagonal covariance matrix.

The matrix notation makes clear one particular feature of VAR models: all variables depend only on past values of themselves and other variables, meaning that contemporaneous dependencies are not explicitly modeled. This feature allows us to estimate the model by ordinary least squares, applied equation-by-equation. Such models are called reduced form VAR models, as opposed to structural form models, discussed in the next section.

Obviously, assuming that there are no contemporaneous effects would be an oversimplification, and the resulting impulse-response relationships, that is, changes in the processes followed by a shock hitting a particular variable, would be misleading and not particularly useful. This motivates the introduction of structured VAR (SVAR) models, which explicitly models the contemporaneous effects among variables:

$$\mathrm{A}\boldsymbol{y}_t = \mathrm{A}_1^*\boldsymbol{y}_{t-1} + \cdots + \mathrm{A}_p^*\boldsymbol{y}_{t-p} + B\boldsymbol{\epsilon}_t$$

Here, $\mathrm{A}_i^* = AA_i$ and $B\boldsymbol{\epsilon}_t = A\boldsymbol{u}_t$; thus, the structural form can be obtained from the reduced form by multiplying it with an appropriate parameter matrix A, which reflects the contemporaneous, structural relations among the variables.

 In the notation, as usual, we follow the technical documentation of the vars package, which is very similar to that of *Lütkepohl (2007)*.

In the reduced form model, contemporaneous dependencies are not modeled; therefore, such dependencies appear in the correlation structure of the error term, that is, the covariance matrix of $\boldsymbol{u}_t$, denoted by $\sum_{u_t} = E(\boldsymbol{u}_t\boldsymbol{u}_t')$. In the SVAR model, contemporaneous dependencies are explicitly modelled (by the A matrix on the left-hand side), and the disturbance terms are defined to be uncorrelated, so the $E(\boldsymbol{\epsilon}_t\boldsymbol{\epsilon}_t') = \Sigma_\epsilon$ covariance matrix is diagonal. Here, the disturbances are usually referred to as structural shocks.

What makes the SVAR modeling interesting and difficult at the same time is the so-called identification problem; the SVAR model is not identified, that is, parameters in matrix A cannot be estimated without additional restrictions.

 How should we understand that a model is not identified? This basically means that there exist different (infinitely many) parameter matrices, leading to the same sample distribution; therefore, it is not possible to identify a unique value of parameters based on the sample.

Given a reduced form model, it is always possible to derive an appropriate parameter matrix, which makes the residuals orthogonal; the covariance matrix $E(u_t u_t') = \Sigma_u$ is positive semidefinitive, which allows us to apply the LDL decomposition (or alternatively, the Cholesky decomposition). This states that there always exists an L lower triangle matrix and a D diagonal matrix such that $\Sigma_u = LDL^T$. By choosing $A = L^{-1}$, the covariance matrix of the structural model becomes $\Sigma_\epsilon = E\left(L^{-1} u_t u_t' \left(L'\right)^{-1}\right) = L^{-1} \Sigma_u \left(L'\right)^{-1}$, which gives $\Sigma_u L \Sigma_\epsilon L^T$. Now, we conclude that Σ_ϵ is a diagonal, as we intended. Note that by this approach, we essentially imposed an arbitrary recursive structure on our equations. This is the method followed by the `irf()` function by default.

There are multiple ways in the literature to identify SVAR model parameters, which include short-run or long-run parameter restrictions, or sign restrictions on impulse responses (see, for example, *Fry-Pagan (2011)*). Many of them have no native support in R yet. Here, we only introduce a standard set of techniques to impose short-run parameter restrictions, which are respectively called A-model, B-model, and AB-model, each of which are supported natively by package `vars`:

- In the case of an A-model, $B = I_n$, and restrictions on matrix A are imposed such that $\Sigma_\epsilon = AE\left(u_t u_t'\right)A' = A\Sigma_u A'$ is a diagonal covariance matrix. To make the model "just identified", we need $n(n+1)/2$ additional restrictions. This is reminiscent of imposing a triangle matrix (but that particular structure is not required).

- Alternatively, it is possible to identify the structural innovations based on the restricted model residuals by imposing a structure on the matrix **B** (B-model), that is, directly on the correlation structure, in this case, $A = I_n$ and $u_t = B\epsilon_t$.

- The AB-model places restrictions on both A and B, and the connection between the restricted and structural model is determined by $Au_t = B\epsilon_t$.

Impulse-response analysis is usually one of the main goals of building a VAR model. Essentially, an impulse-response function shows how a variable reacts (response) to a shock (impulse) hitting any other variable in the system. If the system consists of K variables, K^2 impulse response functions can be determined. Impulse responses can be derived mathematically from the Vector Moving Average representation (VMA) of the VAR process, similar to the univariate case (see the details in *Lütkepohl (2007)*).

VAR implementation example

As an illustrative example, we build a three-component VAR model from the following components:

- Equity return: This specifies the Microsoft price index from January 01, 2004 to March 03, 2014

- Stock index: This specifies the S&P500 index from January 01, 2004 to March 03, 2014

- US Treasury bond interest rates from January 01, 2004 to March 03, 2014

Our primary purpose is to make a forecast for the stock market index by using the additional variables and to identify impulse responses. Here, we suppose that there exists a hidden long term relationship between a given stock, the stock market as a whole, and the bond market. The example was chosen primarily to demonstrate several of the data manipulation possibilities of the R programming environment and to illustrate an elaborate concept using a very simple example, and not because of its economic meaning.

We use the vars and quantmod packages. Do not forget to install and load those packages if you haven't done this yet:

```
install.packages('vars');library('vars')
install.packages('quantmod');library('quantmod')
```

The Quantmod package offers a great variety of tools to obtain financial data directly from online sources, which we will frequently rely on throughout the book. We use the getSymbols() function:

```
getSymbols('MSFT', from='2004-01-02', to='2014-03-31')
getSymbols('SNP', from='2004-01-02', to='2014-03-31')
getSymbols('DTB3', src='FRED')
```

By default, yahoofinance is used as a data source for equity and index price series (src='yahoo' parameter settings, which are omitted in the example). The routine downloads open, high, low, close prices, trading volume, and adjusted prices. The downloaded data is stored in an xts data class, which is automatically named by default after the ticker (MSFT and SNP). It's possible to plot the closing prices by calling the generic plot function, but the chartSeries function of quantmod provides a much better graphical illustration.

The components of the downloaded data can be reached by using the following shortcuts:

```
Cl(MSFT)        #closing prices
Op(MSFT)        #open prices
Hi(MSFT)        #daily highest price
Lo(MSFT)        #daily lowest price
ClCl(MSFT)      #close-to-close daily return
Ad(MSFT)        #daily adjusted closing price
```

Thus, for example, by using these shortcuts, the daily close-to-close returns can be plotted as follows:

```
chartSeries(ClCl(MSFT))   #a plotting example with shortcuts
```

The screenshot for the preceding command is as follows:

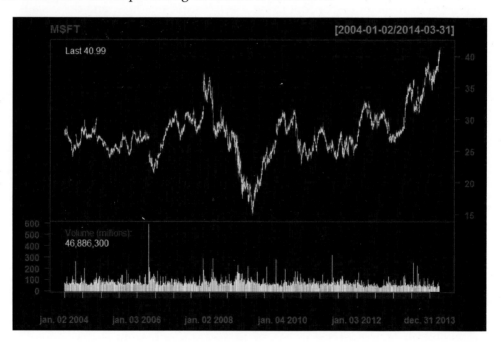

Interest rates are downloaded from the **FRED (Federal Reserve Economic Data)** data source. The current version of the interface does not allow subsetting of dates; however, downloaded data is stored in an `xts` data class, which is straightforward to subset to obtain our period of interest:

```
DTB3.sub <- DTB3['2004-01-02/2014-03-31']
```

The downloaded prices (which are supposed to be nonstationary series) should be transformed into a stationary series for analysis; that is, we will work with log returns, calculated from the adjusted series:

```
MSFT.ret <- diff(log(Ad(MSFT)))
SNP.ret  <- diff(log(Ad(SNP)))
```

To proceed, we need a last data-cleansing step before turning to VAR model fitting. By eyeballing the data, we can see that missing data exists in T-Bill return series, and the lengths of our databases are not the same (on some dates, there are interest rate quotes, but equity prices are missing). To solve these data-quality problems, we choose, for now, the easiest possible solution: merge the databases (by omitting all data points for which we do not have all three data), and omit all NA data. The former is performed by the inner join parameter (see help of the merge function for details):

```
dataDaily <- na.omit(merge(SNP.ret,MSFT.ret,DTB3.sub), join='inner')
```

Here, we note that VAR modeling is usually done on lower frequency data. There is a simple way of transforming your data to monthly or quarterly frequencies, by using the following functions, which return with the opening, highest, lowest, and closing value within the given period:

```
SNP.M  <- to.monthly(SNP.ret)$SNP.ret.Close
MSFT.M <- to.monthly(MSFT.ret)$MSFT.ret.Close
DTB3.M <- to.monthly(DTB3.sub)$DTB3.sub.Close
```

A simple reduced VAR model may be fitted to the data by using the VAR() function of the vars package. The parameterization shown in the following code allows a maximum of 4 lags in the equations, and choose the model with the best (lowest) Akaike Information Criterion value:

```
var1 <- VAR(dataDaily, lag.max=4, ic="AIC")
```

For a more established model selection, you can consider using VARselect(), which provides multiple information criteria (output omitted):

```
>VARselect(dataDaily,lag.max=4)
```

The resulting object is an object of the varest class. Estimated parameters and multiple other statistical results can be obtained by the summary() method or the show() method (that is, by just typing the variable):

```
summary(var1)
var1
```

There are other methods worth mentioning. The custom plotting method for the `varest` class generates a diagram for all variables separately, including its fitted values, residuals, and autocorrelation and partial autocorrelation functions of the residuals. You need to hit *Enter* to get the new variable. Plenty of custom settings are available; please consult the `vars` package documentation:

```
plot(var1)         #Diagram of fit and residuals for each variables
coef(var1)         #concise summary of the estimated variables
residuals(var1)    #list of residuals (of the corresponding ~lm)
fitted(var1)       #list of fitted values
Phi(var1)          #coefficient matrices of VMA representation
```

Predictions using our estimated VAR model can be made by simply calling the `predict` function and by adding a desired confidence interval:

```
var.pred <- predict(var1, n.ahead=10, ci=0.95)
```

Impulse responses should be first generated numerically by `irf()`, and then they can be plotted by the `plot()` method. Again, we get different diagrams for each variable, including the respective impulse response functions with bootstrapped confidence intervals as shown in the following command:

```
var.irf <- irf(var1)
plot(var.irf)
```

Now, consider fitting a structural VAR model using parameter restrictions described earlier as an A-model. The number of required restrictions for the SVAR model that is identified is $\frac{K(K-1)}{2}$; in our case, this is 3.

See *Lütkepohl (2007)* for more details. The number of additional restrictions required is $\frac{K(K+1)}{2}$, but the diagonal elements are normalized to unity, which leaves us with the preceding number.

The point of departure for an SVAR model is the already estimated reduced form of the VAR model (var1). This has to be amended with an appropriately structured restriction matrix.

For the sake of simplicity, we will use the following restrictions:

- S&P index shocks do not have a contemporaneous effect on Microsoft
- S&P index shocks do not have a contemporaneous effect on interest rates
- T-Bonds interest rate shocks have no contemporaneous effect on Microsoft

These restrictions enter into the SVAR model as 0s in the **A** matrix, which is as follows:

$$\begin{matrix} 1 & a_{12} & a_{13} \\ 0 & 1 & 0 \\ 0 & a_{32} & 1 \end{matrix}$$

When setting up the **A** matrix as a parameter for SVAR estimation in R, the positions of the to-be estimated parameters should take the NA value. This can be done with the following assignments:

```
amat <- diag(3)
amat[2, 1] <- NA
amat[2, 3] <- NA
amat[3, 1] <- NA
```

Finally, we can fit the SVAR model and plot the impulse response functions (the output is omitted):

```
svar1 <- SVAR(var1, estmethod='direct', Amat = amat)
irf.svar1 <- irf(svar1)
plot(irf.svar1)
```

Cointegrated VAR and VECM

Finally, we put together what we have learned so far, and discuss the concepts of Cointegrated VAR and **Vector Error Correction Models (VECM)**.

Our starting point is a system of cointegrated variables (for example, in a trading context, this indicates a set of similar stocks that are likely to be driven by the same fundamentals). The standard VAR models discussed earlier can only be estimated when the variables are stationary. As we know, the conventional way to remove unit root model is to first differentiate the series; however, in the case of cointegrated series, this would lead to overdifferencing and losing information conveyed by the long-term comovement of variable levels. Ultimately, our goal is to build up a model of stationary variables, which also incorporates the long-term relationship between the original cointegrating nonstationary variables, that is, to build a cointegrated VAR model. This idea is captured by the Vector Error Correction Model (VECM), which consists of a VAR model of the order *p - 1* on the differences of the variables, and an error-correction term derived from the known (estimated) cointegrating relationship. Intuitively, and using the stock market example, a VECM model establishes a short-term relationship between the stock returns, while correcting with the deviation from the long-term comovement of prices.

Formally, a two-variable VECM, which we will discuss as a numerical example, can be written as follows. Let $\mathbf{y}_t$ be a vector of two nonstationary unit root series $y_t^{(1)}, y_t^{(2)}$ where the two series are cointegrated with a cointegrating vector $\beta = (1, \beta)$. Then, an appropriate VECM model can be formulated as follows:

$$\Delta y_t = \alpha\beta' y_{t-1} + \psi_1 \Delta y_{t-1} + \cdots + \psi_1 \Delta y_{t-p+1} + \in_t$$

Here, $\Delta y_t = y_t - y_{t-1}$ and the first term are usually called the error correction terms.

In practice, there are two approaches to test cointegration and build the error correction model. For the two-variable case, the Engle-Granger method is quite instructive; our numerical example basically follows that idea. For the multivariate case, where the maximum number of possible cointegrating relationships is $(n-1)$, you have to follow the Johansen procedure. Although the theoretical framework for the latter goes far beyond the scope of this book, we briefly demonstrate the tools for practical implementation and give references for further studies.

To demonstrate some basic R capabilities regarding VECM models, we will use a standard example of three months and six months T-Bill secondary market rates, which can be downloaded from the FRED database, just as we discussed earlier. We will restrict our attention to an arbitrarily chosen period, that is, from 1984 to 2014. Augmented Dickey Fuller tests indicate that the null hypothesis of the unit root cannot be rejected.

```
library('quantmod')
getSymbols('DTB3', src='FRED')
getSymbols('DTB6', src='FRED')
DTB3.sub = DTB3['1984-01-02/2014-03-31']
DTB6.sub = DTB6['1984-01-02/2014-03-31']
plot(DTB3.sub)
lines(DTB6.sub, col='red')
```

We can consistently estimate the cointegrating relationship between the two series by running a simple linear regression. To simplify coding, we define the variables x1 and x2 for the two series, and y for the respective vector series. The other variable-naming conventions in the code snippets will be self-explanatory:

```
x1=as.numeric(na.omit(DTB3.sub))
x2=as.numeric(na.omit(DTB6.sub))
y = cbind(x1,x2)
cregr <- lm(x1 ~ x2)
r = cregr$residuals
```

The two series are indeed cointegrated if the residuals of the regression (variable r), that is, the appropriate linear combination of the variables, constitute a stationary series. You could test this with the usual ADF test, but in these settings, the conventional critical values are not appropriate, and corrected values should be used (see, for example *Phillips and Ouliaris (1990)*).

It is therefore much more appropriate to use a designated test for the existence of cointegration, for example, the Phillips and Ouliaris test, which is implemented in the `tseries` and in the `urca` packages as well. The most basic `tseries` version is demonstrated as follows:

```
install.packages('tseries');library('tseries');
po.coint <- po.test(y, demean = TRUE, lshort = TRUE)
```

The null hypothesis states that the two series are not cointegrated, so the low p value indicates rejection of null and presence of cointegration.

The Johansen procedure is applicable for more than one possible cointegrating relationship; an implementation can be found in the `urca` package:

```
yJoTest = ca.jo(y, type = c("trace"), ecdet = c("none"), K = 2)


######################
# Johansen-Procedure #
######################

Test type: trace statistic , with linear trend

Eigenvalues (lambda):
[1] 0.0160370678 0.0002322808

Values of teststatistic and critical values of test:

          test 10pct  5pct  1pct
r <= 1 |   1.76  6.50  8.18 11.65
r = 0  | 124.00 15.66 17.95 23.52

Eigenvectors, normalised to first column:
(These are the cointegration relations)
```

```
          DTB3.12     DTB6.12
DTB3.12  1.000000   1.000000
DTB6.12 -0.994407  -7.867356
Weights W:
(This is the loading matrix)


          DTB3.12          DTB6.12
DTB3.d -0.037015853  3.079745e-05
DTB6.d -0.007297126  4.138248e-05
```

The test statistic for *r = 0* (no cointegrating relationship) is larger than the critical values, which indicates the rejection of the null. For $r \leq 1$, however, the null cannot be rejected; therefore, we conclude that one cointegrating relationship exists. The cointegrating vector is given by the first column of the normalized eigenvectors below the test results.

The final step is to obtain the VECM representation of this system, that is, to run an OLS regression on the lagged differenced variables and the error correction term derived from the previously calculated cointegrating relationship. The appropriate function utilizes the `ca.jo` object class, which we created earlier. The *r = 1* parameter signifies the cointegration rank which is as follows:

```
>yJoRegr = cajorls(dyTest, r=1)
>yJoRegr


$rlm


Call:
lm(formula = substitute(form1), data = data.mat)


Coefficients:
           x1.d        x2.d
ect1      -0.0370159  -0.0072971
constant  -0.0041984  -0.0016892
x1.dl1     0.1277872   0.1538121
x2.dl1     0.0006551  -0.0390444
```

```
$beta
           ect1
x1.l1  1.000000
x2.l1 -0.994407
```

The coefficient of the error-correction term is negative, as we expected; a short-term deviation from the long-term equilibrium level would push our variables back to the zero equilibrium deviation.

You can easily check this in the bivariate case; the result of the Johansen procedure method leads to approximately the same result as the step-by-step implementation of the ECM following the Engle-Granger procedure. This is shown in the uploaded R code files.

Volatility modeling

It is a well-known and commonly accepted stylized fact in empirical finance that the volatility of financial time series varies over time. However, the non-observable nature of volatility makes the measurement and forecasting a challenging exercise. Usually, varying volatility models are motivated by three empirical observations:

- **Volatility clustering**: This refers to the empirical observation that calm periods are usually followed by calm periods while turbulent periods by turbulent periods in the financial markets.

- **Non-normality of asset returns**: Empirical analysis has shown that asset returns tend to have fat tails relative to the normal distribution.

- **Leverage effect**: This leads to an observation that volatility tends to react differently to positive or negative price movements; a drop in prices increases the volatility to a larger extent than an increase of similar size.

In the following code, we demonstrate these stylized facts based on S&P asset prices. Data is downloaded from yahoofinance, by using the already known method:

```
getSymbols("SNP", from="2004-01-01", to=Sys.Date())
chartSeries(Cl(SNP))
```

Our purpose of interest is the daily return series, so we calculate log returns from the closing prices. Although it is a straightforward calculation, the Quantmod package offers an even simpler way:

```
ret <- dailyReturn(Cl(SNP), type='log')
```

Volatility analysis departs from eyeballing the autocorrelation and partial autocorrelation functions. We expect the log returns to be serially uncorrelated, but the squared or absolute log returns to show significant autocorrelations. This means that Log returns are not correlated, but not independent.

Notice the `par(mfrow=c(2,2))` function in the following code; by this, we overwrite the default plotting parameters of R to organize the four diagrams of interest in a convenient table format:

```
par(mfrow=c(2,2))
acf(ret, main="Return ACF");
pacf(ret, main="Return PACF");
acf(ret^2, main="Squared return ACF");
pacf(ret^2, main="Squared return PACF")
par(mfrow=c(1,1))
```

The screenshot for preceding command is as follows:

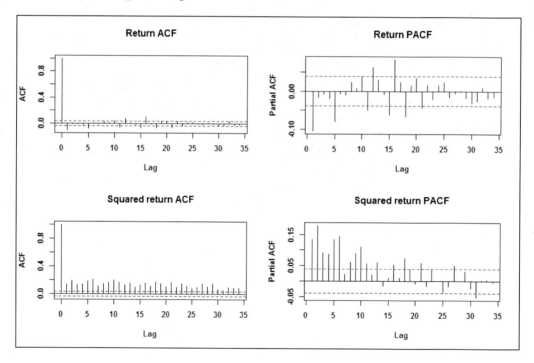

Next, we look at the histogram and/or the empirical distribution of daily log returns of S&P and compare it with the normal distribution of the same mean and standard deviation. For the latter, we use the function `density(ret)`, which computes the nonparametric empirical distribution function. We use the function `curve()` with an additional parameter `add=TRUE` to plot a second line to an already existing diagram:

```
m=mean(ret);s=sd(ret);

par(mfrow=c(1,2))

hist(ret, nclass=40, freq=FALSE, main='Return histogram');curve(dnorm(x,
mean=m,sd=s), from = -0.3, to = 0.2, add=TRUE, col="red")

plot(density(ret), main='Return empirical distribution');curve(dnorm(x,
mean=m,sd=s), from = -0.3, to = 0.2, add=TRUE, col="red")

par(mfrow=c(1,1))
```

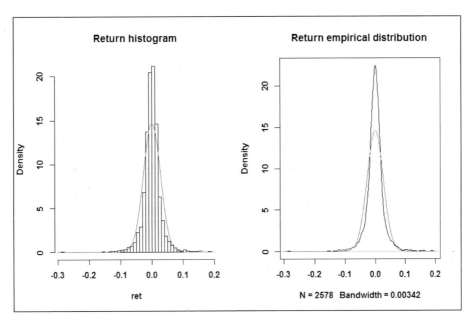

The excess kurtosis and fat tails are obvious, but we can confirm numerically (using the `moments` package) that the kurtosis of the empirical distribution of our sample exceeds that of a normal distribution (which is equal to 3). Unlike some other software packages, R reports the nominal value of kurtosis, and not excess kurtosis which is as follows:

```
> kurtosis(ret)
daily.returns
     12.64959
```

It might be also useful to zoom in to the upper or the lower tail of the diagram. This is achieved by simply rescaling our diagrams:

```
# tail zoom
plot(density(ret), main='Return EDF - upper tail', xlim = c(0.1, 0.2),
ylim=c(0,2));
curve(dnorm(x, mean=m,sd=s), from = -0.3, to = 0.2, add=TRUE, col="red")
```

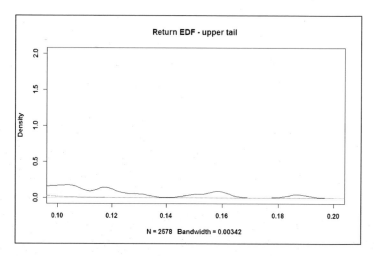

Another useful visualization exercise is to look at the **Density on log-scale** (see the following figure, left), or a **QQ-plot** (right), which are common tools to comparing densities. **QQ-plot** depicts the empirical quantiles against that of a theoretical (normal) distribution. In case our sample is taken from a normal distribution, this should form a straight line. Deviations from this straight line may indicate the presence of fat tails:

```
# density plots on log-scale
plot(density(ret), xlim=c(-5*s,5*s),log='y', main='Density on log-scale')
curve(dnorm(x, mean=m,sd=s), from=-5*s, to=5*s, log="y", add=TRUE,
col="red")

# QQ-plot
qqnorm(ret);qqline(ret);
```

The screenshot for preceding command is as follows:

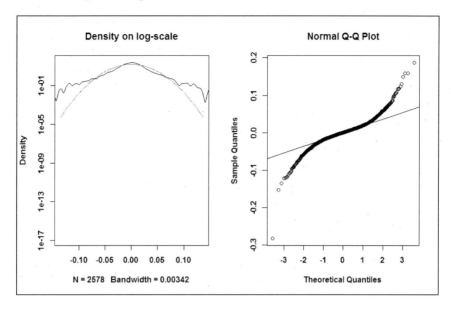

Now, we can turn our attention to modeling volatility.

Broadly speaking, there are two types of modeling techniques in the financial econometrics literature to capture the varying nature of volatility: the **GARCH-family** approach (*Engle, 1982* and *Bollerslev, 1986*) and the **stochastic volatility (SV)** models. As for the distinction between them, the main difference between the GARCH-type modeling and (genuine) SV-type modeling techniques is that in the former, the conditional variance given in the past observations is available, while in SV-models, volatility is not measurable with respect to the available information set; therefore, it is hidden by nature, and must be filtered out from the measurement equation (see, for example, *Andersen – Benzoni (2011)*). In other words, GARCH-type models involve the estimation of volatility based on past observations, while in SV-models, the volatility has its own stochastic process, which is hidden, and return realizations should be used as a measurement equation to make inferences regarding the underlying volatility process.

In this chapter, we introduce the basic modeling techniques for the GARCH approach for two reasons; first of all, it is much more proliferated in applied works. Secondly, because of its diverse methodological background, SV models are not yet supported by R packages natively, and a significant amount of custom development is required for an empirical implementation.

GARCH modeling with the rugarch package

There are several packages available in R for GARCH modeling. The most prominent ones are `rugarch`, `rmgarch` (for multivariate models), and `fGarch`; however, the basic `tseries` package also includes some GARCH functionalities. In this chapter, we will demonstrate the modeling facilities of the `rugarch` package. Our notations in this chapter follow the respective ones of the `rugarch` package's output and documentation.

The standard GARCH model

A GARCH (p,q) process may be written as follows:

$$\epsilon_t = \sigma_t \eta_t$$

$$\sigma_t^2 = \omega + \sum_{i=1}^{q} \alpha_i \, \epsilon_{t-i}^2 + \sum_{j=1}^{q} \beta_j \sigma_{t-j}^2$$

Here, ϵ_t is usually the disturbance term of a conditional mean equation (in practice, usually an ARMA process) and $\eta_t \sim \text{i.i.d.}(0,1)$. That is, the conditional volatility process is determined linearly by its own lagged values σ_{t-j}^2 and the lagged squared observations (the values of ϵ_t). In empirical studies, GARCH (1,1) usually provides an appropriate fit to the data. It may be useful to think about the simple GARCH (1,1) specification as a model in which the conditional variance is specified as a weighted average of the long-run variance $\frac{\omega}{1-\alpha-\beta}$, the last predicted variance σ_{t-1}^2, and the new information ϵ_{t-1}^2 (see *Andersen et al. (2009)*). It is easy to see how the GARCH (1,1) model captures autoregression in volatility (volatility clustering) and leptokurtic asset return distributions, but as its main drawback, it is symmetric, and cannot capture asymmetries in distributions and leverage effects.

The emergence of volatility clustering in a GARCH-model is highly intuitive; a large positive (negative) shock in η_t increases (decreases) the value of ϵ_t, which in turn increases (decreases) the value of σ_{t+1}, resulting in a larger (smaller) value for ϵ_{t+1}. The shock is persistent; this is volatility clustering. Leptokurtic nature requires some derivation; see for example Tsay (2010).

Our empirical example will be the analysis of the return series calculated from the daily closing prices of Apple Inc. based on the period from Jan 01, 2006 to March 31, 2014. As a useful exercise, before starting this analysis, we recommend that you repeat the exploratory data analysis in this chapter to identify stylized facts on Apple data.

Obviously, our first step is to install a package, if not installed yet:

```
install.packages('rugarch');library('rugarch')
```

To get the data, as usual, we use the `quantmod` package and the `getSymbols()` function, and calculate return series based on the closing prices.

```
#Load Apple data and calculate log-returns
getSymbols("AAPL", from="2006-01-01", to="2014-03-31")
ret.aapl <- dailyReturn(Cl(AAPL), type='log')
chartSeries(ret.aapl)
```

The programming logic of `rugarch` can be thought of as follows: irrespective of whatever your aim is (fitting, filtering, forecasting, and simulating), first, you have to specify a model as a system object (variable), which in turn will be inserted into the respective function. Models can be specified by calling `ugarchspec()`. The following code specifies a simple GARCH (1,1) model, (sGARCH), with only a constant μ in the mean equation:

```
garch11.spec = ugarchspec(variance.model = list(model="sGARCH",
garchOrder=c(1,1)), mean.model = list(armaOrder=c(0,0)))
```

An obvious way to proceed is to fit this model to our data, that is, to estimate the unknown parameters by maximum likelihood, based on our time series of daily returns:

```
aapl.garch11.fit = ugarchfit(spec=garch11.spec, data=ret.aapl)
```

The function provides, among a number of other outputs, the parameter estimations $\mu, \omega, \alpha_1, \beta_1$:

```
> coef(aapl.garch11.fit)
          mu         omega       alpha1         beta1
1.923328e-03 1.027753e-05 8.191681e-02 8.987108e-01
```

Estimates and various diagnostic tests can be obtained by the `show()` method of the generated object (that is, by just typing the name of the variable). A bunch of other statistics, parameter estimates, standard error, and covariance matrix estimates can be reached by typing the appropriate command. For the full list, consult the `ugarchfit` object class; the most important ones are shown in the following code:

```
coef(msft.garch11.fit)          #estimated coefficients
vcov(msft.garch11.fit)          #covariance matrix of param estimates
infocriteria(msft.garch11.fit)  #common information criteria list
newsimpact(msft.garch11.fit)    #calculate news impact curve
signbias(msft.garch11.fit)      #Engle - Ng sign bias test
fitted(msft.garch11.fit)        #obtain the fitted data series
residuals(msft.garch11.fit)     #obtain the residuals
uncvariance(msft.garch11.fit)   #unconditional (long-run) variance
uncmean(msft.garch11.fit)       #unconditional (long-run) mean
```

Standard GARCH models are able to capture fat tails and volatility clustering, but to explain asymmetries caused by the leverage effect, we need more advanced models. To approach the asymmetry problem visually, we will now describe the concept of news impact curves.

News impact curves, introduced by Pagan and Schwert (1990) and Engle and Ng (1991), are useful tools to visualize the magnitude of volatility changes in response to shocks. The name comes from the usual interpretation of shocks as news influencing the market movements. They plot the change in conditional volatility against shocks in different sizes, and can concisely express the asymmetric effects in volatility. In the following code, the first line calculates the news impacts numerically for the previously defined GARCH(1,1) model, and the second line creates the visual plot:

```
ni.garch11 <- newsimpact(aapl.garch11.fit)
plot(ni.garch11$zx, ni.garch11$zy, type="l", lwd=2, col="blue",
main="GARCH(1,1) - News Impact", ylab=ni.garch11$yexpr, xlab=ni.
garch11$xexpr)
```

The screenshot for the preceding command is as follows:

As we expected, no asymmetries are present in response to positive and negative shocks. Now, we turn to models to be able to incorporate asymmetric effects as well.

The Exponential GARCH model (EGARCH)

Exponential GARCH models were introduced by Nelson (1991). This approach directly models the logarithm of the conditional volatility:

$$\epsilon_t = \sigma_t \eta_t$$

$$\log \sigma_t^2 = \omega + \sum_{i=1}^{q} \left(\alpha_i \eta_{t-i} + \gamma \left(|\eta_{t-i}| - E|\eta_{t-i}| \right) \right) + \sum_{j=1}^{q} \beta_j \log \left(\sigma_{t-j}^2 \right)$$

where, E is the expectation operator. This model formulation allows multiplicative dynamics in evolving the volatility process. Asymmetry is captured by the α_i parameter; a negative value indicates that the process reacts more to negative shocks, as observable in real data sets.

To fit an EGARCH model, the only parameter to be changed in a model specification is to set the EGARCH model type. By running the `fitting` function, the additional parameter will be estimated (see `coef()`):

```
# specify EGARCH(1,1) model with only constant in mean equation
egarch11.spec = ugarchspec(variance.model = list(model="eGARCH",
garchOrder=c(1,1)), mean.model = list(armaOrder=c(0,0)))
aapl.egarch11.fit = ugarchfit(spec=egarch11.spec, data=ret.aapl)
```

```
> coef(aapl.egarch11.fit)
         mu         omega         alpha1         beta1         gamma1
 0.001446685  -0.291271433  -0.092855672   0.961968640   0.176796061
```

News impact curve reflects the strong asymmetry in response of conditional volatility to shocks and confirms the necessity of asymmetric models:

```
ni.egarch11 <- newsimpact(aapl.egarch11.fit)
plot(ni.egarch11$zx, ni.egarch11$zy, type="l", lwd=2, col="blue",
main="EGARCH(1,1) - News Impact",
ylab=ni.egarch11$yexpr, xlab=ni.egarch11$xexpr)
```

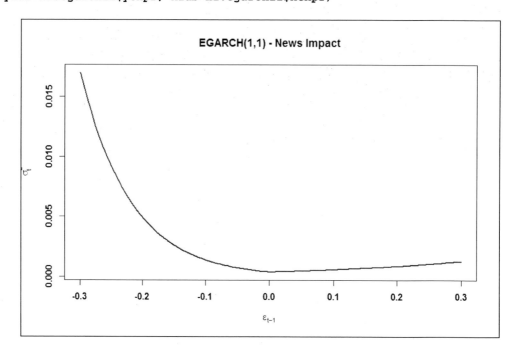

The Threshold GARCH model (TGARCH)

Another prominent example is the TGARCH model, which is even easier to interpret. The TGARCH specification involves an explicit distinction of model parameters above and below a certain threshold. TGARCH is also a submodel of a more general class, the asymmetric power ARCH class, but we will discuss it separately because of its wide penetration in applied financial econometrics literature.

The TGARCH model may be formulated as follows:

$$\epsilon_t = \sigma_t \eta_t$$

$$\sigma_t^2 = \omega + \sum_{i=1}^{q} \left(\alpha_i + \gamma_i I_{t-i} \right) \epsilon_{t-i}^2 + \sum_{j=1}^{q} \beta_j \sigma_{t-j}^2$$

where $I_{t-i} = \begin{cases} 1 \; if \; \epsilon_{t-1} < 0 \\ 0 \; if \; \epsilon_{t-1} \geq 0 \end{cases}$

The interpretation is straightforward; the ARCH coefficient depends on the sign of the previous error term; if γ_1 is positive, a negative error term will have a higher impact on the conditional volatility, just as we have seen in the leverage effect before.

In the R package, `rugarch`, the threshold GARCH model is implemented in a framework of an even more general class of GARCH models, called the Family GARCH model *Ghalanos (2014)*.

```
# specify TGARCH(1,1) model with only constant in mean equation
tgarch11.spec = ugarchspec(variance.model = list(model="fGARCH",
submodel="TGARCH", garchOrder=c(1,1)),
        mean.model = list(armaOrder=c(0,0)))
aapl.tgarch11.fit = ugarchfit(spec=tgarch11.spec, data=ret.aapl)


> coef(aapl.egarch11.fit)
          mu        omega      alpha1        beta1       gamma1
 0.001446685 -0.291271433 -0.092855672  0.961968640  0.176796061
```

Thanks to the specific functional form, the news impact curve for a Threshold-GARCH is less flexible in representing different responses, there is a kink at the zero point which can be seen when we run the following command:

```
ni.tgarch11 <- newsimpact(aapl.tgarch11.fit)
```

```
plot(ni.tgarch11$zx, ni.tgarch11$zy, type="l", lwd=2, col="blue",
main="TGARCH(1,1) - News Impact",
```

```
ylab=ni.tgarch11$yexpr, xlab=ni.tgarch11$xexpr)
```

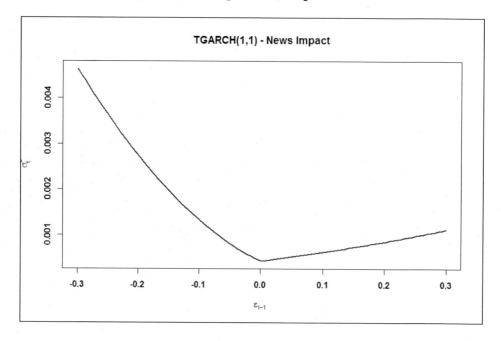

Simulation and forecasting

The Rugarch package allows an easy way to simulate from a specified model. Of course, for simulation purposes, we should also specify the parameters of the model within ugarchspec(); this could be done by the fixed.pars argument. After specifying the model, we can simulate a time series with a given conditional mean and GARCH specification by using simply the ugarchpath() function:

```
garch11.spec = ugarchspec(variance.model = list(garchOrder=c(1,1)),
   mean.model = list(armaOrder=c(0,0)),
      fixed.pars=list(mu = 0, omega=0.1, alpha1=0.1,
         beta1 = 0.7))
garch11.sim = ugarchpath(garch11.spec, n.sim=1000)
```

Once we have an estimated model and technically a fitted object, forecasting the conditional volatility based on that is just one step:

```
aapl.garch11.fit = ugarchfit(spec=garch11.spec, data=ret.aapl, out.
sample=20)
```

```
aapl.garch11.fcst = ugarchforecast(aapl.garch11.fit, n.ahead=10,
n.roll=10)
```

The plotting method of the forecasted series provides the user with a selection menu; we can plot either the predicted time series or the predicted conditional volatility.

```
plot(aapl.garch11.fcst, which='all')
```

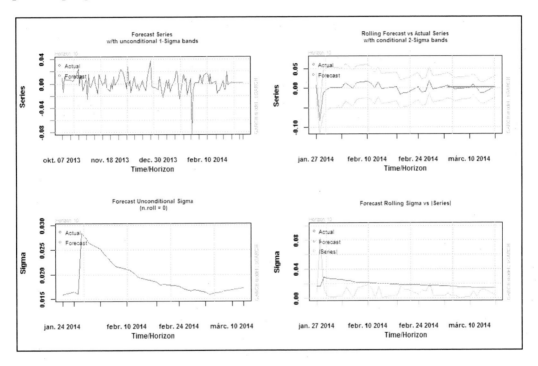

Summary

In this chapter, we reviewed some important concepts of time series analysis, such as cointegration, vector-autoregression, and GARCH-type conditional volatility models. Meanwhile, we have provided a useful introduction to some tips and tricks to start modeling with R for quantitative and empirical finance. We hope that you find these exercises useful, but again, it should be noted that this chapter is far from being complete both from time series and econometric theory, and from R programming's point of view. The R programming language is very well documented on the Internet, and the R user's community consists of thousands of advanced and professional users. We encourage you to go beyond books, be a self-learner, and do not stop if you are stuck with a problem; almost certainly, you will find an answer on the Internet to proceed. Use the documentation of R packages and the help files heavily, and study the official R-site, `http://cran.r-project.org/`, frequently. The remaining chapters will provide you with numerous additional examples to find your way in the plethora of R facilities, packages, and functions.

References and reading list

- Andersen, Torben G; Davis, Richard A.; Kreiß, Jens-Peters; Mikosh, Thomas (ed.) (2009). Handbook of Financial Time Series

- Andersen, Torben G. and Benzoni, Luca (2011). Stochastic volatility. Book chapter in Complex Systems in Finance and Econometrics, Ed.: Meyers, Robert A., Springer

- Brooks, Chris (2008). Introductory Econometrics for Finance, Cambridge University Press

- Fry, Renee and Pagan, Adrian (2011). Sign Restrictions in Structural Vector Autoregressions: A Critical Review. Journal of Economic Literature, American Economic Association, vol. 49(4), pages 938-60, December.

- Ghalanos, Alexios (2014) Introduction to the rugarch package `http://cran.r-project.org/web/packages/rugarch/vignettes/Introduction_to_the_rugarch_package.pdf`

- Hafner, Christian M. (2011). Garch modelling. Book chapter in Complex Systems in Finance and Econometrics, Ed.: Meyers, Robert A., Springer

- Hamilton, James D. (1994). Time Series Analysis, Princetown, New Jersey

- Lütkepohl, Helmut (2007). New Introduction to Multiple Time Series Analysis, Springer

- Murray, Michael. P. (1994). A drunk and her dog: an illustration of cointegration and error correction. *The American Statistician*, *48*(1), 37-39.

- Martin, Vance; Hurn, Stan and Harris, David (2013). Econometric Modelling with Time Series. Specification, Estimation and Testing, Cambridge University Press

- Pfaff, Bernard (2008). Analysis of Integrated and Cointegrated Time Series with R, Springer

- Pfaff, Bernhard (2008). VAR, SVAR and SVEC Models: Implementation Within R Package vars. Journal of Statistical Software, 27(4)

- Phillips, P. C., & Ouliaris, S. (1990). Asymptotic properties of residual based tests for cointegration. *Econometrica: Journal of the Econometric Society*, 165-193.

- Pole, Andrew (2007). Statistical Arbitrage. Wiley

- Rachev, Svetlozar T., Hsu, John S.J., Bagasheva, Biliana S. and Fabozzi, Frank J. (2008). Bayesian Methods in Finance. John Wiley & Sons.

- Sims, Christopher A. (1980). Macroeconomics and reality. *Econometrica: Journal of the Econometric Society*, 1-48.

- Tsay, Ruey S. (2010). Analysis of Financial Time Series, 3rd edition, Wiley

2

Factor Models

In most of the cases in finance, valuation of financial assets is based on the discounted cash flow method; hence, the present value is calculated as the discounted value of the expected future cash flows. Therefore, in order to be able to value assets, we need to know the appropriate rate of return that reflects the time value of money and also the risk of the given asset. There are two main approaches to determine expected returns: the **capital asset pricing model (CAPM)** and the **arbitrage pricing theory (APT)**. CAPM is an equilibrium model, while APT builds on the no-arbitrage principle; thus, these approaches have quite different starting points and inner logic. However, the final pricing formula we get can be quite similar, depending on the market factors we use. For the comparison of CAPM and APT, see *Bodie-Kane-Marcus (2008)*. When we test any of these theoretical models on real-world data, we perform linear regressions. This chapter focuses on APT, since we have discussed CAPM in more detail in *Daróczi et al. (2013)*.

This chapter is divided into two parts. In the first part, we introduce the theory of APT in general, and then we present a special three-factor model published in a seminal paper of *Fama and French*. In the second part, we show how to use R for data selection and how to estimate the pricing coefficients from real market data, and finally we re-examine the famous Fama-French model on a more recent sample.

Arbitrage pricing theory

APT relies on the assumption that asset returns in the market are determined by macroeconomic and firm-specific factors, and asset returns are generated by the following linear factor model:

$$r_i = E(r_i) + \sum_{j=1}^{n} \beta_{ij} F_j + e_i$$

Equation 1

Here, $E(r_i)$ is the expected return of asset i, F_j stands for the unexpected change of the jth factor, and β_{ij} shows the ith security's sensitivity for that factor, while e_i is the return caused by unexpected firm-specific events. So $\sum_{j=1}^{n}\beta_{ij}F_j$ represents the random systemic effect, and e_i represents the non-systemic (that is idiosyncratic) effect, which is not captured by the market factors. Being unexpected, both $\sum_{j=1}^{n}\beta_{ij}F_j$ and e_i have a zero mean. In this model, factors are independent of each other and the firm-specific risk. Thus, asset returns are derived from two sources: the systemic risk of the factors that affect all assets in the market and the non-systematic risk that impacts only that special firm. A non-systemic risk can be diversified by holding more assets in the portfolio. In contrast, a systemic risk cannot be diversified, as it is caused by economy-wide sources of risks that affect the overall stock market (*Brealey-Myers, 2005*).

As a consequence of the model, the realized return of an asset is the linear combination of multiple random factors (*Wilmott, 2007*).

Other important assumptions of APT are as follows:

- There are a finite number of investors on the market who optimize their portfolio for the next period. They are equally informed and have no market power.

- There is a riskless asset and an infinite number of risky assets traded continuously; thus, firm-specific risks can be totally eliminated by diversification. A portfolio that has zero firm-specific risks is called a well-diversified portfolio.

- Investors are rational in the sense that if an arbitrage opportunity occurs (financial assets are mispriced relative to each other), then investors immediately buy the underpriced security/securities and sell the overpriced one(s), and they will take an infinitely large position in order to earn as much riskless profit as possible. Consequently, any mispricing will disappear on the spot.

- Factor portfolios exist, and they are continuously tradable. A factor portfolio is a well-diversified portfolio that reacts only to one of the factors; specifically, it has a beta of 1 for that specified factor and a beta of 0 for all other factors.

From the preceding assumptions, it can be shown that any portfolio's risk premium equals the weighted sum of the factor portfolios' risk premium *(Medvegyev-Száz, 2010)*. The following pricing formula can be derived in the case of a two-factor model:

$$E\left(r_i - r_f\right) = \beta_{i1}\left(r_1 - r_f\right) + \beta_{i2}\left(r_2 - r_f\right)$$

Equation 2

Here, r_i is the return of the ith asset, r_f is the risk-free return, β_{i1} is the sensitivity of the ith stock's risk premium to the first systemic factor, and $(r_1\text{-}r_f)$ is the risk premium of this factor. Similarly, β_{i2} is the sensitivity of the ith stock's risk premium to the second factor's excess return $(r_2\text{-}r_f)$.

When we implement APT, we perform a linear regression in the following form:

$$\left(r_i - r_f\right) = \alpha_i + \beta_{i1}\left(r_1 - r_f\right) + \beta_{i2}\left(r_2 - r_f\right) + \varepsilon_i$$

Equation 3

Here, α_i stands for a constant and ε_i is the asset's non-systemic, firm-specific risk. All other variables are the same as mentioned previously.

If there is only one factor in the model, and it is the return of the market portfolio, the pricing equation of the CAPM model and APT model will coincide:

$$E\left(r_i - r_f\right) = \beta_i\left(r_m - r_f\right)$$

Equation 4

In this case, the formula to be tested on real market data is as follows:

$$\left(r_i - r_f\right) = \alpha_i + \beta_i\left(r_m - r_f\right) + \varepsilon_i$$

Equation 5

Here, r_m is the return of a market portfolio represented by a market index (like the S&P 500). This is why we call Equation (5) the index model.

Implementation of APT

The implementation of APT can be split into four steps: identifying the factors, estimating the factor coefficient, estimating the factor premiums, and pricing with APT (*Bodie et al. 2008*):

1. **Identifying the factors**: As APT mentions nothing about the factors, they have to be identified empirically. These factors are usually macroeconomic factors, like stock market return, inflation, business cycle, and so on. The main problem in using macroeconomic factors is that factors are usually not independent of each other. The identification of the factors is often carried out by factor analysis. However, factors identified by factor analysis cannot necessarily be interpreted in an economically meaningful way.

2. **Estimating factor coefficients**: In order to estimate the coefficients in a multivariate linear regression model, a general version of Equation (3) is used.

3. **Estimating the factor premiums**: The estimation of the factor premiums is based on historical data, taking the average of the historical time-series data of the premiums of the factor portfolios.

4. **Pricing with APT**: Equation (2) is used for calculating the expected return of any asset by substituting the appropriate variables into the equation.

Fama-French three-factor model

Fama and French proposed a multifactor model in 1996, in which they used corporate indicators as factors instead of macroeconomic factors, since they found that these factors better describe the systemic risk of assets. Fama and French (1996) extended the index model by adding the firm size and the book-to-market ratio as return-generating factors to the market portfolio returns (*Fama and French, 1996*).

The firm size factor was constructed by taking the difference between the returns of small and large firms (r_{SMB}). The name of the variable was SMB, which is derived from "small minus big". The book-to-market factor was calculated by taking the difference between firms' returns that have a high and low book-to-market ratio (r_{HML}). The name of the variable was HML, which is derived from "high minus low".

Their model was the following:

$$r_i - r_f = \alpha_i + \beta_{iM}\left(r_M - r_f\right) + \beta_{iHML}r_{HML} + \beta_{iSMB}r_{SMB} + e_i$$

Equation 6

Here, α_i is a constant, which shows the abnormal rate of return, r_f is the risk-free return, and β_{iHML} is the ith asset's sensitivity to the book-to-market factor, while β_{iSMB} is the ith asset's sensitivity to the factor of size, β_{iM} is the sensitivity of the ith stock's risk premium to the market index factor, $(r_M\text{-}r_f)$ is the risk premium of this factor, and e_i is the asset's non-systemic, firm-specific risk with zero mean.

Modeling in R

In the following section, we will learn the implementation of the previously described models with the help of R.

Data selection

In *Chapter 4, Big Data – Advanced Analytics*, we will discuss in detail the aspects and methods of getting data from open sources and working with them efficiently. Here, we only present how the time series of stock prices and other relevant information can be acquired and used for the factor model's estimations.

We used the `quantmod` package to collect the database.

Here is how it works in R:

```
library(quantmod)
stocks <- stockSymbols()
```

As a result, we need to wait for a few seconds while data is fetched, and then we can see the output:

```
Fetching AMEX symbols...
Fetching NASDAQ symbols...
Fetching NYSE symbols...
```

Now, we have a data frame R object that contains about 6,500 stocks that are traded on different exchanges such as AMEX, NASDAQ, or NYSE. In order to see the variables that the dataset contains, we can use the `str` command:

```
str(stocks)
'data.frame':    6551 obs. of  8 variables:
 $ Symbol   : chr  "AA-P" "AAMC" "AAU" "ACU" ...
 $ Name     : chr  "Alcoa Inc." "Altisource Asset Management Corp"...
 $ LastSale : num  87 1089.9 1.45 16.58 16.26 ...
 $ MarketCap: num  0.00 2.44e+09 9.35e+07 5.33e+07 2.51e+07 ...
 $ IPOyear  : int  NA NA NA 1988 NA NA NA NA NA NA ...
 $ Sector   : chr  "Capital Goods" "Finance" "Basic Industries"...
 $ Industry : chr  "Metal Fabrications" "Real Estate"...
 $ Exchange : chr  "AMEX" "AMEX" "AMEX" "AMEX" ...
```

We can drop the variables that we don't really need and include the information about market capitalization and the book value of the company coming from a different database as new variables since we will need them to estimate the Fama-French model:

```
stocks[1:5, c(1, 3:4, ncol(stocks))]
      Symbol LastSale   MarketCap BookValuePerShare
1     AA-P     87.30           0              0.03
2     AAMC    985.00  2207480545            -11.41
3     AAU      1.29    83209284              0.68
4     ACU     16.50    53003808             10.95
5     ACY     16.40    25309415             30.13
```

We will also need the time series of the risk-free return, which will be quantified in this calculation by the one-month USD LIBOR rate:

```
library(Quandl)
Warning message:
package 'Quandl' was built under R version 3.1.0
LIBOR <- Quandl('FED/RILSPDEPM01_N_B',
start_date = '2010-06-01', end_date = '2014-06-01')
Warning message:
```

```
In Quandl("FED/RILSPDEPM01_N_B", start_date = "2010-06-01", end_date
= "2014-06-01") : It would appear you aren't using an authentication
token. Please visit http://www.quandl.com/help/r or your usage may be
limited.
```

We can ignore the warning messages as data is still assigned to the LIBOR variable.

The `Quandl` package, the `tseries` package, and other packages that collect data are discussed in *Chapter 4, Big Data – Advanced Analytics*, in more detail.

This can also be used to get the prices of stocks, and the S&P 500 index can be used as the market portfolio.

We have a table with stock prices (a time series of approximately 5,000 stock prices between June 1, 2010 to June 1, 2014). The first and last few columns look like this:

```
d <- read.table("data.csv", header = TRUE, sep = ";")
d[1:7, c(1:5, (ncol(d) - 6):ncol(d))]
          Date     SP500  AAU   ACU   ACY   ZMH    ZNH ZOES ZQK ZTS
ZX
1  2010.06.01 1070.71  0.96 11.30 20.64 54.17 21.55  NA  4.45 NA NA
2  2010.06.02 1098.38  0.95 11.70 20.85 55.10 21.79  NA  4.65 NA NA
3  2010.06.03 1102.83  0.97 11.86 20.90 55.23 21.63  NA  4.63 NA NA
4  2010.06.04 1064.88  0.93 11.65 18.95 53.18 20.88  NA  4.73 NA NA
5  2010.06.07 1050.47  0.97 11.45 19.03 52.66 20.24  NA  4.18 NA NA
6  2010.06.08 1062.00  0.98 11.35 18.25 52.99 20.96  NA  3.96 NA NA
7  2010.06.09 1055.69  0.98 11.90 18.35 53.22 20.45  NA  4.02 NA NA
```

If we have the data saved on our hard drive, we can simply read it with the `read.table` function. In *Chapter 4, Big Data – Advanced Analytics*, we will discuss how to collect data directly from the Internet.

Now, we have all the data we need: the market portfolio (S&P 500), the price of stocks, and the risk-free rates (one-month LIBOR).

We have chosen to delete the variables with missing values and 0 or negative prices, in order to clean the database. The easiest way to do this is the following:

```
d <- d[, colSums(is.na(d)) == 0]
d <- d[, c(T, colMins(d[, 2:ncol(d)]) > 0)]
```

To use the `colMins` function, we apply the `matrixStats` package. Now, we can start working with the data.

Estimation of APT with principal component analysis

In practice, it is not easy to carry out a factor analysis, because identifying the macro variables that have an effect on the securities' return is difficult (*Medvegyev – Száz, 2010, pp. 42*). In many cases, the latent factors that drive the returns are searched by principal component analysis.

From the originally downloaded 6,500 stocks, we can use the data of 4,015 stocks; the rest were excluded because of missing values or 0 prices. Now, we omit the first two columns because we do not need the dates in this section, and the S&P 500 is considered as a separate factor in itself; hence, we do not include it in the principal component analysis (PCA). After this, the log returns are computed.

```
p <- d[, 3:ncol(d)]
r <- log(p[2:nrow(p), ] / p[1:(nrow(p) - 1), ])
```

There exists another way to calculate the log returns of a given asset, that is, by using `return.calculate(data, method="log")` with the `PerformanceAnalytics` library.

As we have too many stocks, in order to carry out PCA, either we have to have data of at least 25 years, or we need to reduce the number of stocks. It's hopeless for factor models to remain stable for decades; hence, for illustration purposes, we choose to select 10 percent of the stocks randomly and compute the model for this sample:

```
r <- r[, runif(nrow(r)) < 0.1]
```

`runif(nrow(r)) < 0.1` is a 4,013 dimension 0-1 vector, which chooses approximately 10 percent of the columns (in our case, 393) from the table. We can also use the following sample function for this, on which you can find further details at `http://stat.ethz.ch/R-manual/R-devel/library/base/html/sample.html`:

```
pca <- princomp(r)
```

As a result, we receive a `princomp` class object, which has eight attributes, of which the most important ones are the loading matrix and the `sdev` attributes, which contain the standard deviations of the components. The first principal component is the vector on which the data set has the maximum variance.

Let's check the standard deviations of the principal component:

```
plot(pca$sdev)
```

The result is as follows:

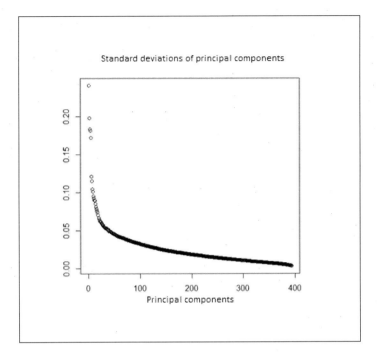

We can see that the first five components are separated; consequently, five factors should be chosen, but other factors also have significant standard deviations, so the market cannot be explained by a few factors.

We can confirm this result by calling the `factanal` function, which estimates the factor model with five factors:

```
factanal(r, 5)
```

We notice that it takes much more time to perform this computation. Factor analysis is related to PCA, but is a little more complicated from a mathematical aspect. As a result, we get an object of class `factanal`, which has many attributes, but now, we are only interested in the following part of the output:

	Factor1	Factor2	Factor3	Factor4	Factor5
SS loadings	56.474	23.631	15.440	12.092	6.257
Proportion Var	0.144	0.060	0.039	0.031	0.016
Cumulative Var	0.144	0.204	0.243	0.274	0.290

Test of the hypothesis that 5 factors are sufficient.

The chi square statistic is 91756.72 on 75073 degrees of freedom.The p-value is 0

This output shows that the factor model with five factors fits, but the explained variance is only approximately 30 percent, which means that the model should be extended with other factors as well.

Estimation of the Fama-French model

We have a data frame with prices of the 4,015 stocks for five years, and the LIBOR data frame with the LIBOR time series. First, we need to compute the returns and combine them with the LIBOR rate.

As a first step, we omit the dates that are not for mathematical computations, and then we compute the log returns for each of the remaining columns:

```
d2 <- d[, 2:ncol(d)]
d2 <- log(tail(d1, -1)/head(d1, -1))
```

After calculating the log returns, we put back the dates to the returns, and then, as a last step, we combine the two data sets:

```
d <- cbind(d[2:nrow(d), 1], d2)
d <- merge(LIBOR, d, by = 1)
```

It is worth mentioning that the merge function operates on data frames equivalent to the (inner) join SQL statement.

The result is as follows:

```
print(d[1:5, 1:5])]
```

Date	LIBOR	SP500	AAU	ACU
2010.06.02	0.4	0.025514387	-0.01047130	0.034786116
2010.06.03	0.4	0.004043236	0.02083409	0.013582552
2010.06.04	0.4	-0.035017487	-0.04211149	-0.017865214
2010.06.07	0.4	-0.013624434	0.04211149	-0.017316450
2010.06.08	0.4	0.010916240	0.01025650	-0.008771986

We adjust the LIBOR rate to the daily returns:

```
d$LIBOR <- d$LIBOR / 36000
```

As the LIBOR rates are quoted on a money-market basis - (actual/360) day-count convention - and the time series contain the rates in percentage, we divided the LIBOR by 36,000. Now, we need to compute the three variables of the Fama-French model. As described in the *Data selection* section, we have the stocks' data frame:

```
d[1:5, c(1,(ncol(d) - 3):ncol(d))]
   Symbol LastSale  MarketCap BookValuePerShare
1    AA-P    87.30          0              0.03
2    AAMC   985.00 2207480545            -11.41
3     AAU     1.29   83209284              0.68
4     ACU    16.50   53003808             10.95
5     ACY    16.40   25309415             30.13
```

We have to drop the stocks for which we do not have price data:

```
> stocks = stocks[stocks$Symbol %in% colnames(d),]
```

We have the market cap as a variable; we still need to compute the book-to-market ratio for each:

```
stocks$BookToMarketRatio <-
  stocks$BookValuePerShare / stocks$LastSale
str(stocks)
'data.frame':   3982 obs. of  5 variables:
 $ Symbol            : Factor w/ 6551 levels "A","AA","AA-P",..: 14
72...
 $ LastSale          : num  1.29 16.5 16.4 2.32 4.05 ...
 $ MarketCap         : num  8.32e+07 5.30e+07 2.53e+07 1.16e+08...
 $ BookValuePerShare : num  0.68 10.95 30.13 0.19 0.7 ...
 $ BookToMarketRatio : num  0.5271 0.6636 1.8372 0.0819 0.1728 ...
```

Now, we need to compute the SMB and HML factors. For simplification, we will define companies as BIG if they are bigger than the average. The same principle is applied for the book-to-market ratio:

```
avg_size <- mean(stocks$MarketCap)
BIG   <- as.character(stocks$Symbol[stocks$MarketCap > avg_size])
SMALL <- as.character(stocks[stocks$MarketCap < avg_size,1])
```

These arrays contain the symbols of the BIG and SMALL companies. Now, we can define the SMB factor:

```
d$SMB <- rowMeans(d[,colnames(d) %in% SMALL]) -
  rowMeans(d[,colnames(d) %in% BIG])
```

We define the HML factor as follows:

```
avg_btm <- mean(stocks$BookToMarketRatio)
HIGH <- as.character(
  stocks[stocks$BookToMarketRatio > avg_btm, 1])
LOW <- as.character(
  stocks[stocks$BookToMarketRatio < avg_btm, 1])
d$HML <- rowMeans(d[, colnames(d) %in% HIGH]) -
  rowMeans(d[, colnames(d) %in% LOW])
```

The third factor is calculated:

```
d$Market <- d$SP500 - d$LIBOR
```

After defining the three factors, we test it on the stock of Citigroup Inc. (Citi) and on Exelixis, Inc. (EXEL):

```
d$C   <- d$C - d$LIBOR
model <- glm( formula = "C ~ Market + SMB + HML" , data = d)
```

The **GLM (general linear model)** function works as follows: it takes the data and formula as arguments. The formula is a string in the form of response ~ terms, where the response is a variable name in the data frame and terms specify the predictors in the model, so it consists of variable names in the data set separated by + operators. This function can also be used for logistic regression, but the default is linear.

The output of the model is as follows:

```
Call:  glm(formula = "C~Market+SMB+HML", data = d)
Coefficients:
(Intercept)        Market           SMB            HML
   0.001476      1.879100      0.401547      -0.263599
Degrees of Freedom: 1001 Total (i.e. Null);  998 Residual
Null Deviance:      5.74
Residual Deviance: 5.364          AIC: -2387
```

The output of the model summary is as follows:

```
summary(model)
Call:
glm(formula = "C~Market+SMB+HML", data = d)
Deviance Residuals:
     Min        1Q     Median        3Q       Max
-0.09344  -0.01104  -0.00289   0.00604   2.26882
Coefficients:
             Estimate Std. Error t value Pr(>|t|)
(Intercept)  0.001476   0.002321   0.636    0.525
Market       1.879100   0.231595   8.114 1.43e-15 ***
SMB          0.401547   0.670443   0.599    0.549
HML         -0.263599   0.480205  -0.549    0.583
---
Signif. codes:  0 '***' 0.001 '**' 0.01 '*' 0.05 '.' 0.1 ' ' 1
(Dispersion parameter for gaussian family taken to be 0.005374535)
    Null deviance: 5.7397  on 1001  degrees of freedom
Residual deviance: 5.3638  on  998  degrees of freedom
AIC: -2387
Number of Fisher Scoring iterations: 2
```

The results show that the only significant factor is the market premium, which means that the stock return of Citigroup seems to moves together with the whole market itself.

To plot the results, this command should be used:

```
estimation <- model$coefficients[1]+
  model$coefficients[2] * d$Market +
  model$coefficients[3]*d$SMB +
  model$coefficients[4]*d$HML
plot(estimation, d$C, xlab = "estimated risk-premium",
  ylab = "observed riks premium",
  main = "Fama-French model for Citigroup")
lines(c(-1, 1), c(-1, 1), col = "red")
```

The following screenshot shows an estimated risk premium of the Fama-French model for Citigroup:

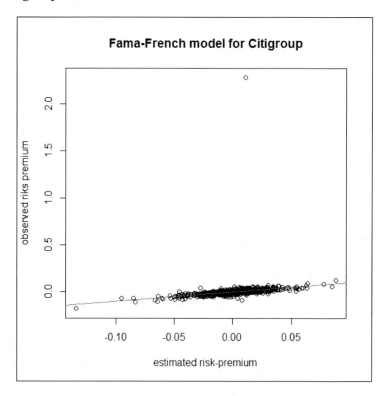

If we have a look at the graph we can see that we have an outlier in the returns. Let's see what happens if we get rid of it, by replacing it with 0.

```
outlier <- which.max(d$C)
d$C[outlier] <- 0
```

If we run the same code again to create the model, and calculate the estimated and observed returns again we get the following results:

```
model_new <- glm( formula = "C ~ Market + SMB + HML" , data = d)
summary(model_new)
Call:
glm(formula = "C ~ Market + SMB + HML", data = d)
```

```
Deviance Residuals:
       Min        1Q     Median        3Q        Max
  -0.091733  -0.007827  -0.000633   0.007972   0.075853
Coefficients:
              Estimate Std. Error t value Pr(>|t|)
(Intercept) -0.0000864  0.0004498  -0.192 0.847703
Market       2.0726607  0.0526659  39.355  < 2e-16 ***
SMB          0.4275055  0.1252917   3.412 0.000671 ***
HML          1.7601956  0.2031631   8.664  < 2e-16 ***
---
Signif. codes:  0 '***' 0.001 '**' 0.01 '*' 0.05 '.' 0.1 ' ' 1
(Dispersion parameter for gaussian family taken to be 0.0001955113)
    Null deviance: 0.55073  on 1001  degrees of freedom
Residual deviance: 0.19512  on  998  degrees of freedom
AIC: -5707.4
Number of Fisher Scoring iterations: 2
```

According to the results, the all the three factors are significant.

The GLM function does not return R^2. For linear regression, the lm function can be used exactly the same way, and we can get from model summary r.squared = 0.6446.

This result indicates that the variables explain more than 64 percent of the variance of the risk-premium of Citi. Let's plot the new results:

```
estimation_new <- model_new$coefficients[1]+
  model_new$coefficients[2]  * d$Market +
  model_new$coefficients[3]*d$SMB +
  model_new$coefficients[4]*d$HML
dev.new()
plot(estimation_new, d$C, xlab = "estimated risk-premium",ylab =
"observed riks premium",main = "Fama-French model for Citigroup")
lines(c(-1, 1), c(-1, 1), col = "red")
```

The output in this case is the following:

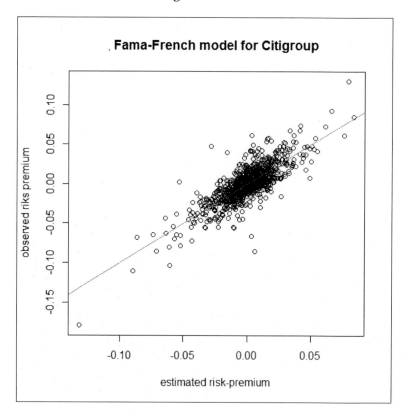

We test the model on another stock, EXEL, as well:

```
d$EXEL <- d$EXEL - d$LIBOR
model2 <- glm( formula = "EXEL~Market+SMB+HML" , data = d)
Call:  glm(formula = "EXEL~Market+SMB+HML", data = d)
Coefficients:
(Intercept)        Market            SMB            HML
  -0.001048      2.038001       2.807804      -0.354592
Degrees of Freedom: 1001 Total (i.e. Null);  998 Residual
Null Deviance:       1.868
Residual Deviance: 1.364          AIC: -3759
```

The output for the model summary is as follows:

```
summary(model2)
Call:
glm(formula = "EXEL~Market+SMB+HML", data = d)
Deviance Residuals:
     Min         1Q     Median         3Q        Max
-0.47367   -0.01480   -0.00088    0.01500    0.25348
Coefficients:
              Estimate Std. Error t value Pr(>|t|)
(Intercept) -0.001773   0.001185  -1.495  0.13515
Market       1.843306   0.138801  13.280  < 2e-16 ***
SMB          2.939550   0.330207   8.902  < 2e-16 ***
HML         -1.603046   0.535437  -2.994  0.00282 **
---
Signif. codes:  0 '***' 0.001 '**' 0.01 '*' 0.05 '.' 0.1 ' ' 1


(Dispersion parameter for gaussian family taken to be 0.001357998)
    Null deviance: 1.8681  on 1001  degrees of freedom
Residual deviance: 1.3553  on  998  degrees of freedom
AIC: -3765.4
Number of Fisher Scoring iterations: 2
```

According to the results, all of the three factors are significant.

The GLM function does not contain R^2. For linear regression, the lm function can be used exactly the same way, and we get r.squared = 0.2723 from model summary. Based on the results, the variables explain more than 27 percent of the variance of the risk premium of EXEL.

To plot the results, the following command can be used:

```
estimation2 <- model2$coefficients[1] +
  model2$coefficients[2] * d$Market +
  model2$coefficients[3] * d$SMB + model2$coefficients[4] * d$HML
plot(estimation2, d$EXEL, xlab = "estimated risk-premium",
  ylab = "observed riks premium",
```

```
main = "Fama-French model for EXEL")
lines(c(-1, 1), c(-1, 1), col = "red")
```

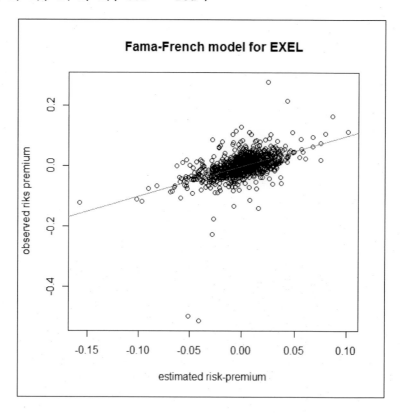

Summary

In this chapter, we saw how a multifactor model can be built and implemented. As a result of a principal component analysis, we identified five independent factors that explained asset returns, but they seemed to be insufficient, given that they explained only 30 percent of the variance. For illustration, we also reproduced the famous Fama-French model on real market data, where, apart from the market factor, two additional firm-specific factors (SMB and HML) were also used. We used built-in functions for principal component analysis and factor analysis, and we have shown how to use a general linear model for regression analysis.

We found that the three factors were significant. Hence, we can conclude that on a more recent sample, the Fama-French factors have explanatory power. We encourage you to develop and test new multifactor pricing formulas that work as the classical ones, or even better.

References

- E.F. Fama, and K.R. French (1996), Multifactor Explanations of asset Pricing Anomalies, Journal of Finance 51, pp. 55-84

- Z. Bodie, A. Kane, and A. Marcus (2008), Essentials of Investment, Edition 7, McGraw-Hill Irwin

- P. Medvegyev, and J. Száz (2010), A meglepetések jellege a pénzügyi piacokon, Bankárképző, Budapest

- P. Wilmott (2007), Paul Wilmott Introduces Quantitative Finance, Edition 2, John Wiley & Sons Ltd, West Sussex

- G. Daróczi, M. Puhle, E. Berlinger, P. Csóka, D. Havran, M, Michaletzky, Zs. Tulassay, K. Váradi and A. Vidovics-Dancs (2013), Introduction to R for Quantitative Finance, Packt Publishing, Birmingham-Mumbai

- S.A. Ross (1976), Return, Risk and Arbitrage: in: Risk and Return in Finance, Cambridge, Mass, Ballinger

- Gy .Walter, E. Berlinger (1999), Faktormodellek az értékpapírpiacokon (Factormodels on securities' markets), Bankszemle, 43(4), pp. 34-43. ISSN 0133-0519

3
Forecasting Volume

Price formation on stock exchanges has been the center of attention of many researchers for several decades now. As a result, there is an abundance of theories, models, and empirical evidence on the price, and although there are always new aspects to discover, we believe that the financial knowledge is fairly comprehensive on the subject. We understand the dynamics of the price reasonably well, and most of us agree that it is rather difficult to forecast.

In contrast, the trading volume, which is another fundamental measure of the trading process on stock exchanges, has been much less researched. The most common equilibrium models on price do not even include volume in their framework of explaining trading activities. It is only recently that researchers appear to be paying increasing attention to volume, and they have already found that its stylized facts allow for much better forecasts compared to price.

This chapter aims to introduce an intra-day forecasting model selected from the available literature, and to provide its implementation in R.

Motivation

The motivation behind gaining a better understanding of volume is not merely theoretical, but it equally has a great practical relevance. On order-driven markets, if a submitted buy (sell) market order is relatively large compared to the market, it will possibly swipe out several price levels; thus, the achieved average price on the entire trade will be higher (lower) than the best price level at the moment of order submission, and the submitter loses money. This phenomenon is often referred to as price impact, and it is well worth making an effort to avoid or at least minimize it.

One way to do this is to perform order splitting, that is, splitting a market order into smaller chunks and submitting them gradually. Among the numerous logics behind splitting, a popular one is the **volume weighted average price (VWAP)** strategy that aims to obtain the daily weighted average price where weights are determined by the volume transacted relative to the total daily volume. Long-term investors would happily settle for an average execution price equal to the daily VWAP, which is considered to be a neutral trading result. However, some investors find it tricky to split their trades throughout the day in a fashion that results in reaching the VWAP, which can only be calculated at the end of the day, so they delegate the problem to brokers. Brokers guarantee to trade on the VWAP, and are paid a fee for this service. This fee also serves as a buffer for tracking errors, which means that the broker that has the most precise forecast of the daily volumes will be the one who can charge the clients the least, because all they have to do is split their trades in similar proportions to their forecasts, and then (assuming the forecasts are perfect) the VWAP will be reached regardless of the price evolution. For brokers, therefore, accurate volume forecasts are considered a valuable business asset that directly affects their profits.

The intensity of trading

The intensity of trading activities can be measured in a number of ways. The most common measure in use is volume, which is simply the number of shares traded during a certain time interval. Given that the liquidity (which shows how easy it is to trade an asset) and therefore the absolute trading activity in each stock is different, the volume expressed in percentage form is a more convenient choice for modeling purposes. This measure is called turnover, which is formally computed from volume, as follows:

$$x_{i,t} = \frac{V_{i,t}}{TSO_{i,t}} \quad (1)$$

Here, x stands for turnover, V for volume, and TSO for the total shares outstanding; the latter indicates the total number of shares available for public trading. The index i indicates the actual stock, and index t indicates the time interval.

As mentioned earlier, there are several stylized facts documented in volume. An obvious one is that volume is non-negative, given that it measures the number of traded shares. This number is zero, if there are no trades at all, and positive otherwise. Another important stylized fact is the intra-daily U shape registered on several different markets (see *Hmaied, D. M., Sioud, O. B., and Grar, A. (2006)* and *Hussain, S. M. (2011)* for a good overview).

This means that the trading activity tends to be more intense after opening and before closure of the market, than during the rest of the day. There are several possible explanations for this phenomenon, but its existence is very clear.

 The enthusiastic reader might be interested in *Kaastra, I. and Boyd, M. S. (1995)* and *Lux, T. and Kaizoji, T. (2004)*, which propose volume-forecasting models using monthly and daily data respectively. *Brownlees, C. T., Cipollini, F., and Gallo, G. M. (2011)* builds a volume forecasting model for intra-day data, which is of direct relevance to this chapter. Our empirical investigations found that the model detailed in the following section (proposed by *Bialkowski, J., Darolles, S., and Le Fol, G. (2008)*) provides a more precise forecast, so merely due to length limitations, this chapter only elaborates on the latter.

This chapter addresses the intra-day forecasting of stock volumes. There are a few models that can be found in the literature, among which we found that the one presented in *Bialkowski, J., Darolles, S., and Le Fol, G. (2008)* is the most accurate. The following section briefly summarizes the model, providing enough detail to understand the implementation later on.

The volume forecasting model

This section explains the intra-day volume forecasting model proposed by *Bialkowski, J., Darolles, S., and Le Fol, G. (2008)*.

They use CAC40 data to test their model, including the turnover of every stock in the index as of September 2004. Trades are aggregated into 20-minute time slots, resulting in 25 observations each day.

Turnover is decomposed into two additive components. The first one is the seasonal component (the U shape) that represents the expected level of turnover on an average day for each stock. Given that every day is a little different from the average, there is a second one, the dynamic component, which shows the expected deviation from the average on a specific day.

The decomposition is carried out using the factor model of *Bai, J. (2003)*. The initial problem is as follows:

$$X = F\Lambda' + e = K + e \quad (2)$$

Here, the X *(TxN)*-sized matrix contains the initial data, F *(Txr)* is the factor matrix, Λ' *(Nxr)* is the matrix of factor loadings, and e *(TxN)* is the error term. K stands for the common term, T stands for the number of observations, N stands for the number of stocks, and r stands for the number of factors.

The dimension of the XX' matrix is *(TxT)*. After determining its eigenvalues and eigenvectors, Eig contains the eigenvectors that are related to the r largest eigenvalues. The estimated factor matrix is then determined as:

$$\tilde{F} = \sqrt{T}\,Eig\,(3)$$

The transpose of the estimated loadings matrix is calculated as:

$$\tilde{\Lambda}' = \frac{\tilde{F}X}{T}\,(4)$$

Finally, the estimated common component will be:

$$\tilde{K} = \tilde{F}\tilde{\Lambda}'\,(5)$$

Given that the model is additive, the estimated dynamic component simply becomes:

$$\tilde{e} = X - \tilde{K}\,(6)$$

Now that the estimated common and dynamic components are both obtained, the next step is to generate their forecasts. The authors assume that the seasonal (U shape) component is constant throughout the 20-day estimation period (but differs among stocks), so they forecast it according to:

$$\tilde{K}_{t+1,i} = \frac{1}{L}\sum_{l=1}^{L} K_{t+1-25\cdot l,i}\,(7)$$

Knowing that 25 is the number of time slots (data points) each day, this means that for stock i, the forecast for the first time slot tomorrow will be the average of the first time slots during the last L days.

The forecast of the dynamic component is obtained in two different ways. One way is by fitting an AR(1) model, specified as follows:

$$\tilde{e}_{t,i} = c + \phi_1 \tilde{e}_{t-1,i} + \varepsilon_{t,i} \quad (8)$$

Another way is by fitting a SETAR model, specified as:

$$\tilde{e}_{t,i} = \left(c_{1,1} + \phi_{1,2}\tilde{e}_{t-1,i}\right) \cdot I\left(\tilde{e}_{t-1,i}\right) + \left(c_{2,1} + \phi_{2,2}\tilde{e}_{t-1,i}\right) \cdot \left(1 - I\left(\tilde{e}_{t-1,i}\right)\right) + \varepsilon_{t,i} \quad (9)$$

Here, the indicator function is the following:

$$I(x) = \begin{cases} 1 & if \ x \leq \tau \\ 0 & if \ x > \tau \end{cases} \quad (10)$$

This means that if the previous observation does not exceed the τ threshold specified within the model, then the forecast is carried out by using one AR(1) model, and if it does, then the other AR(1) model is used.

After having forecasted both the seasonal and the dynamic components, the forecasted turnover will be the sum of the two:

$$\tilde{X}_{t+1,i} = \tilde{K}_{t+1,i} + \tilde{e}_{t+1,i} \quad (11)$$

Note that we have forecasted the dynamic component in two different ways; therefore, we will have two different forecast results depending on which one we add to the forecast of the seasonal component.

Implementation in R

In this section, we show how to implement the model of *Bialkowski, J., Darolles, S., and Le Fol, G. (2008)* in R. We cover every detail, from loading the data to estimating the model parameters and producing the actual forecasts.

The data

The data we use consists of 10 different stocks from the Dow Jones Industrial Average index (see the next table for an overview). We use the 21 trading days between 06/01/2011 and 06/29/2011. Trading on NYSE and NASDAQ is continuous between 09:30 and 16:00. After aggregating the data into 15-minute time slots, we receive 26 observations every day, and a total of *26 * 21 = 546* observations overall.

We divided the trading day into 26 time slots, whereas the original article defined 25. This is due to the difference in the opening hours of the different markets from where data was drawn. This only changes one single parameter in the model, but some attention must be paid to this detail.

All the used stocks are liquid enough to have positive turnover in each time slot throughout the observed period. However, it should be noted that since the model has an additive structure, zero turnover in some of the slots would not cause any difficulties.

The following table is taken from the source `http://kibot.com/`:

	Ticker	Company	Industry	Sector	Exchange
1	AA	Alcoa, Inc.	Aluminum	Basic Materials	NYSE
2	AIG	American International Group, Inc.	Property and Casualty Insurance	Financial	NYSE
3	AXP	American Express Company	Credit Services	Financial	NYSE
4	BA	Boeing Co.	Aerospace/Defense Products and Services	Industrial Goods	NYSE
5	BAC	Bank of America	Regional - Mid-Atlantic Banks	Financial	NYSE
6	C	Citigroup, Inc.	Money Center Banks	Financial	NYSE
7	CAT	Caterpillar, Inc.	Farm and Construction Machinery	Industrial Goods	NYSE
8	CSCO	Cisco Systems, Inc.	Networking and Communication Devices	Technology	NASDAQ

	Ticker	Company	Industry	Sector	Exchange
9	CVX	Chevron Corporation	Major Integrated Oil and Gas	Basic Materials	NYSE
10	DD	E.I. Du Pont De Nemours and Company	Chemicals - Major Diversified	Basic Materials	NYSE

Stocks included in the data set

Out of the 546 observations, we will use the first 520 (20 days) as the estimation period, and the last 26 (one day) as the forecast period. It is important to keep the actual data for the forecast period so that we can assess the precision of our forecast and compare it to the actual realizations.

As an illustration of the data, see *Figure 3.1* that depicts the first five days (130 observations) of Alcoa.

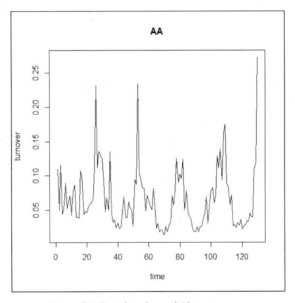

Figure 3.1: First five days of Alcoa turnover

Although every day is a little different, we can clearly see the five separate days indicated by the five U shapes in the turnover graph.

Loading the data

We organized the data in a `.csv` file with the tickers in the header field. The dimension of the data matrix is 546 x 10. The following code loads the data and prints the first five rows and six columns:

```
turnover_data <- read.table("turnover_data.csv", header = T, sep = ";")
format(turnover_data[1:5, 1:6],digits = 3)
```

The output for the top-left segment of the data matrix is shown below. Given that our data shows turnover values (in a percentage form), and not volume, each value is below unity. We can see, for example, that within the first 15 minutes of the sample, 0.11 percent of the total shares outstanding of Alcoa were traded (see Equation (1)).

```
      AA     AIG     AXP     BA     BAC      C
1 0.1101 0.0328 0.0340 0.0310 0.0984 0.0826
2 0.0502 0.0289 0.0205 0.0157 0.0635 0.0493
3 0.1157 0.0715 0.0461 0.0344 0.1027 0.1095
4 0.0440 0.1116 0.0229 0.0228 0.0613 0.0530
5 0.0514 0.0511 0.0202 0.0263 0.0720 0.0836
```

The following code plots the first day of Alcoa turnover. The graph is shown in *Figure 3.2*.

```
plot(turnover_data$AA[1:26], type = "l", main = "AA", xlab = "time",
ylab="turnover")
```

We can recognize the U shape of the first day, but we need to rely a little on our imagination at this point. This is because the U shape is a stylized fact that is only observed on a statistical basis.

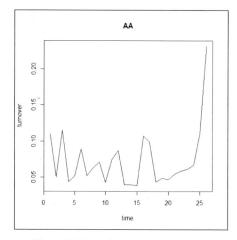

Figure 3.2: First day of Alcoa turnover

We therefore expect the U shape to be more definite on average. The following code plots the average Alcoa turnover throughout the 21 days of the sample. To this end, we transform the first column of the data matrix into a 26*21 matrix, and plot the row averages.

```
AA_average <- matrix(turnover_data$AA, 26, 546/26)
```

```
plot(rowMeans(AA_average), type = "l", main = "AA" , xlab = "time", ylab
= "turnover")
```

The result is shown in *Figure 3.3*, where the U shape is very clearly drawn.

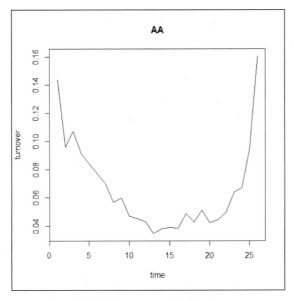

Figure 3.3: 21-day average of Alcoa turnover

Now that the data is loaded, we are ready to implement the model.

The seasonal component

The first step is to determine the seasonal component. As mentioned earlier, we will use the first 520 observations for estimation. The following code creates the appropriate sample matrix from the data frame:

```
n <- 520
m <- ncol(turnover_data)
sample <- as.matrix(turnover_data[1:n, ])
```

Now, we can start the factor decomposition (see Equations (2) to (6)) of *Bai, J. (2003)*. After creating the $S = XX'$ matrix (of dimension 520 x 520), we find its eigenvalues and eigenvectors.

```
S <- sample %*% t(sample)
D <- eigen(S)$values
V <- eigen(S)$vectors
```

Next, we have to determine the number of factors to use (r). The following code plots the eigenvalues in diminishing order:

```
plot(D, main = "Eigenvalues", xlab = "", ylab = "")
```

The result is shown in *Figure 3.4*, where the first eigenvalue clearly dominates all the others. This means that the variance explained by the first eigenvector explains the majority of the variance, so we choose to use a single factor in our model ($r = 1$). As a rule of thumb, we can use as many factors as the number of eigenvalues that are greater than one, but it always remains a subjective decision.

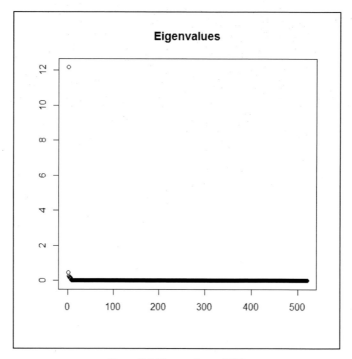

Figure 3.4: Eigenvalues of **XX'**

Using the eigenvector that corresponds to this largest eigenvalue, we can now compute the estimated factor matrix (see Equation (3)).

```
Eig <- V[, 1]
F <- sqrt(n) * Eig
```

Then, we calculate the transpose of the estimated loadings matrix according to Equation (4), and the estimated common (seasonal) component according to Equation (5). Finally, the dynamic (idiosyncratic) component is also calculated (see Equation (6)).

```
Lambda <- F %*% sample / n
K <- F %*% Lambda
IC <- sample - K
```

The dynamic component will be forecasted in the following two subsections, but we still need to forecast the seasonal component here. This will be done according to Equation (7).

```
K26 <- matrix(0, 26, m)

for (i in 1:m) {
    tmp <- matrix(K[,i], 26, n/26)
    K26[,i] <- rowMeans(tmp)
}
```

The previous code calculates 20-day averages for all 26 slots, dealing with one stock at a time, resulting in a 26 x 10 matrix, including one-day seasonal component forecasts for all 10 stocks.

Now, we have the forecasts of the dynamic component left, which will be done in two different ways: by fitting an AR(1) and a SETAR model.

AR(1) estimation and forecasting

In this subsection, we fit AR(1) models to the dynamic component. We will need to specify 10 models, one for each stock. The following code performs the parameter estimations:

```
library(forecast)

models <- lapply(1:m, function(i)
    Arima(IC[, i], order = c(1, 0, 0), method = "CSS"))
coefs <- sapply(models, function(x) x$coef)
round(coefs, 4)
```

Coefficients are collected in the `coefs` variable and printed in the following output, rounded to 4 digits. Coefficients need not necessarily be saved (saving the model would be sufficient) because the `forecast` package has a built-in `forecast` function, and we will make use of this in the following example:

```
       [,1]    [,2]    [,3]    [,4]    [,5]    [,6]    [,7]    [,8]    [,9]   [,10]
[1,] 0.4745 0.4002  0.3171 0.4613 0.4139  0.5091  0.4072 0.4149  0.2643  0.3940
[2,] 0.0000 0.0004 -0.0007 0.0000 -0.0005 -0.0005 0.0002 0.0017 -0.0004 -0.0007
```

AR coefficients for each stock

There are several ways to estimate an AR(1) model in R. Apart from the method mentioned earlier, which is suitable for any ARIMA model, the code below (using the example of Alcoa only) reproduces the same results, but with the use of a different package, which can only handle ARMA (and not ARIMA) models.

```
library("tseries")
arma_mod <- arma(IC[, 1], order = c(1, 0))
```

So the next step is to produce the forecasts for the next day, that is, for the next 26 time slots using the AR(1) models estimated previously. The following code performs this for us:

```
ARf <- sapply(1:m, function(i) forecast(models[[i]], h = 26)$mean)
```

In order to receive the complete forecasts (including both the seasonal and the dynamic components), we simply refer to Equation (11).

```
AR_result <- K26+ARf
```

The full forecasts are now stored in the `AR_result` variable.

SETAR estimation and forecasting

The second method for obtaining forecasts of the dynamic component is through a SETAR model. Again, we need 10 different models for each stock. There is also a package in R for SETAR estimation, so the code becomes as simple as this:

```
library(tsDyn)
setar_mod <- apply(IC,2,setar, 1);
setar_coefs <-  sapply(setar_mod, FUN = coefficients)
round(setar_coefs, 4)
```

Unlike the AR model, we do have to save the coefficients explicitly for the forecast, which is also done by the previous code. The 4-digit rounded values are printed in the following output:.

	[,1]	[,2]	[,3]	[,4]	[,5]	[,6]	[,7]	[,8]	[,9]	[,10]
[1,]	0.0018	-0.0003	-0.0004	0.0001	-0.0163	-0.0062	-0.0067	0.0016	-0.0003	-0.0001
[2,]	0.5914	0.5843	0.4594	0.6160	-0.1371	0.3108	0.1946	0.4541	0.3801	0.5930
[3,]	-0.0016	0.0180	0.0046	0.0061	0.0001	0.0033	0.0011	-0.0040	0.0021	0.0086
[4,]	0.4827	-0.0720	-0.0003	0.1509	0.4315	0.3953	0.3635	0.5241	0.0441	-0.0854
[5,]	0.0063	0.0092	0.0026	0.0036	-0.0141	-0.0054	-0.0103	0.0130	0.0018	0.0057

SETAR coefficients for each stock

The five parameters from top to bottom are the following (see Equation (9)) for details):

1. Intercept (lower regime).
2. AR coefficient (lower regime).
3. Intercept (upper regime).
4. AR coefficient (upper regime).
5. Threshold.

Now, all we have left to do is to forecast the dynamic component for the next 26 time slots using the SETAR model we just described. This is done using the following code:

```
SETARf <- matrix(0, 27, m)
SETARf[1,] <- sample[520,]

for (i in 2:27){
SETARf[i,] <-
(setar_coefs[1,]+SETARf[i-1,]*setar_coefs[2,])*
(SETARf[i-1,] <= setar_coefs[5,]) +
(setar_coefs[3,]+SETARf[i-1,]*setar_coefs[4,])*
(SETARf[i-1,] >  setar_coefs[5,])
}
```

Although we are looking to have forecasts for 26 time slots (that is, for one entire day) for each stock, the SETARf variable has 27 rows because we have to store the last known observation in the first one in order to be able to calculate recursively. Also, note that we calculate row-by-row here, that is, we calculate the next forecast for every stock at the same time, and only then do we move on to the next time slot.

Finally, referring to Equation (11) again, the full forecast for the turnover is as follows:

```
SETAR_result = K26 + SETARf[2:27,]
```

The full forecasts are now stored in the `SETAR_result` variable.

Interpreting the results

We have obtained the turnover forecasts of all 10 stocks for the next day based on the last 20 days. Depending on how we forecast the dynamic component, we have two different results for each stock.

We excluded the last day of our data set from the estimation in order to be able to compare the actual values to the forecasts. The following code helps us do this by generating 10 different plots, one for every stock, using AR(1) for the dynamic component forecasts. The output is shown in *Figure 3.5*.

```
par(mfrow = c(2, 5))
for (i in 1:10) {matplot(cbind(AR_result[, i], turnover_data[521:546,
i]), type = "l", main = colnames(turnover_data)[i], xlab = "", ylab = "",
col = c("red", "black"))}
```

On each plot, the black dotted line depicts the realized turnover of that specific stock, while the red solid line shows the forecasted turnover. As mentioned before, the actual realizations can notably deviate from the stylized fact of the U shape.

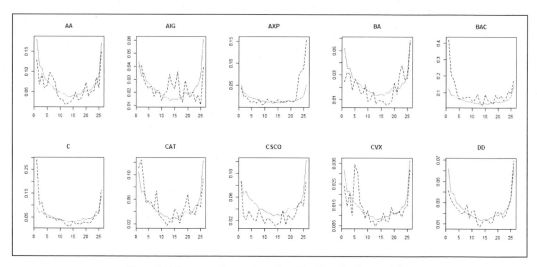

Figure 3.5: Turnover forecasts and realizations for the next day
AR(1) is used on the dynamic component

We can conclude that the forecasts appear fairly precise visually. When the realization resembles a more regular U shape, the forecasts can better approximate it (Alcoa, Caterpillar, Chevron, and Du Pont De Nemours), but the one-off large values will always be unpredictable (like the fifth observation in Chevron). The forecasts perform poorly when the realization becomes unusually asymmetric; that is, either the first few or the last few trades are much larger than the rest (American Express, Bank of America, and Citigroup), but even in those cases, the rest of the day is reasonably well approximated.

This time, we refrain from numerically evaluating the errors of the estimation because we will first need a benchmark to do it, and more importantly, because we only forecasted for one single day; therefore, the results will not be robust anyway.

We can use some code similar to what we used earlier in order to plot the results of the SETAR-based estimation. The output is shown in *Figure 3.6*.

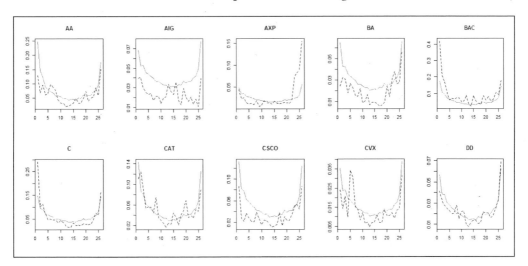

Figure 3.6: Turnover forecasts and realizations for the next day
SETAR is used on the dynamic component

At first glance, the results appear very similar to the previous case, which is understandable, because the forecast of the seasonal component is the same in both of them, and apparently, this dominates the forecast; the rest is merely due to individual deviations. The difference between the AR-based and SETAR-based forecasts is more pronounced towards the beginning of the day.

If we observe the first and the last data points of the day in *Figures 3.5* and *Figure 3.6*, we can find a number of stocks (Alcoa, Bank of America, Citigroup, Caterpillar, Cisco, and Du Pont De Nemours) where the forecast for the last point (and mostly throughout the day) is similar, while the forecast for the first point is significantly larger in the case of SETAR. The most noticeable difference between the two forecasts is in the American International and Boeing stocks, where SETAR produces higher values throughout the day.

Summary

In this chapter, we presented an intra-day volume forecasting model and its implementation in R using data from the DJIA index. Due to length limitations, we selected the one model from the literature that we believe is the most accurate when used to predict stock volumes. The model uses turnover instead of volume for convenience, and separates a seasonal component (U shape) and a dynamic component, and forecasts these two separately. The dynamic component is forecasted in two different ways, fitting an AR(1) and a SETAR model. Similarly to the original article, we do not declare one to be better than the other, but we visually show the results and find them to be acceptably accurate. The original article convincingly proves the model to be better than a carefully selected benchmark, but we leave it to the reader to examine that, because we only used a short data set for illustration, which is not suitable to obtain robust results.

References

- **Bai, J. (2003)**: Inferential theory for factor models of large dimensions. Econometrica, 71:135-171.

- **Bialkowski, J., Darolles, S., and Le Fol, G. (2008)**: Improving VWAP strategies: A dynamic volume approach. Journal of Banking & Finance, 32:1709-1722.

- **Brownlees, C. T., Cipollini, F., and Gallo, G. M. (2011)**: Intra-daily volume modeling and prediction for algorithmic trading. Journal of Financial Econometrics, 9:489-518.

- **Hmaied, D. M., Sioud, O. B., and Grar, A. (2006)**: Intra-daily and weekly patterns of bid-ask spreads, trading volume and volatility on the Tunisian Stock Exchange. Banque & Marchés, 84:35-44.

- **Hussain, S. M. (2011)**: The intraday behavior of bid-ask spreads, trading volume, and return volatility: Evidence from DAX30. International Journal of Economics and Finance, 3:23-34.

- **Kaastra, I. and Boyd, M. S. (1995)**: Forecasting futures trading volume using neural networks. The Journal of Futures Markets, Vol. 15, No. 8,:953-970.

- **Lux, T. and Kaizoji, T. (2004)**: Forecasting volatility and volume in the Tokyo stock market: The advantage of long memory models. Economics working paper, Christian-Albrechts-Universität Kiel, Department of Economics.

4
Big Data – Advanced Analytics

In this chapter, we will deal with one of the biggest challenges of high-performance financial analytics and data management; that is, how to handle large datasets efficiently and flawlessly in R.

Our main objective is to give a practical introduction on how to access and manage large datasets in R. This chapter does not focus on any particular financial theorem, but it aims to give practical, hands-on examples to researchers and professionals on how to implement computationally - intensive analyses and models that leverage large datasets in the R environment.

In the first part of this chapter, we explained how to access data directly for multiple open sources. R offers various tools and options to load data into the R environment without any prior data-management requirements. This part of the chapter will guide you through practical examples on how to access data using the `Quandl` and `qualtmod` packages. The examples presented here will be a useful reference for the other chapters of this book. In the second part of this chapter, we will highlight the limitation of R to handle big data and show practical examples on how to load a large amount of data in R with the help of big memory and `ff` packages. We will also show how to perform essential statistical analyses, such as K-mean clustering and linear regression, using large datasets.

Getting data from open sources

Extraction of financial time series or cross-sectional data from open sources is one of the challenges of any academic analysis. While several years ago, the accessibility of public data for financial analysis was very limited, in recent years, more and more open access databases are available, providing huge opportunities for quantitative analysts in any field.

In this section, we will present the Quandl and quantmod packages, two specific tools that can be used to seamlessly access and load financial data in the R environment. We will lead you through two examples to showcase how these tools can help financial analysts to integrate data directly from sources without any prior data management.

Quandl is an open source website for financial time series, indexing over millions of financial, economic, and social datasets from 500 sources. The Quandl package interacts directly with the Quandl API to offer data in a number of formats usable in R. Besides downloading data, users can also upload and edit their own data, as well as search in any of the data sources directly from R.upload and search for any data.

In the first simple example, we will show you how to retrieve and plot exchange rate time series with Quandl in an easy way. Before we can access any data from Quandl, we need to install and load the Quandl package using the following commands:

```
install.packages("Quandl")
library(Quandl)
library(xts)
```

We will download the currency exchange rates in EUR for USD, CHF, GBP, JPY, RUB, CAD, and AUD between January 01, 2005 and May 30, 2014. The following command specifies how to select a particular time series and period for the analysis:

```
currencies <- c( "USD", "CHF", "GBP", "JPY", "RUB", "CAD", "AUD")
currencies <- paste("CURRFX/EUR", currencies, sep = "")
currency_ts <- lapply(as.list(currencies), Quandl, start_date="2005-01-
01",end_date="2013-06-07", type="xts")
```

As the next step, we will visualize the exchange rate evolution of four selected exchange rates, USD, GBP, CAD, and AUD, using the matplot() function:

```
Q <- cbind(
currency_ts[[1]]$Rate,currency_ts[[3]]$Rate,currency_
ts[[6]]$Rate,currency_ts[[7]]$Rate)
```

```
matplot(Q, type = "l", xlab = "", ylab = "", main = "USD, GBP, CAD, AUD",
xaxt = 'n', yaxt = 'n')
ticks = axTicksByTime(currency_ts[[1]])
abline(v = ticks,h = seq(min(Q), max(Q), length = 5), col = "grey", lty =
4)
axis(1, at = ticks, labels = names(ticks))
axis(2, at = seq(min(Q), max(Q), length = 5), labels = round(seq(min(Q),
max(Q), length = 5), 1))
legend("topright", legend = c("USD/EUR", "GBP/EUR", "CAD/EUR", "AUD/
EUR"), col = 1:4, pch = 19)
```

The following screenshot displays the output of the preceding code:

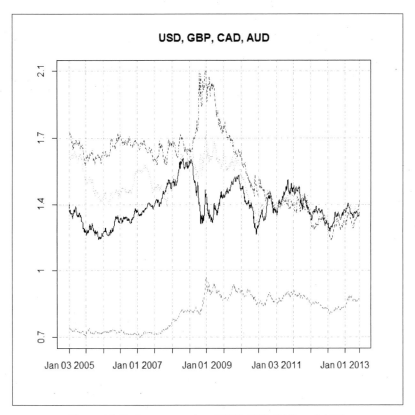

Figure 4.1: Exchange rate plot of USD, GBP, CAD, and AUD

In the second example, we will demonstrate the usage of the `quantmod` package to access, load, and investigate data from open sources. One of the huge advantages of the quantmod package is that it works with a variety of sources and accesses data directly for Yahoo! Finance, Google Finance, **Federal Reserve Economic Data (FRED)**, or the Oanda website.

In this example, we will access the stock price information of BMW and analyze the performance of the car-manufacturing company since 2010:

```
library(quantmod)
```

From the Web, we will obtain the price data of BMW stock from Yahoo! Finance for the given time period. The `quantmod` package provides an easy-to-use function, `getSymbols()`, to download data from local or remote sources. As the first argument of the function, we need to define the character vector by specifying the name of the symbol loaded. The second one specifies the environment where the object is created:

```
bmw_stock<- new.env()
getSymbols("BMW.DE", env = bmw_stock, src = "yahoo", from =
as.Date("2010-01-01"), to = as.Date("2013-12-31"))
```

As the next step, we need to load the `BMW.DE` variable from the `bmw_stock` environment to a vector. With the help of the `head()` function, we can also show the first six rows of the data:

```
BMW<-bmw_stock$BMW.DE
head(BMW)
```

	BMW.DE.Open	BMW.DE.High	BMW.DE.Low	BMW.DE.Close	BMW.DE.Volume
2010-01-04	31.82	32.46	31.82	32.05	1808100
2010-01-05	31.96	32.41	31.78	32.31	1564100
2010-01-06	32.45	33.04	32.36	32.81	2218600
2010-01-07	32.65	33.20	32.38	33.10	2026100
2010-01-08	33.33	33.43	32.51	32.65	1925800
2010-01-11	32.99	33.05	32.11	32.17	2157800

	BMW.DE.Adjusted
2010-01-04	29.91
2010-01-05	30.16
2010-01-06	30.62
2010-01-07	30.89
2010-01-08	30.48
2010-01-11	30.02

The `quantmod` package is also equipped with a finance charting ability. The `chartSeries()` function allows us to not only visualize but also interact with the charts. With its expanded functionality, we can also add a wide range of technical and trading indicators to a basic chart; this is a very useful functionality for technical analysis.

In our example, we will add the Bollinger Bands using the `addBBands()` command and the MACD trend-following momentum indicator using the `addMACD()` command to get more insights on the stock price evolution:

```
chartSeries(BMW,multi.col=TRUE,theme="white")
addMACD()
addBBands()
```

The following screenshot displays the output of the preceding code:

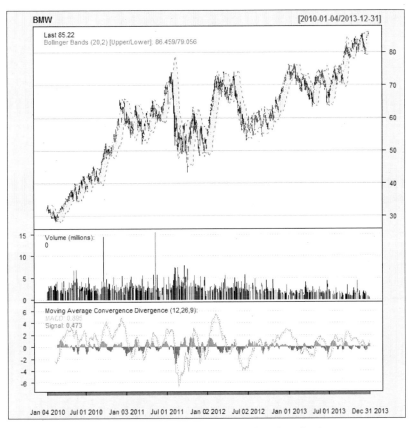

Figure 4.2: BMW stock price evolution with technical indicators

Finally, we will calculate the daily log return of the BMW stock for the given period. We would also like to investigate whether the returns have normal distribution. The following figure shows the daily log returns of the BMW stock in the form of a normal Q-Q plot:

```
BMW_return <-
log(BMW$BMW.DE.Close/BMW$BMW.DE.Open)
qqnorm(BMW_return, main = "Normal Q-Q Plot of BMW daily log return",
 xlab = "Theoretical Quantiles",
        ylab = "Sample Quantiles", plot.it = TRUE, datax = FALSE
 )
qqline(BMW_return, col="red")
```

The following screenshot displays the output of the preceding code. It shows the daily log returns of the BMW stock in the form of a normal Q-Q plot:

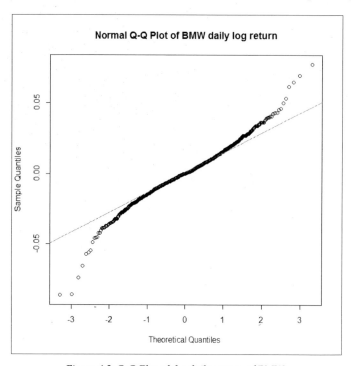

Figure 4.3: Q-Q Plot of the daily return of BMW

Introduction to big data analysis in R

Big data refers to the situations when volume, velocity, or a variety of data exceeds the abilities of our computation capacity to process, store, and analyze them. Big data analysis has to deal not only with large datasets but also with computationally intensive analyses, simulations, and models with many parameters.

Leveraging large data samples can provide significant advantages in the field of quantitative finance; we can relax the assumption of linearity and normality, generate better perdition models, or identify low-frequency events.

However, the analysis of large datasets raises two challenges. First, most of the tools of quantitative analysis have limited capacity to handle massive data, and even simple calculations and data-management tasks can be challenging to perform. Second, even without the capacity limit, computation on large datasets may be extremely time consuming.

Although R is a powerful and robust program with a rich set of statistical algorithms and capabilities, one of the biggest shortcomings is its limited potential to scale to large data sizes. The reason for this is that R requires the data that it operates on to be first loaded into memory. However, the operating system and system architecture can only access approximately 4 GB of memory. If the dataset reaches the RAM threshold of the computer, it can literally become impossible to work with on a standard computer with a standard algorithm. Sometimes, even small datasets can cause serious computation problems in R, as R has to store the biggest object created during the analysis process.

R, however, has a few packages to bridge the gap to provide efficient support for big data analysis. In this section, we will introduce two particular packages that can be useful tools to create, store, access, and manipulate massive data.

First, we will introduce the `bigmemory` package that is a widely used option for large-scale statistical computing. The package and its sister packages (`biganalytics`, `bigtabulate`, and `bigalgebra`) address two challenges in handling and analyzing massive datasets: data management and statistical analysis. The tools are able to implement massive matrices that do not fit in the R runtime environment and support their manipulation and exploration.

An alternative for the bigmemory package is the `ff` package. This package allows R users to handle large vectors and matrices and work with several large data files simultaneously. The big advantage of `ff` objects is that they behave as ordinary R vectors. However, the data is not stored in the memory; it is a resident on the disk.

In this section, we will showcase how these packages can help R users overcome the limitations of R to cope with very large datasets. Although the datasets we use here are simple in size, they effectively shows the power of big data packages.

K-means clustering on big data

Data frames and matrices are easy-to-use objects in R, with typical manipulations that execute quickly on datasets with a reasonable size. However, problems can arise when the user needs to handle larger data sets. In this section, we will illustrate how the `bigmemory` and `biganalytics` packages can solve the problem of too large datasets, which is impossible to handle by data frames or data tables.

 The latest updates of `bigmemory`, `biganalytics`, and `biglm` packages are not available on Windows at time of writing this chapter. The examples shown here assume that R Version 2.15.3 is the current state-of-the-art version of R for Windows.

In the following example, we will perform K-means clustering on large datasets. For illustrative purposes, we will use the Airline Origin and Destination Survey data of the U.S. Bureau of Transportation Statistics. The datasets contain the summary characteristics of more than 3 million domestic flights, including the itinerary fare, number of passengers, originating airport, roundtrip indicator, and miles flown, in a `csv` format.

Loading big matrices

Reading dataset from `csv` files can be easily executed by the `read.csv()` file. However, when we have to handle larger datasets, the reading time of any file can become quite substantial. With some careful options, however, the data-loading functionality of R can be significantly improved.

One option is to specify correct types in `colClasses = argument` when loading data to R; this will result in a faster conversion of external data. Also, the NULL specification of columns that are not needed for the analysis can significantly decrease the time and memory consumed to load the data.

However, if the dataset reaches the RAM threshold of the computer, we need to adopt more memory-efficient data-leading options. In the following example, we will show how the bigmemory package can handle this task.

First of all, we will install and load the required `bigmemory` and `biganalytics` packages to perform the K-means cluster analysis on big data:

```
install.packages("bigmemory")
install.packages("biganalytics")
library(bigmemory)
library(biganalytics)
```

We used the `read.big.matrix` function to import the downloaded dataset in R from the local system. The function handles data not as a data frame but as matrix-like objects, which we need to turn into a matrix with the `as.matrix` function:

```
x<-read.big.matrix( "FlightTicketData.csv", type='integer', header=TRUE,
backingfile="data.bin",descriptorfile="data.desc")
xm<-as.matrix(x)
nrow(x)
[1] 3156925
```

Big data K-means clustering analysis

The format of the big data K-means function in R is `bigkmeans` (*x, centers*), where *x* is a numeric dataset (big data matrix object), and centers is the number of clusters to extract. The function returns the cluster memberships, centroids, **within cluster sum of squares (WCSS)**, and cluster sizes. The `bigkmeans()` function works either on regular R matrix objects or on `big.matrix` objects.

We will determine the number of clusters based on the percentage of variance explained by each cluster; therefore, we will plot the percentage of variance explained by the clusters versus the number of clusters:

```
res_bigkmeans <- lapply(1:10, function(i) {
 bigkmeans(x, centers=i,iter.max=50,nstart=1)
 })
```

```
lapply(res_bigkmeans, function(x) x$withinss)
var <- sapply(res_bigkmeans, function(x) sum(x$withinss))
plot(1:10, var, type = "b", xlab = "Number of clusters", ylab =
"Percentage of variance explained")
```

The following screenshot displays the output of the preceding code:

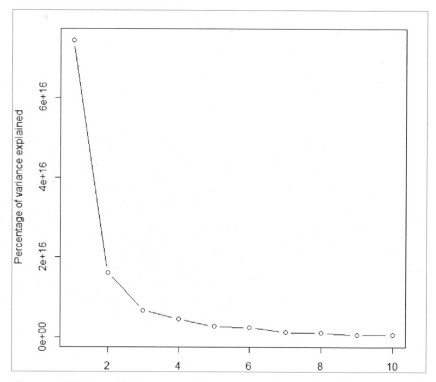

Figure 4.4: Plot the within cluser sums of squares versus the number of clusters extracted

The sharp decrease from 1 to 3 clusters (with little decrease thereafter) suggests a three-cluster solution. Therefore, we will perform the big data K-means cluster analysis with three clusters:

```
res_big<-bigkmeans(x, centers=3,iter.max=50,nstart=1)
res_big
K-means clustering with 3 clusters of sizes 919959, 1116275, 1120691
```

```
Cluster means:
         [,1]      [,2]     [,3]     [,4]      [,5]       [,6]      [,7]
[,8]
[1,] 2.663235 12850.78 1285081 32097.61 0.6323662 0.03459393 2.084982
2305.836
[2,] 2.744241 14513.19 1451322 32768.11 0.6545699 0.02660276 1.974971
2390.292
[3,] 2.757645 11040.08 1104010 30910.66 0.6813850 0.03740460 1.989817
2211.801
         [,9]
[1,] 1.929160
[2,] 1.930394
[3,] 1.949151


Clustering vector:
[1] 3 3 3 3 3 3 1 1 1 1 1 1 1 1 1 1 1 1 1 2 2 2 2 2 2 2 2 3 3 3 3 3 3 3
3
[37] 3 3 3 3 3 3 3 3 3 3 1 1 1 1 1 1 2 2 2 2 3 3 3 3 3 1 1 1 1 1 1 1 1 1
1 1
[73] 1 2 2 2 2 2 2 3 3 3 1 2 2 3 3 3 1 1 1 1 1 1 2 2
Within cluster sum of squares by cluster:
[1] 2.010160e+15 2.466224e+15 2.183142e+15


Available components:

[1] "cluster"  "centers"  "withinss" "size"
```

The bigkmeans() function also works with ordinary matrix objects, offering a faster calculation than the kmeans() function.

To test this hypothesis, we will measure the average execution time of the bigkmeans() and kmeans() functions with different dataset sizes:

```
size<-round(seq(10,2500000,length=20))
nsize<-length(size)
calc.time <- matrix(NA, nrow=nsize, ncol=2)
for (i in 1:nsize) {
 size.i<-size[i]
```

```
 xm.i<-xm[1:size.i,]
vec1=rep(0,10)
vec2=rep(0,10)
for (j in 1:10) {
vec1[j]<-system.time(kmeans(xm.i,centers=3,iter.max=50,nstart=1))[3]
vec2[j]<-system.time(bigkmeans(xm.i,centers=3,iter.max=50,nstart=1))[3]
}
calc.time[i,1]<-mean(vec1)
calc.time[i,2]<-mean(vec2)
}
```

The following screenshot displays the output of the preceding code:

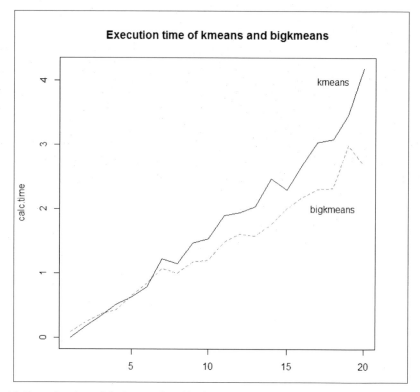

Figure 4.5: Execution time of the kmeans() and bigkmeans() function according to the size of the dataset

Calculating the average execution time of the two functions takes substantial time. The preceding figure, however, reveals that bigkmeans() works more efficiently with larger datasets than the kmeans() function, thus reducing the calculation time of R in the analysis.

Big data linear regression analysis

In this section, we will illustrate how to load large datasets directly from a URL with the help of the `ff` package and how to interact with a `biglm` package to fit a general linear regression model to the datasets that are larger than the memory. The `biglm` package can effectively handle datasets even if they overload the RAM of the computer, as it loads data into memory in chunks. It processes the last chunk and updates the sufficient statistics required for the model. It then disposes the chunk and loads the next one. This process is repeated until all the data is processed in the calculation.

The following example examines the unemployment compensation amount as a linear function of a few social-economic data.

Loading big data

To perform a big data linear regression analysis, we first need to install and load the `ff` packages, which we will use to open large files in R, and the `biglm` package, which we will use to fit the linear regression model on our data:

```
install.packages("ff")
install.packages("biglm")
library(ff)
library(biglm)
```

For the big data linear regression analysis, we used the Individual Income Tax ZIP Code Data provided by the U.S government agency, **Internal Revenue Service (IRS)**. ZIP code-level data shows selected income and tax items classified by the state, ZIP code, and income classes. We used the 2012 data of the database; this database is reasonable in size but allows us to highlight the functionality of the big data packages.

We will directly load the required dataset into R from the URL with the following command:

```
download.file("http://www.irs.gov/file_source/pub/irs-soi/12zpallagi.
csv","soi.csv")
```

Once we have downloaded the data, we will use the `read.table.ffdf` function that reads the files into an `ffdf` object that is supported by the `ff` package. The `read.table.ffdf` function works very much like the `read.table` function. It also provides convenient options to read other file formats, such as `csv`:

```
x <- read.csv.ffdf(file="soi.csv",header=TRUE)
```

After we have converted the dataset into an `ff` object, we will load the `biglm` package to perform the linear regression analysis.

Leveraging the dataset of almost 1,67,000 observations along 77 different variables, we will investigate whether the location-level amount of unemployment compensation (defined as variable A02300) can be explained by the total salary and wages amount (A00200), the number of residents by income category (AGI_STUB), the number of dependents (the NUMDEP variable), and the number of married people (MARS2) in the given location.

Fitting a linear regression model on large datasets

For the linear regression analysis, we will use the `biglm` function; therefore, before we specify our model, we need to load the package:

```
require(biglm)
```

As the next step, we will define the formula and fit the model on our data. With the summary function, we can obtain the coefficients and the significance level of the variable of the fitted model. As the model output does not include the R-square value, we need to load the R-square value of the model with a separate command:

```
mymodel<-biglm(A02300 ~ A00200+AGI_STUB+NUMDEP+MARS2,data=x)
summary(mymodel)
Large data regression model: biglm(A02300 ~ A00200 + AGI_STUB + NUMDEP +
MARS2, data = x)
Sample size =  166904
              Coef     (95%      CI)      SE       p
(Intercept) 131.9412  44.3847 219.4977 43.7782 0.0026
A00200       -0.0019  -0.0019  -0.0018  0.0000 0.0000
AGI_STUB    -40.1597 -62.6401 -17.6794 11.2402 0.0004
NUMDEP        0.9270   0.9235   0.9306  0.0018 0.0000
MARS2        -0.1451  -0.1574  -0.1327  0.0062 0.0000
A00200       -0.0019  -0.0019  -0.0018  0.0000 0.0000
summary(mymodel)$rsq
[1] 0.8609021
```

We can conclude from the regression model coefficient output that all the variables contribute significantly to the model. The independent variables explain 86.09 percent of the total variance of the unemployment compensation amount, indicating a good fit of the model.

Summary

In this chapter, we applied R to access data from open sources and perform various analyses on large datasets. The examples presented here aimed to be a practical guide to empirical researchers who handle a large amount of data.

First, we introduced useful methods for open source data integration. R has powerful options to directly access data for financial analysis without any prior data-management requirement. Second, we discussed how to handle big data in an R environment. Although R has fundamental limitations in handling large datasets and performing computationally intensive analyses and simulations, we introduced specific tools and packages that can bridge this gap. We presented two examples on how to perform K-means clustering and how to fit linear regression models on big data. This is the last chapter of the first part in this book. Next we will look at FX derivatives.

References

- **Adler, D., Nenadic, O., Zucchini, W.,Gläser, C. (2007)**: The ff package: Handling Large Data Sets in R with Memory Mapped Pages of Binary Flat Files

- **Enea, M. (2009)**: Fitting Linear Models and Generalized Linear Models with large data sets in R. In book of short papers, conference on "Statistical Methods for the analysis of large data-sets", Italian Statistical Society, Chieti-Pescara, 23-25 September 2009, 411-414.

- **Kane, M.,Emerson, JW., Weston (2010)**: The Bigmemory Project, Yale University

- **Kane, M.,Emerson, JW., Weston, S. (2013)**: Scalable Strategies for Computing with Massive Data. Journal of Statistical Software , Vol. 55, Issue 14

- **Lumley, T. (2009) biglm**: bounded memory linear and generalized linear models. R package version 0.7

5
FX Derivatives

FX derivatives (or foreign exchange derivatives) are financial derivative products whose payoff is a function of the exchange rate of two (or more) currencies. Like derivatives in general, FX derivatives can be grouped in three main categories: futures, swaps, and options. In this chapter, we will only deal with option-type derivatives. We will start with a straightforward generalization of the basic Black-Scholes model, and will show how to price a simple European call or put currency option. Afterwards, we will discuss the pricing of exchange options and quanto options.

Throughout this chapter, we will assume that you have some basic knowledge about derivative pricing, especially the Black-Scholes model and risk-neutral valuation. Occasionally, we will refer to some mathematic relationships often used in quantitative finance (such as Itô's lemma or Girsanov theorem), but a deep understanding of these theorems is not essential for this chapter. However, those interested in the pure mathematical background of this topic can check out *Medvegyev (2007)*.

Terminology and notations

As we will work with FX rates, it is important to clarify some related terms. Generally, we will denote spot FX rates by S, which measures the price of one currency (called base currency) in terms of another currency (called variable or quote currency). In other words, one unit of the base currency is equivalent to S unit of the variable currency. It is also important to understand how to read FX market quotes. An FX quote on a currency pair is denoted by the abbreviations of the two currencies: a three-letter code for the base currency, followed by another three-letter code for the variable currency. For example, EURUSD=1.25 means that 1 euro is worth 1.25 dollars. This is equivalent to the quote USDEUR=0.8, which means that 1 dollar is worth 0.8 euros. Usually, it depends on historical market conventions that decide which currency is treated as the base currency in a given FX-pair.

In *Chapter 4, Big Data – Advanced Analytics*, we have already seen how to download currency rates from the Internet, so we can use what we have learned to check this on real data.

This short code plots the EURUSD and USDEUR rates to the same plot window:

```
library(Quandl)
library(xts)


EURUSD <- Quandl("QUANDL/EURUSD",
    start_date="2014-01-01",end_date="2014-07-01", type="xts")
USDEUR <- Quandl("QUANDL/USDEUR",
    start_date="2014-01-01",end_date="2014-07-01", type="xts")


dev.new(width = 15, height = 8)
par(mfrow = c(1, 2))
plot(USDEUR)
plot(EURUSD)
```

Here, we can see the result in the following image:

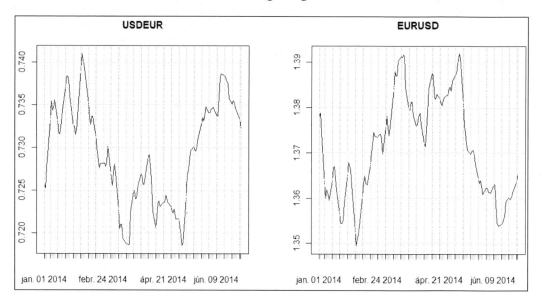

We can also check out the first few lines of the data:

```
USDEUR[1:5,]
```

	Rate	High (est)	Low (est)
2014-01-01	0.725711	0.73392	0.71760
2014-01-02	0.725238	0.73332	0.71725
2014-01-03	0.727714	0.73661	0.71892
2014-01-06	0.733192	0.00000	0.00000
2014-01-07	0.735418	0.00000	0.00000

```
EURUSD[1:5,]
```

	Rate	High (est)	Low (est)
2014-01-01	1.37791	0.0000	0.0000
2014-01-02	1.37876	1.3949	1.3628
2014-01-03	1.37434	0.0000	0.0000
2014-01-06	1.36346	1.3799	1.3473
2014-01-07	1.35990	1.3753	1.3447

Here, we have to say something about notations. So far, we have denoted FX rates by S. However, the price of the underlying asset in derivatives pricing is generally denoted by S, regardless of whether it is a stock or a currency. On the other hand, FX rates are usually denoted by X or sometimes by E (both come from the word "exchange"). Furthermore, the strike or exercise price of an option is also abbreviated by X or E. Now, as the reader, you may have some idea about how challenging it is to use a consistent notation system in this chapter, where the underlying might be a stock or a currency as well, and where stock prices, FX rates, and strike prices might appear at the same time. We decided to adopt the notations of R-functions as much as possible, so in this chapter, the notations we will follow are as follows:

- The price of the underlying will always be S, but if it is not necessarily a currency, we will use numeric or alphabetic indices such as S_1 or S_A
- The strike price will always be X
- The expected value operator will be denoted by E

We strongly recommend that you be careful when reading other literature on this topic, because their notation might differ from ours.

Currency options

European currency options grant the holder the right to buy (call option) or sell (put option) currency at a predetermined exchange rate (strike price or exercise price, *X*), on a specified date (maturity, *T*). These financial assets are also called foreign exchange options (or FX options), but to avoid confusion with the term "exchange option", we prefer the "currency option" terminology.

A basic assumption of the original Black-Scholes model (*Black and Sholes, 1973,* see also *Merton, 1973*) is that the underlying is a stock that pays no dividend. More generally, the results of the model are held only if the underlying does not grant any kind of yield and does not generate any kind of cost either. However, this assumption might be relaxed easily, and an extended version of the Black-Scholes formula is valid for currency options as well, while all the logic and argumentation of the model is unchanged.

The closed form formula for the price of a European currency call option (c_0) is the following:

$$c_0 = S_0 e^{-qT} N(d_1) - X e^{-rT} N(d_2)$$

In the preceding formula, the values of d_1 and d_2 are as follows:

$$d_1 = \frac{\ln\left(\frac{S_0}{X}\right) + \left(r - q + \frac{\sigma^2}{2}\right)T}{\sigma\sqrt{T}} \quad \text{and} \quad d_2 = \frac{\ln\left(\frac{S_0}{X}\right) + \left(r - q - \frac{\sigma^2}{2}\right)T}{\sigma\sqrt{T}}.$$

In the preceding formulas, S_0 is the spot FX rate (the price of one unit of the base currency, expressed in the variable currency), *X* is the strike price, *T* is the time to maturity of the option (in years), σ is the volatility of the FX-rate, *r* and *q* are the risk-free log returns of the variable and the base currency respectively, and *N* denotes the cumulative distribution function of the standard normal distribution. It is easy to see from put-call parity that the price of a European currency put option (p_0) with the same parameters is as follows:

$$p_0 = X e^{-rT} N(-d_2) - S_0 e^{-qT} N(-d_1)$$

The Black-Scholes formula and other option pricing models are available in the `fOptions` package. We can use the `BlackScholesOption` or the `GBSOption` function, both of which are practically the same, and the latter is a shorthand alias for the prior function.

```
BlackScholesOption(TypeFlag, S, X, Time, r, b, sigma,...)
```

Here, `TypeFlag` is either the character `c`, which stands for call or `p` (put). `S` is the current price and `sigma` is the volatility of the underlying. `X` is the strike price and `Time` is the time to maturity.

The other two parameters are a bit tricky because `r` and `b` are the risk-free rates, but the second one is meaningless when pricing options for stocks with the original BS model. This indicates that we must set `b = r` to get the BS stock option model, and set `b = r-q` to get the currency option model or the stock option model with continuous dividend yield. The other parameters of the function are optional and we do not need them.

To see how it works, let's say we have an option for EUR with five years' maturity, and the strike price is 0.7. The USD risk-free rate is `r = 3%` and the EUR risk-free rate is `q = 2%`. 1 USD is currently 0.7450 EUR, so this is the spot price of the underlying. Let the EUR volatility be 20 percent. If we call the `BlackSholesOption` function with the given parameters, we will get the following result:

```
BlackScholesOption ("c", 0.7450, 0.7, 5, 0.03, 0.01, 0.2)

Title:
 Black Scholes Option Valuation

Call:
 GBSOption(TypeFlag = "c", S = 0.745, X = 0.7, Time = 5, r = 0.03,
     b = 0.01, sigma = 0.2)

Parameters:
           Value:
 TypeFlag c
 S         0.745
 X         0.7
 Time      5
 r         0.03
 b         0.01
 sigma     0.2

Option Price:
 0.152222
```

Description:
Thu Aug 07 20:13:28 2014

We can also check out the price of the put option:

```
BlackScholesOption("p", 0.7450, 0.7, 5, 0.03, 0.01, 0.2)
```

Title:
Black Scholes Option Valuation

Call:
```
GBSOption(TypeFlag = "p", S = 0.745, X = 0.7, Time = 5, r = 0.03,
    b = 0.01, sigma = 0.2)
```

Parameters:

	Value:
TypeFlag	p
S	0.745
X	0.7
Time	5
r	0.03
b	0.01
sigma	0.2

Option Price:
0.08061367

Description:
Thu Aug 07 20:15:11 2014

Then, we can also check the consistency with the put-call parity, which takes the following form for the currency options:

```
c - p = S*exp(-r*T)-X*exp(-q*T)
```

Substituting the data, on the left hand-side we have:

```
c - p = 0.152222 - 0.08061367 = 0.07160833,
```

On the right-hand side, we have:

```
0.745*exp(-0.02*5)-0.7*exp(-0.03*5) = 0.07160829.
```

Prices of options are rounded to eight digits, so there is a slight difference.

It is important to mention that pricing a currency option is equivalent to pricing an option with any kind of underlying asset that grants continuous yield. For example, if the underlying is a stock or stock index with dividend yield q per annum, then the pricing formulas are the same as mentioned earlier.

Exchange options

Exchange options grant the holder the right to exchange one risky asset to another risky asset at maturity. It is easy to see that simple options are special forms of exchange options where one of the risky assets is a constant amount of money (the strike price).

The pricing formula of an exchange option was first derived by *Margrabe, 1978*. The model assumptions, the pricing principles, and the resultant formula of `Margrabe` are very similar to (more precisely, the generalization of) those of Black, Scholes, and Merton. Now we will show how to determine the value of an exchange option.

Let's denote the spot prices of the two risky assets at time t by S_{1t} and S_{2t}.

We assume that these prices under the risk neutral probability measure (Q) follow geometric Brownian motion with drifts equal to the risk-free rate (r), shown as

$$dS_1 = rS_1 dt + \sigma_1 S_1 dW_1 \text{ and } dS_2 = rS_2 dt + \sigma_2 S_2 dW_2.$$

Here, W_1 and W_2 are standard Wiener processes under Q, with correlation ρ. You may observe that here, the assets have no yield (for example, stocks that pay no dividend). It is well known (and easy to see with Itô's lemma) that the solutions of the earlier mentioned stochastic differential equations are

$$S_{1t} = S_{10} \exp\left[\left(r - \sigma_1^2 / 2\right)t + \sigma_1 W_{1t}\right] \text{ and } S_{2t} = S_{20} \exp\left[\left(r - \sigma_2^2 / 2\right)t + \sigma_2 W_{2t}\right] \quad (1)$$

We assume that you are familiar with the basics of stochastic processes in one dimension. However, in the case of exchange options, we have a two-dimensional Wiener process, so it is useful to illustrate how this looks.

Two-dimensional Wiener processes

The 2D Wiener process is like a random walk in two dimensions and continuous time. We can easily generate such a process with a few lines of code when the coordinates are independent Wiener processes (not bothering ourselves with scaling the process because it looks the same).

```
D2_Wiener <- function() {
    dev.new(width = 10, height = 4)
    par(mfrow = c(1, 3), oma = c(0, 0, 2, 0))
    for(i in 1:3) {
        W1 <- cumsum(rnorm(100000))
        W2 <- cumsum(rnorm(100000))
        plot(W1,W2, type= "l", ylab = "", xlab = "")
    }
    mtext("2-dimensional Wiener-processes with no correlation",
        outer = TRUE, cex = 1.5, line = -1)
}
```

If we call this function, the output is something like this:

```
 D2_Wiener()
```

Here, we can see the result in the following image:

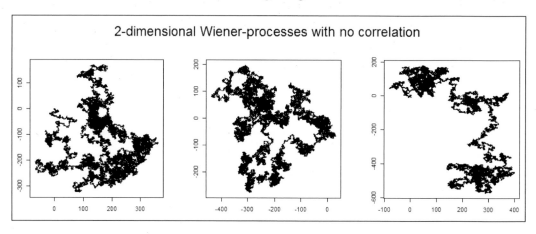

Correlation between the Wiener processes changes the picture dramatically. In the case of positive correlation, the two Wiener processes look like they are moving in the same direction; in the case of negative correlation, they look like they are moving in the opposite direction.

We can modify our function to get correlated Wiener processes. It is easy to see that the following code does the job:

```
Correlated_Wiener <- function(cor) {
    dev.new(width = 10, height = 4)
    par(mfrow = c(1, 3), oma = c(0, 0, 2, 0))
    for(i in 1:3) {
        W1 <- cumsum(rnorm(100000))
        W2 <- cumsum(rnorm(100000))
        W3 <- cor * W1 + sqrt(1 - cor^2) * W2
        plot(W1, W3, type= "l", ylab = "", xlab = "")
    }
    mtext(paste("2-dimensional Wiener-processes (",cor," correlation)",
        sep = ""), outer = TRUE, cex = 1.5, line = -1)
}
```

The result depends on the generated random numbers, but it is pretty much like this:

```
Correlated_Wiener(0.6)
```

Here, we can see the result in the following image:

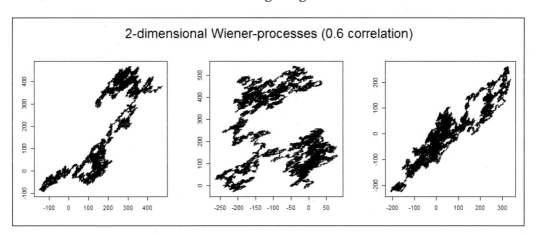

In the previous example, we set the correlation coefficient to 0.6. Now, let's see what happens when it is -0.7:

```
Correlated_Wiener(-0.7)
```

Here, we can see the result in the following image:

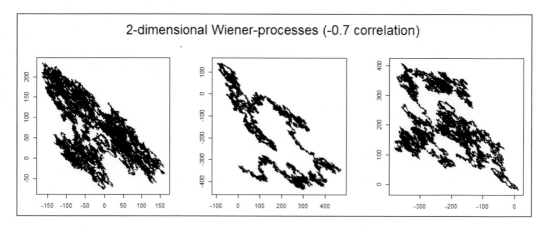

We can clearly see the difference between the processes with different correlations. Now, let's turn our attention back to exchange options.

The Margrabe formula

The payoff H_T of the exchange option at maturity is defined by $H_T = \max\left(S_{1T} - S_{2T}; 0\right)$. According to the basic risk-neutral pricing principle, the value of this payoff (or equivalently, the price of the exchange option, denoted by $\pi(H_T)$) is as follows:

$$\pi\left(H_T\right) = exp\left(-rT\right) \boldsymbol{E}^Q\left[\max\left(S_{1T} - S_{2T}; 0\right)\right]$$

$$= exp\left(-rT\right) \boldsymbol{E}^Q\left[\max\left(S_{2T}\left(\frac{S_{1T}}{S_{2T}} - 1\right); 0\right)\right] =$$

$$= exp\left(-rT\right) \boldsymbol{E}^Q\left[\max\left(S_{2T}\left(S_T - 1\right); 0\right)\right] \quad (2)$$

In Equation (2), S_t (without number 1 or 2 in the index) is defined as the S_{1t}/S_{2t} quotient. In other words, S is the price of S_1 in terms of S_2. If the two risky assets are two currencies, then S is an FX rate, and that is why we use this notation.

To calculate the earlier mentioned expected value, we need to introduce a new measure (R), defined by the following Radon-Nikodym derivative:

$$\frac{dR}{dQ} = \exp\left(\sigma_2 W_{2T} - \frac{1}{2}\sigma_2^2 T\right) = \exp(-rT)\frac{S_{2T}}{S_{20}}$$

Here, the right-hand side of the earlier equation comes from Equation (1) for S_2.

Then, the price of the exchange option will take the following form:

$$\pi\left(H_T\right) = \exp(-rT)\, \boldsymbol{E}^R\left[\max\left(S_{2T}\left(S_T - 1\right);0\right)\frac{dQ}{dR}\right] =$$

$$= S_{20}\, \boldsymbol{E}^R\left[\max\left(S_T - 1;0\right)\right] \ (3)$$

Now, we have to determine what kind of process S follows under R. From Girsanov's theorem, we know that $\hat{W}_{1t} = W_{1t} - \sigma_2\rho t$ and $\hat{W}_{2t} = W_{2t} - \sigma_2 t$ are Wiener processes under R, and their correlation is still ρ. Let's introduce the following two notations:

$$\sigma = \sqrt{\sigma_1^2 + \sigma_2^2 - 2\sigma_1\sigma_2\rho}$$

$$W_t = \frac{1}{\sigma}\left(\sigma_1\hat{W}_{1t} - \sigma_2\hat{W}_{2t}\right)$$

From Lévy's characterisation, we know that W is a Wiener process under R. Now we can determine the equation of S:

$$S_t = \frac{S_{1t}}{S_{2t}} = \frac{S_{10} exp\left[\left(r - \sigma_1^2/2\right)t + \sigma_1 W_{1t}\right]}{S_{20} exp\left[\left(r - \sigma_2^2/2\right)t + \sigma_2 W_{2t}\right]} =$$

$$= \frac{S_{10}}{S_{20}} exp\left[-\frac{1}{2}\left(\sigma_1^2 - \sigma_2^2\right)t + \sigma_1 W_{1t} - \sigma_2 W_{2t}\right] =$$

$$= \frac{S_{10}}{S_{20}} exp\left[-\frac{1}{2}\left(\sigma_1^2 - \sigma_2^2 - \sigma^2 + \sigma^2\right)t + \sigma_1 W_{1t} - \sigma_2 W_{2t}\right] =$$

$$= \frac{S_{10}}{S_{20}} exp\left[\left(\sigma_1^2 - \sigma_1\sigma_2\rho - \frac{1}{2}\sigma^2\right)t + \sigma_1 W_{1t} - \sigma_2 W_{2t}\right] =$$

$$= \frac{S_{10}}{S_{20}} exp\left(-\frac{1}{2}\sigma^2 t + \sigma_1 \hat{W}_{1t} - \sigma_2 \hat{W}_{2t}\right) =$$

$$= \frac{S_{10}}{S_{20}} exp\left(-\frac{1}{2}\sigma^2 t + \sigma W_t\right)$$

This means that S under R is a geometric Brownian motion with zero drift, that is $dS = \sigma S dW$.

Now, if you remember, in Equation (3), we had the following equation for the price of the exchange option:

$$\pi\left(H_T\right) = S_{20} \mathbf{E}^R\left[max\left(S_T - 1; 0\right)\right]$$

Using this relationship for S, the expected value at the right-hand side is the value of a simple call option with an underlying asset S, r is equal to 0, and X is equal to 1. Let's denote the price of this call option simply with c_0. Then $\pi(H_T) = S_{20}c_0$.

Here, c_0 might be determined with the help of the basic Black-Scholes formula, substituting the parameters we just discussed:

$$c_0 = S_0 N(d_1) - 1e^{-0T} N(d_2) =$$

$$= \frac{S_{10}}{S_{20}} N(d_1) - N(d_2)$$

Hence $\pi(H_T) = S_{10} N(d_1) - S_{20} N(d_2)$

where $d_1 = \dfrac{\ln\left(\dfrac{S_{10}}{S_{20}}\right) + \dfrac{\sigma^2}{2}T}{\sigma\sqrt{T}}$ and $d_2 = \dfrac{\ln\left(\dfrac{S_{10}}{S_{20}}\right) - \dfrac{\sigma^2}{2}T}{\sigma\sqrt{T}}$

The previously mentioned formula for $\pi(H_T)$, which is the pricing formula for the exchange option, is called the Margrabe formula. Continuous dividend yields, if applicable, might be inserted into the formula as simply as in the case of the Black-Scholes formula. Without repeating the calculations, we give only the results for this case.

So, let's assume that the risky assets to be exchanged have positive continuous dividend yields denoted by δ_1 and δ_2 respectively. In this case, the processes of their prices under measure Q are as follows:

$$dS_1 = (r - \delta_1)S_1 dt + \sigma_1 S_1 dW_1 \text{ and } dS_2 = (r - \delta_2)S_2 dt + \sigma_2 S_2 dW_2$$

In this case, the Margrabe formula will take the following form:

$$\pi(H_T) = S_{10}e^{-\delta_1 T} N(d_1) - S_{20}e^{-\delta_2 T} N(d_2) \quad (4)$$

Here, $d_1 = \dfrac{\ln\left(\dfrac{S_{10}}{S_{20}}\right) + \left(\delta_2 - \delta_1 + \dfrac{\sigma^2}{2}\right)T}{\sigma\sqrt{T}}$ and $d_2 = \dfrac{\ln\left(\dfrac{S_{10}}{S_{20}}\right) + \left(\delta_2 - \delta_1 - \dfrac{\sigma^2}{2}\right)T}{\sigma\sqrt{T}}$.

Application in R

R has no built-in function for the Margrabe formula. However, it is much more difficult to understand the complex theory behind it than implement the result. Here, we present the `Margrabe` function only in a few lines, which calculates the price of the exchange option based on the parameters shown in the following code:

```
Margrabe <- function(S1, S2, sigma1, sigma2, Time, rho, delta1 = 0,
    delta2 = 0) {
    sigma <- sqrt(sigma1^2 + sigma2^2 - 2 * sigma1 * sigma2 * rho)
    d1 <- ( log(S1/S2) + ( delta2-delta1 + sigma^2/2 ) * Time ) /
        (sigma*sqrt(Time))
    d2 <- ( log(S1/S2) + ( delta2-delta1 - sigma^2/2 ) * Time ) /
        (sigma*sqrt(Time))
    M <- S1*exp(-delta1*Time)*pnorm(d1) - S2*exp(-delta2*Time)*pnorm(d2)
    return(M)
}
```

This is the core body of the function. If we are more demanding or want to develop a user-friendly application, we need to catch possible errors and exceptions. For example, we should include something like this:

```
if min(S1, S2) <= 0) stop("prices must be positive")
```

The execution should also be stopped when volatility is negative, but user-experience and related software design are beyond the scope of this book. We can use this function with valid parameters to see an example of how it works. Let's say we have two risky assets that pay no dividend, one with a price of 100 USD and 20 percent volatility, and the other with a price of 120 USD and 30 percent volatility, and the maturity is two years. At first, let the correlation be 15 percent.

We simply call the `Margrabe` function with the given parameters:

```
Margrabe(100, 120, .2, .3, 2, .15)
[1] 12.05247
```

The result is 12 USD. Now, let's see what happens if one of the assets is riskless, that is, its volatility is 0. Let's call the function with the following parameters:

```
Margrabe(100, 120, .2, 0, 2, 0, 0, 0.03)
[1] 6.566047
```

What does this mean? This product grants us the right to change the first risky asset, which is a stock that costs 100 USD with 20 percent volatility, to the second "risky" asset, which has a price of 120 USD, pays a 3 percent dividend, and has 0 volatility, (so it is a fixed cash amount) with 3 percent interest. Practically, in two years, it would be the right to buy the stock for 120 USD when the risk-free rate is 3 percent. Let's compare the price to the BS price of this call option:

```
BlackScholesOption("c", 100, 120, 2, 0.03, 0.03, .2)
Title:
 Black Scholes Option Valuation
Call:
 GBSOption(TypeFlag = "c", S = 100, X = 120, Time = 2, r = 0.03,
     b = 0.03, sigma = 0.2)
Parameters:
           Value:
 TypeFlag c
 S         100
 X         120
 Time      2
 r         0.03
 b         0.03
 sigma     0.2


Option Price:
 6.566058


Description:
 Tue Aug 05 11:29:57 2014
```

Yes, they are indeed the same. If we set the volatility of the first asset to 0, this practically means that we have a put option for the second asset.

```
Margrabe(100, 120, 0, 0.2, 2, 0, 0.03, 0)
[1] 3.247161
```

The result of the BS formula is as follows:

```
BlackScholesOption("p", 120, 100, 2, 0.03, 0.03, .2)
```

```
Title:

 Black Scholes Option Valuation


Call:

 GBSOption(TypeFlag = "p", S = 120, X = 100, Time = 2, r = 0.03,
     b = 0.03, sigma = 0.2)


Parameters:

           Value:

 TypeFlag p

 S         120

 X         100

 Time      2

 r         0.03

 b         0.03

 sigma     0.2


Option Price:

 3.247153


Description:

 Fri Aug 08 17:38:04 2014
```

In both cases, there is only a numeric error from the fifth digit.

We can also use the Margrabe formula to get the price of the currency option we discussed in the section *Currency Options*. We can check whether the BS formula provided the same price:

```
Margrabe(0.745, 0.7, 0.2, 0, 5, 0.15, 0.02, 0.03)
[1] 0.152222
```

The last thing we need to discuss is how correlation affects the price of the option. To illustrate this, we calculate the Margrabe price of the option for different values of correlation. This can be done with a few lines of code:

```
x <- seq(-1, 1, length = 1000)
y <- rep(0, 1000)
```

```
for (i in 1:1000)
    y[i] <- Margrabe(100, 120, .2, 0.3, 2, x[i])
plot(x, y, xlab = "correlation", ylab = "price",
    main = "Price of exchange option", type = "l", lwd = 3)
```

Here, we can see the result in the following image:

The result is not surprising. When correlation is high, we have the right to switch between identical stocks, which, clearly, is worth nothing. When the correlation is high on the negative side, we have better chances to make a good deal with the option if things go wrong (which means that if our asset decreases, the higher the negative correlation, the higher the chance that the price of the other asset increases and saves us from loss). In other words, in this case, the option is for insurance rather than speculation; we do not have to bear the risk from the price change of the other asset. This is why the option is more valuable when correlation is negative.

Quanto options

The term "**quanto**" is the abbreviation of **quantity adjusting option**. The payoff of quanto derivatives is determined by an asset denominated in one currency, but is paid in another currency.

The best way to understand a quanto product (or any kind of derivative) is to examine its payoff function. It is well known that assuming the underlying asset is a stock that pays no dividend, the payoff of a European call option is as follows:

$$c_T = \max\left(S_{AT} - X; 0\right)$$

Here, S_A is the price of the stock and X is the strike price. Here, c, S_{AT}, and X are denominated in the same currency; let's call it domestic currency.

The payoff of a European call quanto is as follows:

$$H_T = \max\left[S_T\left(S_{AT} - X\right); 0\right]$$

Here, S is a foreign exchange rate. Thus, a call quanto pays the same "quantity" of money as a simple call option, but in another currency — let's call it foreign currency. So, this quantity paid has to be multiplied by an FX rate so that we get the payoff's value in domestic currency. Of course, S has to be the price of the foreign currency in terms of domestic currency. In other words, in the quotation of S, the base currency is the foreign one.

Pricing formula for a call quanto

Pricing a call quanto means determining the value of the earlier payoff. As usual, we will assume that the price of the underlying asset under the risk neutral measure (Q) follows geometric Brownian motion with drift equal to the risk-free domestic rate (r), that is:

$$dS_A = rS_A dt + \sigma_1 S_A dW_1$$

Furthermore, we assume that the FX rate follows a similar process:

$$dS = \mu S dt + \sigma_2 S dW_2$$

In these equations, W_1 and W_2 are standard Wiener processes under Q, with correlation ρ. Let q denote the risk-free foreign rate. This means that the value of one unit of foreign bank deposit at time t is $exp(qt)$. In terms of the domestic currency, this value is as follows:

$$S_t \exp(qt) = S_0 \exp\left[\left(\mu + q - \frac{1}{2}\sigma_2^2\right)t + \sigma_2 W_{2t}\right]$$

Supposing that this is a traded product in the domestic market, its discounted value has to be a martingale under Q. Let's calculate this discounted value:

$$\exp(-rt)S_t \exp(qt) = S_0 \exp\left[\left(\mu + q - r - \frac{1}{2}\sigma_2^2\right)t + \sigma_2 W_{2t}\right]$$

This process is martingale only if $\mu = r - q$, which is under Q.

$$dS = (r - q)Sdt + \sigma_2 SdW_2$$

Now, we will calculate the SS_A product, which we will denote by Y.

$$Y_t = (SS_A)_t =$$

$$= S_0 S_{A0} \exp\left[\left(r - q - \frac{\sigma_2^2}{2}\right)t + \sigma_2 W_{2t} + \left(r - \frac{\sigma_1^2}{2}\right)t + \sigma_1 W_{1t}\right] =$$

$$= S_0 S_{A0} \exp\left[\left(2r - q + \sigma_1\sigma_2\rho - \frac{\sigma_3^2}{2}\right)t + \sigma_3 W_{3t}\right]$$

Here, $\sigma_3 = \sqrt{\sigma_1^2 + \sigma_2^2 + 2\sigma_1\sigma_2\rho}$ and $W_{3t} = \dfrac{\sigma_1 W_{1t} + \sigma_2 W_{2t}}{\sigma_3}$.

The correlation $\hat{\rho}$ between W_2 and W_3 is $\hat{\rho} = \dfrac{\sigma_1\rho + \sigma_2}{\sigma_3}$.

Consequently, $dY = \left(2r - q + \sigma_1\sigma_2\rho\right)Ydt + \sigma_3 YdW_3$.

Now, it is important to notice that the call quanto is a special exchange option, and hence, might be priced with Margrabe's formula. We only have to identify the two risky assets to be exchanged upon exercising the option, and the related parameters. From the payoff function of the quanto, it is easy to see that the first risky asset is $SS_A = Y$, while the second one is XS (both expressed in domestic currency). Since the drift components of these processes under Q are not simply the risk-free domestic rate, we have to use the `Margrabe` formula with dividend yields. From the earlier calculations, we can see that the Y process should be handled as if the dividend yield was $q - r - \rho\sigma_1\sigma_2$, while in case of XS, it is simply q. The only remaining parameter to be determined is σ. With straightforward substitutions, we have the following calculation:

$$\sigma = \sqrt{\sigma_3^2 + \sigma_2^2 - 2\sigma_3\sigma_2\hat{\rho}} =$$

$$= \sqrt{\sigma_1^2 + \sigma_2^2 + 2\rho\sigma_1\sigma_2 + \sigma_2^2 - 2\sigma_2\left(\sigma_1\rho + \sigma_2\right)} =$$

$$= \sqrt{\sigma_1^2} = \sigma_1$$

Summarizing all these results, we have to use the `Margrabe` formula (given in Equation (4)) with the substitutions $S_1 = Y = SS_A$, $S_2 = XS$, $\delta_1 = q - r - \rho\sigma_1\sigma_2$, $\delta_2 = q$, and $\sigma = \sigma_1$.

Hence, the price of the call quanto is as follows:

$$\pi\left(H_T\right) = S_0 S_{A0} e^{-\left(q - r - \rho\sigma_1\sigma_2\right)T} N\left(d_1\right) - XS_0 e^{-qT} N\left(d_2\right)$$

In the earlier equation, d_1 and d_2 were as follows:

$$d_1 = \frac{\ln\left(\frac{S_{A0}}{X}\right) + \left(r + \rho\sigma_1\sigma_2 + \frac{\sigma_1^2}{2}\right)T}{\sigma_1\sqrt{T}} \text{ and } d_2 = \frac{\ln\left(\frac{S_{A0}}{X}\right) + \left(r + \rho\sigma_1\sigma_2 - \frac{\sigma_1^2}{2}\right)T}{\sigma_1\sqrt{T}}.$$

Pricing a call quanto in R

Let's see an example to price a call quanto in R. Our favorite stock is priced at 100 USD and 20 percent volatility. We need a call option with 90 USD, which is paid in EURs in three years. The USD risk-free rate is `r = 2%` and the EUR risk-free rate is `q = 3%`. Currently, 1 USD is equal to 0.7467 EUR. The EUR volatility is 15%, and the correlation between the stock price and the USDEUR exchange rate is 10%.

If in three years the price of the stock is higher than 90 USD, the difference is paid in EUR. If, for instance, the price is 110 USD in 3 years, we will get 20 EURs. On the current FX rate, it is `20*0.7467 = 26.78093 USD`, but if the EURUSD exchange rate is different in three years, for example, USDEUR is equal to 0.7, this equals 28.57143 USD. So the payoff can be different in USD, but we eliminated the FX rate risk if we want to be paid in EUR.

This seems complicated, but fortunately, we can use the Margrabe formula and our `Margrabe` function to calculate the price of the option.

```
Margrabe = function(S1, S2, sigma1, sigma2, Time, rho, delta1 = 0, delta2
= 0)
```

We need these substitutions $S_1 = Y = SS_A$, $S_2 = XS$, $\delta_1 = q - r - \rho\sigma_1\sigma_2$, $\delta_2 = q$, and $\sigma = \sigma_1$.

`S1` is the stock price in EUR, and `S2` is the strike price in EUR. `delta1` and `delta2` can be calculated easily: `delta1 = 0.03-0.02-0.2*0.15*0.1` and `delta2 = 0.03`. The only problem is that we need to set `sigma = sigma1`, but `sigma` is not a parameter of the Margrabe function; it is calculated inside the function body. Consider the following command:

```
sigma = sqrt(sigma1^2 + sigma2^2 - 2 * sigma1 * sigma2 * rho)
```

To get the *sigma = sigma1* result, we need to set *sigma2 = rho = 0*.

Now, we can call the `Margrabe` function with the given parameters.

```
Margrabe(74.67, 90*0.7467, 0.2, 0,3, 0, 0.007 , 0.03)
[1] 16.23238
```

The result is 16.23. This is the price of the quanto.

Summary

In this chapter, we met the challenge of discussing one of the most beautiful and most difficult parts of financial math: derivative pricing. We learned in theory and in practice about generalizations of the Black-Scholes model for related problems. We learned how to use R and the Black-Scholes formula for currency options. We saw how easy it is to implement our own code for the Margrabe formula, which is an extension of the Black-Scholes model. We used this formula to price stock options, currency options, and exchange options. Finally, we discussed quanto options and realized that quantos can also be priced with the Margrabe formula.

If you found this chapter exciting, you will be enthusiastic about the next one, which is about a related topic, that is, interest rate derivatives.

References

- **Black, F. and Scholes, M. (1973)**: The Pricing of Options and Corporate Liabilities. *The Journal of Political Economy*, 81(3), pp. 637-654.

- **Margrabe, W. (1978)**: The Value of an Option to Exchange One Asset for Another. *Journal of Finance*, 33(1), pp. 177-186.

- **Medvegyev, Péter (2007)**: *Stochastic Integration Theory*. Oxford University Press.

- **Merton, R. (1973)**: Theory of Rational Option Pricing. *The Bell Journal of Economics and Management Science*, 4(1), pp. 141-183.

6

Interest Rate Derivatives and Models

Interest rate derivatives are financial derivative products whose payoff is dependent on the interest rates.

There is a wide range of such products; the basic types include interest rate swaps, forward rate agreements, callable and puttable bonds, bond options, caps and floors, and so on.

In this chapter, we will start with the Black model (also referred to as the Black-76 model), which is a generalized version of the Black-Scholes model, and is often used to price interest rate derivatives. Then, we will show how to apply the Black model to price an interest rate cap.

A shortcoming of the Black model is that it assumes lognormal distribution for some underlying asset (for example, bond price or interest rate), and it neglects how interest rate changes across time. Consequently, Black's formula cannot be used for all kinds of interest rate derivatives. Sometimes, it is necessary to model the term structure of interest rate models. There are plenty of interest rate models that try to capture the main features of this term structure. In the second part of this chapter, we discuss two basic and frequently used interest rate models, namely the Vasicek and the Cox-Ingersoll-Ross models. As in the previous chapter, we will assume that you are familiar with the Black-Scholes model and the basics of risk-neutral valuation.

The Black model

We started this chapter by defining interest rate derivatives as assets with interest-rate-dependent cash flows. It is worth noting that the value of financial products is almost always dependent on some interest rates because of the need to discount the future cash flows. However, in the case of interest rate derivatives, not only the discounted value but the payoff itself depends on the interest rates. This is the main reason why interest rate derivatives are more complicated to price than stock or FX derivatives (*Hull, 2009* discusses these difficulties in detail).

The Black model (*Black, 1976*) was developed to price options on futures contracts. Futures options grant the holder the right to enter into a futures contract at a predetermined futures price (strike price or exercise price, X) on a specified date (maturity, T). In this model, we keep the assumptions of the Black-Scholes model, except that the underlying is the futures price instead of the spot price. Hence, we assume that the futures price (F) follows a geometric Brownian motion:

$$dF = \mu Fdt + \sigma FdW$$

It is easy to see that futures contracts might be handled as products with a continuous growth rate that is equal to the risk-free interest rate (r). Thus, it is not surprising that Black's formula for futures options is exactly the same as the Black-Scholes formula for currency options (discussed in the previous chapter), with q equal to r (as if the domestic and foreign interest rates were the same). So, Black's formula for a European futures call option is as follows:

$$c = e^{-rT} \left[FN(d_1) - XN(d_2) \right]$$

Here, $d_1 = \dfrac{ln\left(\dfrac{F}{X}\right) + \dfrac{\sigma^2}{2}T}{\sigma\sqrt{T}}$ and $d_2 = \dfrac{ln\left(\dfrac{F}{X}\right) - \dfrac{\sigma^2}{2}T}{\sigma\sqrt{T}}$.

The price of a similar put option is as follows:

$$p = e^{-rT} \left[XN(-d_2) - FN(-d_1) \right]$$

It is not a surprise that the `GBSOption` function (or the `BlackScholesOption` function) is useful for the Black model too. It is time to have a closer look at how it actually works.

When a function's name is typed in the R console without parenthesis, the function will not be called, but the source code is returned (except for byte-compiled code). This is not recommended for beginners, but it can be extremely useful for programmers with some experience because these details are usually not included in package documentation. Let's try it:

```
require(fOptions)
GBSOption
function (TypeFlag = c("c", "p"), S, X, Time, r, b, sigma, title = NULL,
    description = NULL)
{
    TypeFlag = TypeFlag[1]
    d1 = (log(S/X) + (b + sigma * sigma/2) * Time)/(sigma * sqrt(Time))
    d2 = d1 - sigma * sqrt(Time)
    if (TypeFlag == "c")
        result = S * exp((b - r) * Time) * CND(d1) - X * exp(-r *
            Time) * CND(d2)
    if (TypeFlag == "p")
        result = X * exp(-r * Time) * CND(-d2) - S * exp((b -
            r) * Time) * CND(-d1)
    param = list()
    param$TypeFlag = TypeFlag
    param$S = S
    param$X = X
    param$Time = Time
    param$r = r
    param$b = b
    param$sigma = sigma
    if (is.null(title))
        title = "Black Scholes Option Valuation"
    if (is.null(description))
        description = as.character(date())
    new("fOPTION", call = match.call(), parameters = param, price =
result,
        title = title, description = description)
}
<environment: namespace:fOptions>
```

Do not worry if this is not totally clear; we are only interested in the computation of the price of the call option. First, d1 is calculated (we will check the formula in a minute). The BS formula has different forms (for stock options, currency options, and stock options with dividend), but the following equation always holds:

$$d_1 - d_2 = \sigma \sqrt{T}$$

In the function, d2 is calculated based on this equation. The final result has the form $aN(d_1) - bN(d_2)$, where *a* and *b* are dependent on the model but are always the discounted value of the price of the underlying and the strike price.

Now, we can see the role of the b parameter in the calculation. As we mentioned in the previous chapter, this is how we can decide which model we want to use. If we carefully check the formulas, we can conclude that by setting b = r, we get the Black-Scholes stock option model; with b = r-q, we get Merton's stock option model with continuous dividend yield q (which is the same as the currency option model, as we saw in the previous chapter); and with b = 0, we get Black's futures option model.

Now, let's see an example of the Black model.

We need an option for an asset with 100 strike price in 5 years. The futures price is 120. Volatility of the asset is assumed to be 20%, and the risk-free rate is 5%. Now, simply call the BS option pricing formula with S = F and b = 0:

```
GBSOption("c", 120, 100, 5, 0.05, 0, 0.2)
```

We get the results in the usual form:

```
Title:
 Black Scholes Option Valuation
Call:
 GBSOption(TypeFlag = "c", S = 120, X = 100, Time = 5, r = 0.05,
    b = 0, sigma = 0.2)
Parameters:
        Value:
 TypeFlag c
 S        120
 X        100
 Time     5
 r        0.05
```

```
b           0
sigma       0.2
```

```
Option Price:
[1] 24.16356
```

The price of the option is about 24 USD, and we can also check from the output that b = 0, from which we must know that the Black model for futures options was used (or we made a serious mistake).

Although it was originally developed for commodity products, the Black model turned out to be a useful tool for pricing interest rate derivatives such as options on bonds or caps and floors. In the next section, we show how to use this model to price an interest rate cap.

Pricing a cap with Black's model

Interest rate caps are interest rate derivatives where the holder receives positive payments throughout a number of time periods if the interest rate exceeds a certain level (the strike price, X). Analogously, the holder of an interest rate floor receives positive payments in each period if the interest rate is below the strike price. It is obvious that caps and floors are efficient products to hedge against interest rate volatility. In this section, we will discuss the pricing of a cap. Let's assume that the underlying rate is the LIBOR, L.

As we discussed in the previous chapter, the best way to understand derivatives is to determine their payoff structure. The payoff of a cap (with one unit of notional amount) at the end of the nth period is as follows:

$$\tau \max \left(L_{n-1} - X ; 0 \right)$$

Here, τ is the time interval between two payments. This single payment is called a caplet, and the cap is, of course, a portfolio of sequential caplets. When pricing a cap, all the caplets must be valued and then their prices have to be summed. Furthermore, the earlier mentioned payoff shows us that pricing the nth caplet is nothing but pricing a call option with the underlying asset of the Libor, strike price X, and maturity τn.

If we assume that the Libor rate at time $n-1$ (L_{n-1}) is a random variable that has lognormal distribution and the volatility is σ_{n-1}, then we can use Black's formula to price the caplet:

$$c_n = \tau e^{-r\tau n}\left[F_{n-1}N(d_1) - XN(d_2)\right]$$

Here, $d_1 = \dfrac{ln\left(\dfrac{F_{n-1}}{X}\right) + \dfrac{\sigma_{n-1}^2}{2}\tau(n-1)}{\sigma_{n-1}\sqrt{\tau(n-1)}}$ and $d_2 = \dfrac{ln\left(\dfrac{F_{n-1}}{X}\right) - \dfrac{\sigma_{n-1}^2}{2}\tau(n-1)}{\sigma_{n-1}\sqrt{\tau(n-1)}}$.

Here, F_{n-1} is the forward Libor rate between $\tau(n-1)$ and τn, and r is the risk-free spot log return with maturity τn. Once we have the value of one single caplet, we can price all of them to get the price of the cap.

Let's see an example to understand this in depth. We have to pay USD LIBOR for 6 months to a business partner between May 2014 and November 2014. A caplet is an easy way to avoid the interest rate risk. Assume that we have a caplet on the LIBOR rate with 2.5% strike price (using the usual terminology).

This means that if the LIBOR rate is higher then 2.5%, we will receive the difference in cash. If, for example, the LIBOR rate turns out to be 3% in May, our payoff on one unit of notional amount is 0.5*max(3% -2.5%, 0).

Now, let's see how to price the caplet. There is nothing new in it; we can simply use the Black-Scholes formula. It is clear that we need to set S = F_{n-1}, Time = 0.5, and b = 0. Assuming that the LIBOR rate follows the geometric Brownian motion with 20% volatility, the forward rate between May 1st and November 1st is 2.2%, and the spot rate is 2%. In this case, the price of the caplet is as follows:

```
GBSOption("c", 0.022, 0.025, 0.5, 0.02, 0, 0.2)
Title:
 Black Scholes Option Valuation
Call:
 GBSOption(TypeFlag = "c", S = 0.022, X = 0.025, Time = 0.5, r = 0.02,
     b = 0, sigma = 0.2)
Parameters:
          Value:
 TypeFlag c
 S        0.022
 X        0.025
 Time     0.5
```

```
r          0.02
b          0
sigma      0.2
Option Price:
 0.0003269133
```

The price of the option is 0.0003269133. We still need to multiply it with $\tau = 0.5$, which makes it 0.0001634567. If we measure everything in million USD, this means that the price of the caplet is about 163 USD.

A cap is simply a sum of caplets, but we can combine them with different parameters if needed. Let's say we need a cap that pays if the LIBOR rate goes above 2.5% in the first 3 months, or if it is higher than 2% in the following 3 months. The forward LIBOR rate can also be different in the May and August period (let's say it is 2.1%), and in the August and November period (let's say it is 2.2%). We simply price both caplets one by one and add their prices:

```
GBSOption("c", 0.021, 0.025, 0.25, 0.02, 0, 0.2)
GBSOption("c", 0.022, 0.02, 0.25, 0.02, 0, 0.2)
```

We do not include all the outputs here, only the prices:

```
Option Price:
 3.743394e-05
Option Price:
 0.002179862
```

Now, we need to multiply both with $\tau = 0.25$ and take the sum of their prices:

```
(3.743394e-05 + 0.002179862 ) * 0.25
0.000554324
```

The price of this cap with a notional amount of 1 million is about 554 USD.

Pricing a floor is very similar. First, we divide the asset's cash flows into single payments, called floorlets. Then, we determine the value of each floorlet with the help of the Black model; the only difference is that floorlets are not call but put options. Finally, we add up the prices of the floorlets to get the value of the floor.

Black's model is applicable when we can assume that the future value of the underlying asset has lognormal distribution. Another approach to value interest rate derivatives is by modeling the term structure of interest rates. Here, we continue by presenting two basic interest rate models and their main characteristics.

The Vasicek model

The Vasicek model (*Vasicek, 1977*) is a continuous, affine, one-factor stochastic interest rate model. In this model, the instantaneous interest rate dynamics are given by the following stochastic differential equation:

$$dr_t = \alpha \left(\beta - r_t \right) dt + \sigma dW_t$$

Here, α, β, and σ are positive constants, r_t is the interest rate, t is time, and W_t denotes the standard Wiener process. In mathematics, this process is called the Ornstein-Uhlenbeck process.

As you may observe, the interest rate in the Vasicek model follows a mean-reverting process with a long-term average β; when $r_t < \beta$, the drift term becomes positive, so the interest rate is expected to increase and vice versa. The speed of adjustment to the long-run mean is measured by α. The volatility term is constant in this model.

Interest rate models are implemented in R, but to understand more deeply what is behind the formulas, let's write a function that directly implements the stochastic differential equation of the Vasicek model:

```r
vasicek <- function(alpha, beta, sigma, n = 1000, r0 = 0.05){
  v <- rep(0, n)
  v[1] <- r0
  for (i in 2:n){
    v[i] <- v[i - 1] + alpha * (beta - v[i - 1]) + sigma * rnorm(1)
        }
    return(v)
}
```

That's it. Now, let's plot some trajectories to see how it looks:

```r
set.seed(123)
r <- replicate(4, vasicek(0.02, 0.065, 0.0003))

matplot(r, type = "l", ylab = "", xlab = "Time", xaxt = "no",  main =
"Vasicek modell trajectories")
lines(c(-1,1001), c(0.065, 0.065), col = "grey", lwd = 2, lty = 1)
```

The following screenshot gives the output of the preceding command:

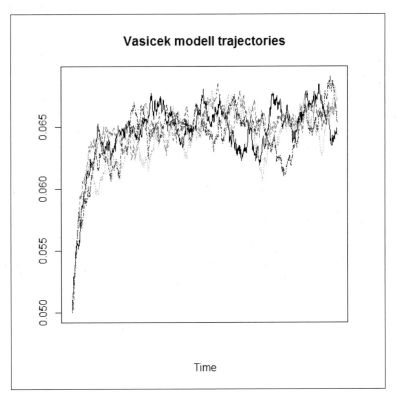

To understand the role of parameters, we plot the same trajectory (that is, the trajectory generated by the same random numbers) with different values of sigma and alpha:

```
r <- sapply(c(0, 0.0002, 0.0006),
function(sigma){set.seed(102323); vasicek(0.02, 0.065, sigma)})


matplot(r, type = "l", ylab = "", xlab = "Time" ,xaxt = "no",  main =
"Vasicek trajectories with volatility 0, 0.02% and 0.06%")
lines(c(-1,1001), c(0.065, 0.065), col = "grey", lwd = 2, lty = 3)
```

The following is the output of the preceding code:

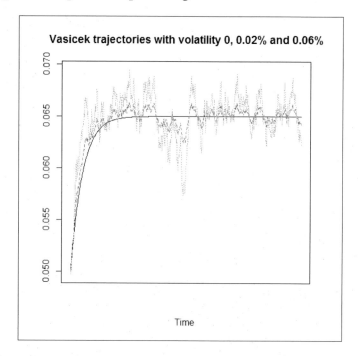

r <- sapply(c(0.002, 0.02, 0.2),

function(alpha){set.seed(2014); vasicek(alpha, 0.065, 0.0002)})

Trajectories have the same shape but different volatility:

```
matplot(r, type = "l", ylab = "", xaxt = "no",  main = "Vasicek
trajectories with alpha = 0.2%, 2% and 20%")
lines(c(-1,1001), c(0.065, 0.065), col = "grey", lwd = 2, lty = 3)
```

The following is the output of the preceding command:

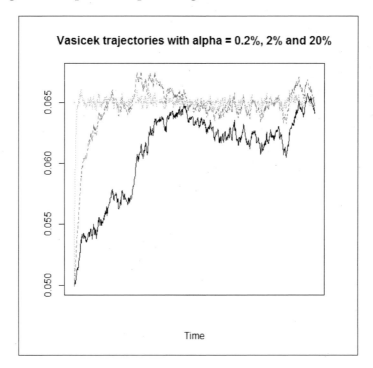

We can see that the higher the value of α, the earlier the trajectory reaches the long-term average.

It can be shown (see, for example, the original paper of Vasicek already cited) that the short rate in the Vasicek model is normally distributed with the following conditional expected value and variance:

$$E\left[r_T \mid r_t\right] = r_t e^{-\alpha(T-t)} + \beta\left(1 - e^{-\alpha(T-t)}\right)$$

$$Var\left[r_T \mid r_t\right] = \frac{\sigma^2}{2\alpha}\left(1 - e^{-2\alpha(T-t)}\right)$$

It is worth observing that the expected value converges to β when T or α goes to infinity. Furthermore, the variance converges to 0 when α goes to infinity. These observations are in line with the parameters' interpretations.

To demonstrate how the coefficients of the equation determine the parameters of the distribution, let's plot the conditional probability density function for different values of α, β, and σ, and see how it changes over time:

```
vasicek_pdf = function(x, alpha, beta, sigma, delta_T, r0 = 0.05){
  e <- r0*exp(-alpha*delta_T)+beta*(1-exp(-alpha*delta_T))
  s <- sigma^2/(2*alpha)*(1-exp(-2*alpha*delta_T))
  dnorm(x, mean = e, sd = s)
}


x <- seq(-0.1, 0.2, length = 1000)
par(xpd = T ,mar = c(2,2,2,2), mfrow = c(2,2))
y <- sapply(c(10, 5, 3, 2), function(delta_T)
        vasicek_pdf(x, .2, 0.1, 0.15, delta_T))
par(xpd = T ,mar = c(2,2,2,2), mfrow = c(2,2))
matplot(x, y, type = "l",ylab ="",xlab = "")
legend("topleft", c("T-t = 2", "T-t = 3", "T-t = 5", "T-t = 10"), lty =
1:4, col=1:4, cex = 0.7)


y <- sapply(c(0.1, 0.12, 0.14, 0.16), function(beta)
        vasicek_pdf(x, .2, beta, 0.15, 5))
matplot(x, y, type = "l", ylab ="",xlab = "")
legend("topleft", c("beta = 0.1", "beta = 0.12", "beta = 0.14", "beta =
0.16"), lty = 1:4, col=1:4,cex = 0.7)


y <- sapply(c(.1, .2, .3, .4), function(alpha)
        vasicek_pdf(x, alpha, 0.1, 0.15, 5))


matplot(x, y, type = "l", ylab ="",xlab = "")
legend("topleft", c("alpha = 0.1", "alpha = 0.2", "alpha = 0.3", "alpha =
0.4"), lty = 1:4, col=1:4, cex = 0.7)


y <- sapply(c(.1, .12, .14, .15), function(sigma)
        vasicek_pdf(x, .1, 0.1, sigma, 5))
```

```
matplot(x, y, type = "l", ylab ="",xlab = "")
legend("topleft", c("sigma = 0.1", "sigma = 0.12", "sigma = 0.14", "sigma
= 0.15"), lty = 1:4, col=1:4, cex = 0.7)
```

The following screenshot is the result of the of preceding code:

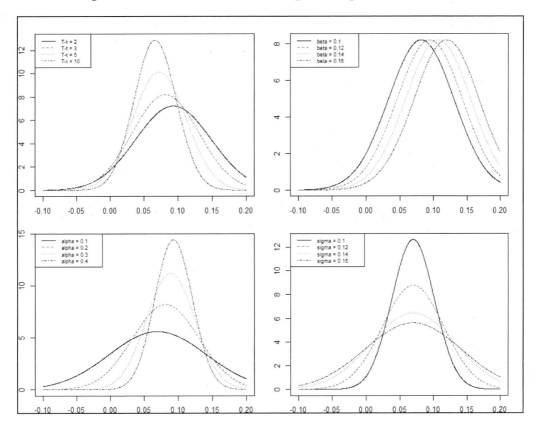

We can see that the variance of the distribution increases over time. β affects only the mean of the probability distribution. It is clear that with a higher value of α, the process reaches its long-term mean sooner and has less variance, and with greater volatility, we get a flatter density function, that is, greater variance.

Pricing a zero-coupon bond when the interest rate follows a Vasicek model results in the following formula (for a derivation of this formula, see, for example, *Cairns [2004]*):

$$P(t, r_t, T) = e^{A(T-t) - B(T-t)r_t}$$

Here, $B(\tau) = \dfrac{1 - e^{-\alpha\tau}}{\alpha}$ and $A(\tau) = \left(B(\tau) - \tau\right)\left(\beta - \dfrac{\sigma^2}{2\alpha^2}\right) - \dfrac{\sigma^2 B^2(\tau)}{4\alpha}$.

In the preceding formula, P denotes the price of the zero-coupon bond, t is the time when we price the bond, and T is the maturity (hence, T-t is the time to maturity). If we have the zero-coupon bond prices, we can determine the spot yield curve with the following simple relationship:

$$R(t, T) = -\frac{1}{T - t} \ln P(t, T) = -\frac{A(T - t)}{T - t} + \frac{B(T - t)}{T - t} r_t$$

The Cox-Ingersoll-Ross model

Like the Vasicek model, the Cox-Ingersoll-Ross model (*Cox at al., 1985*), which is often cited as the CIR model, is a continuous, affine, one-factor stochastic interest rate model. In this model, the instantaneous interest rate dynamics are given by the following stochastic differential equation:

$$dr_t = \alpha(\beta - r_t)dt + \sigma\sqrt{r_t}dW_t$$

Here, α, β, and σ are positive constants, r_t is the interest rate, t is the time, and W_t denotes the standard Wiener process. It is easy to see that the drift component is the same as in the Vasicek model; hence, the interest rate follows a mean-reverting process again, β is the long-run average, and α is the rate of adjustment. The difference is that the volatility term is not constant but is proportional to the square root of the interest rate level. This 'small' difference has dramatic consequences regarding the probability distribution of the future short rates. In the CIR model, the interest rate has non-central chi-squared distribution, with the following density function (f):

$$f\left[r_T \mid r_t\right] = 2c * \chi^2_{2q+2, 2u}\left[2cr_t\right]$$

Here, $q = \dfrac{2\alpha\beta}{\sigma^2} - 1$, $u = cr_t e^{-\alpha(T-t)}$, and $c = \dfrac{2\alpha}{\sigma^2\left(1-e^{-\alpha(T-t)}\right)}$.

Here, $\chi^2_{n,m}$ denotes the probability density function of the chi-squared distribution with n degrees of freedom and m denoting the non-centrality parameter. As the expected value and the variance of such a random variable is $n+m$ and $2(n+2m)$ respectively, we have the following moments for the interest rate:

$$E[r_T \mid r_t] = r_t e^{-\alpha(T-t)} + \beta\left(1-e^{-\alpha(T-t)}\right)$$

$$Var[r_T \mid r_t] = \frac{\sigma^2 r_t}{\alpha}\left(e^{-\alpha(T-t)} - e^{-2\alpha(T-t)}\right) + \frac{\sigma^2\beta}{2\alpha}\left(1-e^{-\alpha(T-t)}\right)^2$$

We might observe that the conditional expected value is exactly the same as in the Vasicek model. It is important to notice that the short rate, as a normally distributed variable, might become negative in the Vasicek model, but this cannot happen in the CIR model.

Like in the case of the Vasicek model, we can see how the coefficients determine the shape of the probability density function if we plot it with different parameter sets. The following code does this job by comparing the probability density functions under various parameter specifications:

```
CIR_pdf = function(x, alpha, beta, sigma, delta_T, r0 = 0.1){
  q = (2*alpha*beta)/(sigma^2) - 1
  c = (2*alpha)/(sigma^2*(1-exp(-alpha*delta_T)))
  u = c*r0*exp(-alpha*delta_T)
  2*c*dchisq(2*c*x, 2*q+2, ncp = 2*u)
              }


x <- seq(0, 0.15, length = 1000)
y <- sapply(c(1, 2, 5, 50), function(delta_T)
        CIR_pdf(x, .3, 0.05,0.1,delta_T))
```

```
par(mar = c(2,2,2,2), mfrow = c(2,2))

matplot(x, y, type = "l",ylab ="",xlab = "")

legend("topright", c("T-t = 1", "T-t = 2", "T-t = 5", "T-t = 50"), lty =
1:4, col = 1:4, cex = 0..7)


y <- sapply(c(.2, .4, .6, 1), function(alpha)
       CIR_pdf(x, alpha, 0.05,0.1,1))
  matplot(x, y, type = "l",ylab ="",xlab = "")

legend("topright", c("alpha = 0.2", "alpha = 0.4", "alpha = 0.6", "alpha
= 1"), lty = 1:4, col = 1:4, cex = 0.7)


y <- sapply(c(.1, .12, .14, .16), function(beta)
       CIR_pdf(x, .3, beta,0.1,1))


matplot(x, y, type = "l",ylab ="",xlab = "")

legend("topleft", c("beta = 0.1", "beta = 0.12", "beta = 0.14", "beta =
0.16"), lty = 1:4, col = 1:4, cex = 0.7)


x <- seq(0, 0.25, length = 1000)

y <- sapply(c(.03, .05, .1, .15), function(sigma)
        CIR_pdf(x, .3, 0.05,sigma,1))


matplot(x, y, type = "l",ylab ="",xlab = "")

legend("topright", c("sigma = 1", "sigma = 5", "sigma = 10", "sigma =
15"), lty = 1:4, col = 1:4, cex = 0.7)
```

Here, we can see the result. We come to the same conclusion as we did in the case of the Vasicek model, except that here, β changes the shape of the density function and not just shifts it.

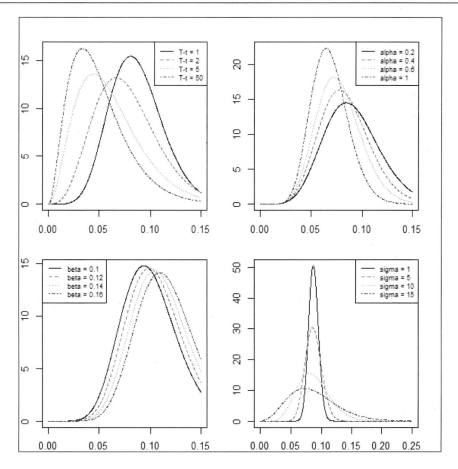

Pricing a zero-coupon bond in the CIR model yields the following formula (see, for example, *Cairns [2004]*):

$$P(t, r_t, T) = e^{A(T-t) - B(T-t)r_t}$$

Here, $B(\tau) = \dfrac{2(e^{\gamma\tau} - 1)}{(\gamma + \alpha)(e^{\gamma\tau} - 1) + 2\gamma}$, $A(\tau) = \dfrac{2\alpha\beta}{\sigma^2} ln\dfrac{2\gamma e^{\frac{(\gamma + \alpha)\tau}{2}}}{(\gamma + \alpha)(e^{\gamma\tau} - 1) + 2\gamma}$, and $\gamma = \sqrt{\alpha^2 + 2\sigma^2}$.

Determining the yield curve from the bond prices is exactly the same as in the Vasicek model.

Parameter estimation of interest rate models

When using the interest rate models for pricing or simulation purposes, it is important to calibrate their parameters to real data properly. Here, we present a possible method to estimate the parameters. This method was developed by *Chan et al, 1992*, and is often referred to as the CKLS method. The procedure was elaborated to estimate the parameters of the following interest rate model with the help of the econometric procedure called Generalized Method of Moments (GMM; see *Hansen, 1982*, for more details):

$$dr_t = \alpha(\beta - r_t)dt + \sigma r_t^\gamma dW_t$$

It is easy to see that this process gives the Vasicek model when $\gamma = 0$, and the CIR model when $\gamma = 0.5$. As the first step of the parameter estimation, we discretize this equation with the Euler approximation (see *Atkinson, 1989*):

$$r_t = \alpha\beta\delta_t + (1 - \alpha\delta_t)r_{t-1} + \sigma r_{t-1}^\gamma \sqrt{\delta_t} e_t$$

Here, δ_t is the time interval between two observations of the interest rate and e_t is independent, standard normal random variables. The parameters are estimated with the following null hypothesis:

$$r_t - r_{t-1} = \alpha\beta\delta_t - \alpha\delta_t r_{t-1} + \varepsilon_t$$

$$E(\varepsilon_t) = 0$$

$$E(\varepsilon_t^2) = \sigma^2 \delta_t r_{t-1}^{2\gamma}$$

Let Θ be the vector of the parameters to be estimated, that is, $\Theta = (\alpha, \beta, \sigma, \gamma)$.

We consider the following function of the parameter vector:

$$M_t(\Theta) = \begin{bmatrix} \varepsilon_t \\ \varepsilon_t r_{t-1} \\ \varepsilon_t^2 - \sigma^2 r_{t-1}^{2\gamma} \\ \left(\varepsilon_t^2 - \sigma^2 r_{t-1}^{2\gamma} \right) r_{t-1} \end{bmatrix}$$

It is easy to see that under the null hypothesis, $E\big(M_t(\Theta)\big) = 0$.

The first step of GMM is that we consider the sample corresponding to $E\big(M_t(\Theta)\big)$, which is $m_t(\Theta)$:

$$m_t(\Theta) = \frac{\sum_{t=1}^{n} M_t(\Theta)}{n}$$

Here, n is the number of observations.

Finally, GMM determines the parameters by minimizing the following quadratic form:

$$m_t^{'}(\Theta)\Omega(\Theta)m_t(\Theta)$$

Here, Ω is a symmetric, positive definite weight matrix.

There is a `quadprog` package in R for these kinds of problems, or we can use general methods for optimization with the `optim` function.

Using the SMFI5 package

After discussing the math behind interest rate models and after hard programming, let's recommend the SMFI5 package, which provides user-friendly solutions to model and simulate interest rate models (if it is modeled by an Ornstein-Uhlenbeck process), price bonds, and many other applications.

We cannot discuss it in detail, but as a short demonstration, let's call a function that simulates bond prices for different maturities:

```
bond.vasicek(0.5,2.55,0.365,0.3,0,3.55,1080,c(1/12, 3/12, 6/12, 1),365)
```

This returns a spectacular result:

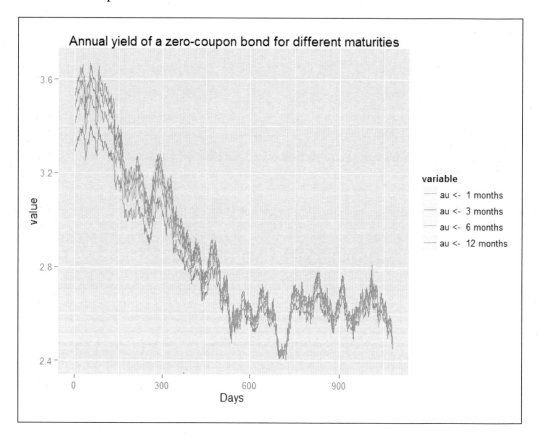

Summary

This chapter was about interest rate models and interest rate derivatives. After introducing the Black model, we used it to price caps and caplets. We also examined the R code for the Black-Scholes model.

Then, we turned our attention to interest rate models such as the Vasicek and CIR models. We discussed the theory of parameter estimation as well. At the end, we briefly demonstrated how the SMFI5 package works. Interest rate models were important for us in this chapter because the pricing of interest rate derivatives starts with assuming something about interest rates and yield curves in the future. With the help of a properly chosen and calibrated model, we have the opportunity to analyze possible future scenarios of the interest rates. Interest rate models are, of course, a much wider topic, which is worth studying in more detail. However, learning the most popular and well-known models is a good start, and we encourage you to study them further or check out the next chapter because some options still have some surprises for us.

References

- **Atkinson, K. [1989]**: An Introduction to Numerical Analysis. John Wiley & Sons, New York.

- **Black, F. [1976]**: The Pricing of Commodity Contracts. *Journal of Financial Economics*, 3(1-2), pp. 167-179.

- **Cairns, A. [2004]**: *Interest Rate Models: An Introduction*. Princeton University Press, Princeton-Oxford.

- **Chan, K., Karolyi, A., Longstaff, A. and Sanders, A. [1992]**: An Empirical Comparison of Alternative Models of the Short-Term Interest Rate. The *Journal of Finance*, No. 3. pp. 1209-1227.

- **Cox, J., Ingersoll, J. and Ross, S. [1985]**: The Theory of the Term Structure of Interest Rates. *Econometrica*, No. 53. pp. 385-407.

- **Hansen, L. [1982]**: Large Sample Properties of Generalized Method of Moment Estimators. *Econometrica*, No. 4. pp. 1029-1054.

- **Hull, J. [2009]**: *Options, Futures, and Other Derivatives*. Pearson Prentice Hall, New Jersey.

- **Vasicek, O. [1977]**: An Equilibrium Characterisation of the Term Structure. *Journal of Financial Economics*, 5(2), pp. 177-188.

7
Exotic Options

All derivatives are financial contracts, and in these contracts, there are far more features that can be agreed on than a simple right to buy or to sell. Complex payout structures can be engineered based on what-if scenarios; thus, the final payout of an exotic contract can be dependent on a whole set of circumstances. Often, even the path of the underlying has a serious influence on the final payout. Compared to these derivatives, the good old call and put options were soon seen simple, earning them a not too impressive nickname: plain vanilla.

Vanilla call and put options are like plain vanilla ice-creams, the simplest possible ice-cream without any fancy optional toppings. The expression "plain vanilla" is so strongly embedded in finance that it is even used in the bond market, where a vanilla bond is the simplest possible coupon-paying bond.

Any option that has some extras over the basic plain vanilla options belong to a very numerous group called exotic options. Exotic options are popular because sell-side bankers are in fierce competition to offer tailor-made products for the clients. Another reason behind the fact that exotics are widely spread is that, interestingly enough, most of the time, quoting a price on an exotic structure is not a much more difficult task for market makers than quoting vanilla prices.

A general pricing approach

Exotic or not, there is one intrinsic feature that is always the same in every derivative product, that is, it is a function of other instruments, hence the name derivative. Thus, the price of a derivative is not independently developed as the outcome of a direct supply and demand; rather, it is given as an estimated construction cost. For example, the one month forward dollar price of a euro is highly dependent on the spot dollar price of the euro; the forward price is just the function of the spot price (and the interest rates).

If exactly the same benefits that are granted by holding a derivative can be constructed by a trading strategy that involves less complex instruments, then the derivative can be replicated. Derivatives are not like unique paintings; the forgery of a derivative has the very same value, while replicas are as good as the original. By using the no-arbitrage argument, *Black and Scholes (1973)* and *Merton (1973)* showed that the price of a derivative should be equal to the expected sum of expenses that arise during the proper implementation of the dynamic replication strategy. *Taleb (1997)* extensively describes that implementing a proper replication strategy under real market circumstances could often be really tricky.

The role of dynamic hedging

Most of the time, replication is a dynamic strategy. You should do more or less trading almost continuously during the lifetime of the derivatives. *Haug (2007b)* shows that the hedging error of non-continuous hedging could be significant even for plain vanilla options. Anyway, continuous hedging is a huge effort, which is often not seen explicitly in the pricing formulas; however, most pricing functions are based on the assumption that dynamic hedging should be done in the background properly all the time. This is also the case whenever we talk about risk-neutral world or the risk-neutral pricing. For further references, see *Wilmott (2006)*.

Luckily, no matter how hard dynamic hedging could be, running an option book is at least a scalable business; hedging thousands of options is not much more difficult than hedging just a couple of them. All options can be decomposed into certain sensitivities, the so-called Greek letters (or simply Greeks). This nickname came from the fact that some crucial sensitivity was named with a letter from the Greek alphabet (delta, gamma, rho, and theta). They are partial derivatives and thus they are additive. Summing up the deltas of the individual options gives the delta of the portfolio and so on. This works not only for the plain vanillas but for the exotics too, thus creating a very strong link between the vanillas and the exotics.

How R can help a lot

We start this chapter by showing some examples for exotic options, giving one possible classification. We will show examples from the fExoticOptions package and how the so-called Black-Scholes surface can be created for any derivative-pricing function. Afterwards, we will focus on the numerical estimation of the Greeks of any exotic derivative. Next, we will show the pricing of an exotic option that is not yet included in the fExoticOptions package.

We have chosen the **Double-no-touch (DNT)** binary option mainly because of its popularity on the foreign exchange (**FX**) markets and the many conclusions that are relevant even for other exotics. We will use AUDUSD as underlying because at the time of writing this chapter, there is a significant interest differential between the AUD and the USD interest rates, and we can show how to put these rates into the pricing functions. We will show a second way of calculating the price of a DNT by using static option replication arguments. We will show a real-life example of a DNT, and in a simulation, we will show a way to estimate the survivorship probability of a DNT. Using this, we can discuss the relationship of real-world and risk-neutral probabilities and the role of risk premium. Finally, we will show some practical fine-tuning tricks to embed exotic options into structured products.

Besides seeing examples to implement complex exotic option-pricing functions and simulations in R, as a side effect, understanding the Greeks as links between exotics and vanillas will be the learning outcome of this chapter. We will use the same terminology that was introduced in *Chapter 5, FX Derivatives*, which also includes much more about currencies and plain vanilla options.

A glance beyond vanillas

Haug (2007a) comprehensively covers the collection of pricing formulas for around 100 exotic derivatives. The `fOptions` and `fExoticOptions` packages are based on this book. *Wilmott (2006)*, *Taleb (1997)*, and *DeRosa (2011)* describe a lot of practical issues about them.

The first impression could be that there are way too many exotic options. There are many ways of classification. Market makers talk about different generations of exotics, such as first generation, second generation, and so on. Their approach is from a hedging point of view. We will use a slightly different angle, the end-user approach, and classify the options based on their main exotic feature.

Asian type exotics are about the average. It could be an average rate or an average strike, and it could also be an arithmetic or geometric average. These options are path dependent; that is, their value at expiry is not purely a function of the underlying price at expiry but the total path. Asian options are cheaper than the vanillas since the volatility of the average price is lower than the volatility of the price itself:

```
library(fOptions)
library(fExoticOptions)
a <- GBSOption("c", 100, 100, 1, 0.02, -0.02, 0.3, title = NULL,
    description = NULL)
(z <- a@price)
```

```
[1] 10.62678
a <- GeometricAverageRateOption("c", 100, 100, 1, 0.02, -0.02, 0.3,
    title = NULL, description = NULL)
(z <- a@price)
[1] 5.889822
```

Barrier type exotics are also path-dependent options. There could be one or two barriers. Each barrier could be either **knock-in (KI)** or **knock-out (KO)**. During the lifetime of the option, the price of the underlying is monitored, and if it is traded at or over the barrier, there will be a knock event. Options with KI barriers become exercisable if the knock event occurs. Options with KO barriers start their life as exercisable options, however, they become non-exercisable if the knock event occurs. If there are two barriers, both of them could be the same type: **double-knock-out (DKO)** and **double-knock-in (DKI)**, or it could be a **knock-in-knock-out (KIKO)** type.

If all other parameters are set to be the same, then the following equation holds:

KI + KO = vanilla.

This is because in this case, KI and KO options are mutually exclusive, but one of them will be exercisable for sure. The first parameters cuo and cui are flags for call-up-and-out and call-up-and-in. Next, we check for the following condition:

vanilla - KO - KI = 0.

The following code illustrates the preceding condition:

```
library(fExoticOptions)
a <- StandardBarrierOption("cuo", 100, 90, 130, 0, 1, 0.02, -0.02, 0.30,
    title = NULL, description = NULL)
x <- a@price
b <- StandardBarrierOption("cui", 100, 90, 130, 0, 1, 0.02, -0.02, 0.30,
    title = NULL, description = NULL)
y <- b@price
c <- GBSOption("c", 100, 90, 1, 0.02, -0.02, 0.3, title = NULL,
    description = NULL)

z <- c@price

v <- z - x - y

v

[1] 0
```

Based on the same logic of *DKO + DKI = vanilla*, we can even state that *KO - DKO = KIKO*. So, the KIKO options start as non-exercisable, and as long as both the short DKO and the long KO are alive, they neutralize each other. Should the short DKO die and the long KO survive, then it is a KI event for the KIKO option. However, the KIKO can still die even after being knocked-in. Naturally, the KIKO + DKO = KO approach leads to the same conclusion.

Also, there are some important convergence features among barrier options. Based on the KO + KI= vanilla equation, the KO converges into vanilla as we push the barrier further from the spot, since KI converges into zero if we push the barrier further from the spot. The next chart will to demonstrate this feature.

```
vanilla <- GBSOption(TypeFlag = "c", S = 100, X = 90, Time = 1,
    r = 0.02, b = -0.02, sigma = 0.3)
KO <- sapply(100:300, FUN = StandardBarrierOption, TypeFlag = "cuo",
    S = 100, X = 90, K = 0, Time = 1, r = 0.02, b = -0.02, sigma = 0.30)
plot(KO[[1]]@price, type = "l",
    xlab = "barrier distance from spot",
    ylab = "price of option",
    main = "Price of KO converges to plain vanilla")
abline(h = vanilla@price, col = "red")
```

The following output is the result of the preceding code:

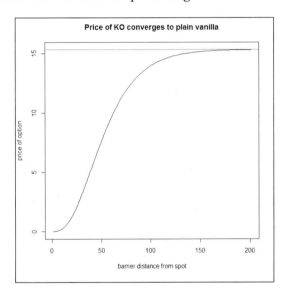

Similarly, double barrier options converge into single barrier ones if one of the barriers starts to get unimportant and converges towards plain vanillas if both the barriers are getting unimportant.

Thanks to the preceding mentioned parities, most of the time, finding pricing formulas for KO options is enough. Although this is of huge help, often, pricing a KO could be still very tricky. Replicating the KO event is based on a technique that tries to build a portfolio made of vanillas that have exactly zero worth when the knock event occurs, so at that point, they can be closed for free. There are two famous methods for this, explained by *Derman-Ergener-Kani (1995)* and *Carr-Ellis-Gupta (1998)*.

The so-called Black-Scholes surface is a 3D chart where the option price can be shown as a function of time to maturity and the underlying price. Since some of the exotic pricing functions can go crazy under extreme input circumstances, it is advisable to use our financial knowledge that an option price can never go below zero.

The following is the code for the Black-Scholes surface:

```
install.packages('plot3D')
BS_surface <- function(S, Time, FUN, ...) {
    require(plot3D)
    n <- length(S)
    k <- length(Time)
    m <- matrix(0, n, k)
    for (i in 1:n){
        for (j in 1:k){
            l <- list(S = S[i], Time = Time[j], ...)
            m[i,j] <- max(do.call(FUN, l)@price, 0)
        }
    }
    persp3D(z = m, xlab = "underlying", ylab = "Remaining time",
        zlab = "option price", phi = 30, theta = 20, bty = "b2")
}
BS_surface(seq(1, 200,length = 200), seq(0, 2, length = 200),
    GBSOption, TypeFlag = "c", X = 90, r = 0.02, b = 0, sigma = 0.3)
```

The preceding code yields the following output:

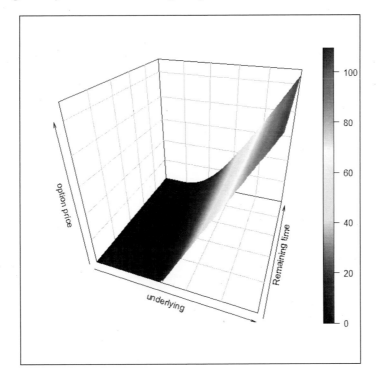

First, we prepared the Black-Scholes surface of a plain vanilla call option. However, the `BS_surface` code can be used for many more purposes. Just like the fact that the concept of the Black-Scholes surface can be used for any kind of single underlying dependent derivative, if we have a pricing function, it can be used as the `FUN` argument:

```
BS_surface(seq(1,200,length = 200), seq(0, 2, length = 200),

    StandardBarrierOption, TypeFlag = "cuo", H = 130, X = 90, K = 0,

    r = 0.02, b = -0.02, sigma = 0.30)
```

The following screenshot is the result of the preceding code:

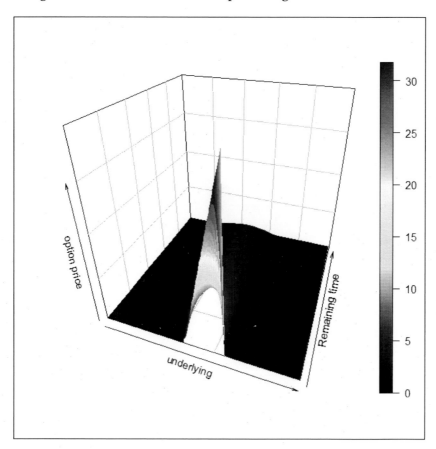

It is easy to see that compared to the plain vanilla call, the up-and-out call option has a limited value.

On [page 156], we use this same function to chart the BS Surface for a Double-no-touch option.

Binary options are exotics that have a fixed contingent payout. The name comes from the feature that they have only two possible outcomes: either pay a fixed amount or don't pay at all. They have the 0-1 relationship in the options world. Binary features could be mixed with the barrier feature; thus, they become path dependent. A One-Touch (OT) option pays only if a knock event occurred during its lifetime, while a No-Touch pays only if no knock event occurred.

There could be two barriers associated with the binaries, thus getting the Double-One-Touch and Double-No-Touch options. Based on no arbitrage arguments, the following equations must hold:

NT + OT = T-Bill

DNT + DOT = T-Bill

Convergence can be seen here too, similar to the cases we have shown for the barriers. A DNT converges to an NT if one of the barriers is far enough, and converges to a T-Bill if both the barriers are far enough. A pricing function for a DNT is the Jack-of-all-trades of the binaries, similar to the DKO option for the barrier type.

Lookback options are also path dependent. The lookback feature is very convenient. At expiry, the holder of the position can look back and choose the best price from the path of the underlying. For a floating rate lookback, the option holder can look back for the strike price. For a fixed rate lookback, the holder can exercise the option against any price on which the underlying was traded during the lifetime of the option. *Taleb (1997)* shows how lookbacks can be replicated by an infinite chain of KIKO options. In this sense, this is at least second generation exotic, since we need exotics as building blocks to be able to replicate a lookback.

More than one underlying is also a common exotic feature. Two examples have already been discussed in the *exchange options* and *quanto options* sections of *Chapter 5*, *FX Derivatives*. However, there are plenty more. Best-of and worst-of (also called rainbow) options are give the best or the worst performing underlying from a basket. The spread option is very similar to a vanilla option with the twist that the underlying of this option is the difference of two assets. These are just a few examples, which are enough to show that not surprisingly, in all of these cases, correlation plays an important role. Also, these features can be mixed with barrier or lookback or Asian features that result in an almost endless number of combinations. In this chapter, we will not be discussing these types any further.

Greeks – the link back to the vanilla world

As we explained in the introductory part of this chapter, Greeks are partial derivatives. Some important Greeks are as follows:

- **delta**: This denotes the DvalueDspot, which is the change of the option price with respect to the change of the underlying spot price
- **gamma**: This denotes the DdeltaDspot

- **vega**: This denotes the DvalueDvolatility
- **theta**: This denotes the DvalueDtime
- **rho**: This denotes the DvalueDinterest rate

In some simple cases, these partial derivatives can be found analytically. For example, the `fOptions` package includes the `GBSGreeks` function that gives the Greeks for vanillas.

Analytical Greeks are convenient; however, there are two problems with them. The first problem is that market-traded parameters are not changing in infinitesimal small increments. For example, on the New York Stock Exchange, the smallest possible change in the stock price is one cent. The stock price either changes at least one cent or there is no change at all. On the OTC (over-the-counter), FX market traders are quoting volatility as an integer multiple of 0.0005. The second problem with analytical Greeks comes from the fact that for many exotics, we have no closed formula. We still need to know the Greeks anyway, because we would like to sum them up to get the Greeks for the portfolio. Adding up analytical Greeks and numerical ones can lead to errors, so using numerical Greeks is a much safer way.

The `GetGreeks` function calculates any Greeks for any pricing function:

```
GetGreeks <- function(FUN, arg, epsilon,...) {
    all_args1 <- all_args2 <- list(...)
    all_args1[[arg]] <- as.numeric(all_args1[[arg]] + epsilon)
    all_args2[[arg]] <- as.numeric(all_args2[[arg]] - epsilon)
    (do.call(FUN, all_args1)@price -
        do.call(FUN, all_args2)@price) / (2 * epsilon)
}
```

OTC market makers do not quote FX volatility in any quantities, but normally, as an integer multiple of 0.0005, a typical quote for AUDUSD at-the-money volatility is 5.95 percent/6.05 percent. Of course, for exchange-traded derivatives that are quoted in price instead of volatility, the price-change-implied volatility change could be smaller than 0.0005.

So when we calculate vega numerically, we should set epsilon to 0.0005 as a market consistent smallest possible change; for example, to calculate a delta of an AUDUSD option, we can set epsilon as 0.0001 (one pip), or for a stock, we can set epsilon as 0.01 (one cent). It is also useful to adjust epsilon to 1/365 (one day) for theta, and to 0.0001 (one basis point) for rho.

The following code plots the delta, vega theta, and rho for a `FloatingStrikeLookbackOption`:

```
x <- seq(10, 200, length = 200)
delta <- vega <- theta <- rho <- rep(0, 200)
for(i in 1:200){
    delta[i] <- GetGreeks(FUN = FloatingStrikeLookbackOption,
        arg = 2, epsilon = 0.01, "p", x[i], 100, 1, 0.02, -0.02, 0.2)
    vega[i]  <- GetGreeks(FUN = FloatingStrikeLookbackOption,
        arg = 7, epsilon = 0.0005, "p", x[i], 100, 1, 0.02, -0.02,
            0.2)
    theta[i] <- GetGreeks(FUN = FloatingStrikeLookbackOption,
        arg = 4, epsilon = 1/365, "p", x[i], 100, 1, 0.02, -0.02,
            0.2)
    rho[i]   <- GetGreeks(FUN = FloatingStrikeLookbackOption,
arg = 5, epsilon = 0.0001, "p", x[i], 100, 1, 0.02, -0.02, 0.2)
}
par(mfrow = c(2, 2))
plot(x, delta, type = "l", xlab = "S", ylab = "", main = "Delta")
plot(x, vega,  type = "l", xlab = "S", ylab = "", main = "Vega")
plot(x, theta, type = "l", xlab = "S", ylab = "", main = "Theta")
plot(x, rho,   type = "l", xlab = "S", ylab = "", main = "Rho")
```

The preceding code gives the following output:

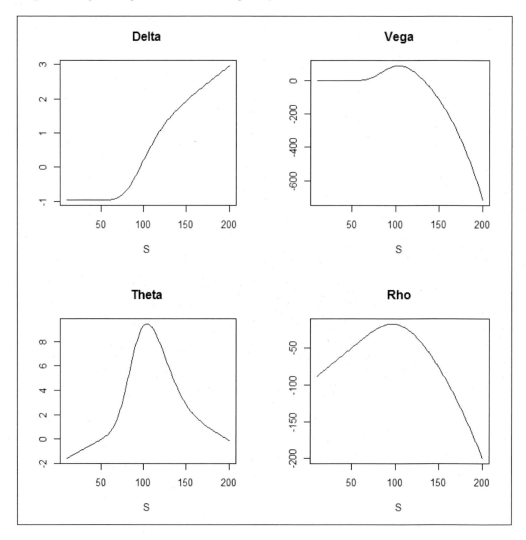

Pricing the Double-no-touch option

A Double-no-touch (DNT) option is a binary option that pays a fixed amount of cash at expiry. Unfortunately, the fExoticOptions package does not contain a formula for this option at present. We will show two different ways to price DNTs that incorporate two different pricing approaches. In this section, we will call the function dnt1, and for the second approach, we will use dnt2 as the name for the function.

Hui (1996) showed how a one-touch double barrier binary option can be priced. In his terminology, "one-touch" means that a single trade is enough to trigger the knock-out event, and "double barrier" binary means that there are two barriers and this is a binary option. We call this DNT as it is commonly used on the FX markets. This is a good example for the fact that many popular exotic options are running under more than one name. In *Haug (2007a)*, the Hui-formula is already translated into the generalized framework. S, r, b, σ, and T have the same meaning as in *Chapter 5, FX Derivatives*. K means the payout (dollar amount) while L and U are the lower and upper barriers.

$$c = \sum_{i=1}^{\infty} \frac{2\pi i K}{Z^2} \left[\frac{\left(\frac{S}{L}\right)^\alpha - (-1)^i \left(\frac{S}{U}\right)^\alpha}{\alpha^2 + \left(\frac{i\pi}{Z}\right)^2} \right] \times \sin\left(\frac{i\pi}{Z}\ln(S/L)\right) e^{-\frac{1}{2}\left[\left(\frac{i\pi}{Z}\right)^2 - \beta\right]\sigma^2 T}$$

Where, $z = \ln(U/L)$, $\alpha = -\frac{1}{2}\left(\frac{2b}{\sigma^2}-1\right)$, $\beta = -\frac{1}{4}\left(\frac{2b}{\sigma^2}-1\right)^2 - 2\frac{r}{\sigma^2}$.

Implementing the *Hui (1996)* function to R starts with a big question mark: what should we do with an infinite sum? How high a number should we substitute as infinity? Interestingly, for practical purposes, small number like 5 or 10 could often play the role of infinity rather well. *Hui (1996)* states that convergence is fast most of the time. We are a bit skeptical about this since α will be used as an exponent. If b is negative and sigma is small enough, the (S/L)ᵃ part in the formula could turn out to be a problem.

First, we will try with normal parameters and see how quick the convergence is:

```
dnt1 <- function(S, K, U, L, sigma, T, r, b, N = 20, ploterror = FALSE){
    if ( L > S | S > U) return(0)
    Z <- log(U/L)
    alpha <- -1/2*(2*b/sigma^2 - 1)
    beta <- -1/4*(2*b/sigma^2 - 1)^2 - 2*r/sigma^2
    v <- rep(0, N)
    for (i in 1:N)
        v[i] <- 2*pi*i*K/(Z^2) * (((S/L)^alpha - (-1)^i*(S/U)^alpha ) /
```

```
                (alpha^2+(i*pi/Z)^2)) * sin(i*pi/Z*log(S/L)) *
                exp(-1/2 * ((i*pi/Z)^2-beta) * sigma^2*T)
        if (ploterror) barplot(v, main = "Formula Error");
        sum(v)

}
print(dnt1(100, 10, 120, 80, 0.1, 0.25, 0.05, 0.03, 20, TRUE))
```

The following screenshot shows the result of the preceding code:

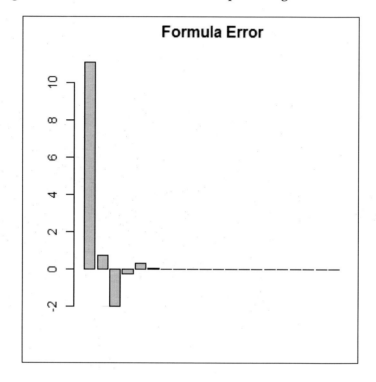

The Formula Error chart shows that after the seventh step, additional steps were not influencing the result. This means that for practical purposes, the infinite sum can be quickly estimated by calculating only the first seven steps. This looks like a very quick convergence indeed. However, this could be pure luck or coincidence.

What about decreasing the volatility down to 3 percent? We have to set N as 50 to see the convergence:

```
print(dnt1(100, 10, 120, 80, 0.03, 0.25, 0.05, 0.03, 50, TRUE))
```

The preceding command gives the following output:

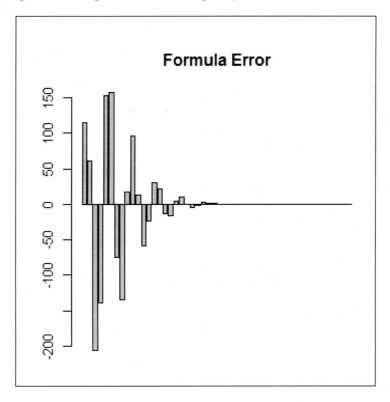

Not so impressive? 50 steps are still not that bad. What about decreasing the volatility even lower? At 1 percent, the formula with these parameters simply blows up. First, this looks catastrophic; however, the price of a DNT was already 98.75 percent of the payout when we used 3 percent volatility. Logic says that the DNT price should be a monotone-decreasing function of volatility, so we already know that the price of the DNT should be worth at least 98.75 percent if volatility is below 3 percent.

Another issue is that if we choose an extreme high U or extreme low L, calculation errors emerge. However, similar to the problem with volatility, common sense helps here too; the price of a DNT should increase if we make U higher or L lower.

There is still another trick. Since all the problem comes from the α parameter, we can try setting b as 0, which will make α equal to 0.5. If we also set r to 0, the price of a DNT converges into 100 percent as the volatility drops.

Anyway, whenever we substitute an infinite sum by a finite sum, it is always good to know when it will work and when it will not. We made a new code that takes into consideration that convergence is not always quick. The trick is that the function calculates the next step as long as the last step made any significant change. This is still not good for all the parameters as there is no cure for very low volatility, except that we accept the fact that if implied volatilities are below 1 percent, than this is an extreme market situation in which case DNT options should not be priced by this formula:

```
dnt1 <- function(S, K, U, L, sigma, Time, r, b) {
  if ( L > S | S > U) return(0)
  z <- log(U/L)
  alpha <- -1/2*(2*b/sigma^2 - 1)
  beta <- -1/4*(2*b/sigma^2 - 1)^2 - 2*r/sigma^2
  p <- 0
  i <- a <- 1
  while (abs(a) > 0.0001){
    a <- 2*pi*i*K/(z^2) * (((S/L)^alpha - (-1)^i*(S/U)^alpha ) /
      (alpha^2 + (i *pi / z)^2) ) * sin(i * pi / z * log(S/L)) *
        exp(-1/2*((i*pi/z)^2-beta) * sigma^2 * Time)
    p <- p + a
    i <- i + 1
  }
  p
}
```

Now that we have a nice formula, it is possible to draw some DNT-related charts to get more familiar with this option. Later, we will use a particular AUDUSD DNT option with the following parameters: L equal to 0.9200, U equal to 0.9600, K (payout) equal to USD 1 million, T equal to 0.25 years, volatility equal to 6 percent, r_AUD equal to 2.75 percent, r_USD equal to 0.25 percent, and b equal to -2.5 percent. We will calculate and plot all the possible values of this DNT from 0.9200 to 0.9600; each step will be one pip (0.0001), so we will use 2,000 steps.

The following code plots a graph of price of underlying:

```
x <- seq(0.92, 0.96, length = 2000)
y <- z <- rep(0, 2000)
```

```
for (i in 1:2000){
    y[i] <- dnt1(x[i], 1e6, 0.96, 0.92, 0.06, 0.25, 0.0025, -0.0250)
    z[i] <- dnt1(x[i], 1e6, 0.96, 0.92, 0.065, 0.25, 0.0025, -0.0250)
}
matplot(x, cbind(y,z), type = "l", lwd = 2, lty = 1,
    main = "Price of a DNT with volatility 6% and 6.5%
", cex.main = 0.8, xlab = "Price of underlying" )
```

The following output is the result of the preceding code:

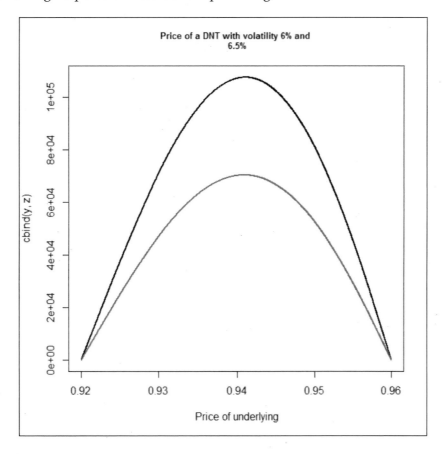

It can be clearly seen that even a small change in volatility can have a huge impact on the price of a DNT. Looking at this chart is an intuitive way to find that vega must be negative. Interestingly enough even just taking a quick look at this chart can convince us that the absolute value of vega is decreasing if we are getting closer to the barriers.

Most end users think that the biggest risk is when the spot is getting close to the trigger. This is because end users really think about binary options in a binary way. As long as the DNT is alive, they focus on the positive outcome. However, for a dynamic hedger, the risk of a DNT is not that interesting when the value of the DNT is already small.

It is also very interesting that since the T-Bill price is independent of the volatility and since the DNT + DOT = T-Bill equation holds, an increasing volatility will decrease the price of the DNT by the exact same amount just like it will increase the price of the DOT. It is not surprising that the vega of the DOT should be the exact mirror of the DNT.

We can use the GetGreeks function to estimate vega, gamma, delta, and theta. For gamma we can use the GetGreeks function in the following way:

```
GetGreeks <- function(FUN, arg, epsilon,...) {
    all_args1 <- all_args2 <- list(...)
    all_args1[[arg]] <- as.numeric(all_args1[[arg]] + epsilon)
    all_args2[[arg]] <- as.numeric(all_args2[[arg]] - epsilon)
    (do.call(FUN, all_args1) -
        do.call(FUN, all_args2)) / (2 * epsilon)
}
Gamma <- function(FUN, epsilon, S, ...) {
    arg1 <- list(S, ...)
    arg2 <- list(S + 2 * epsilon, ...)
    arg3 <- list(S - 2 * epsilon, ...)
    y1 <- (do.call(FUN, arg2) - do.call(FUN, arg1)) / (2 * epsilon)
    y2 <- (do.call(FUN, arg1) - do.call(FUN, arg3)) / (2 * epsilon)
    (y1 - y2) / (2 * epsilon)
}
x = seq(0.9202, 0.9598, length = 200)
delta <- vega <- theta <- gamma <- rep(0, 200)
```

```
for(i in 1:200){
  delta[i] <- GetGreeks(FUN = dnt1, arg = 1, epsilon = 0.0001,
    x[i], 1000000, 0.96, 0.92, 0.06, 0.5, 0.02, -0.02)
  vega[i]  <-   GetGreeks(FUN = dnt1, arg = 5, epsilon = 0.0005,
    x[i], 1000000, 0.96, 0.92, 0.06, 0.5, 0.0025, -0.025)
  theta[i] <- - GetGreeks(FUN = dnt1, arg = 6, epsilon = 1/365,
    x[i], 1000000, 0.96, 0.92, 0.06, 0.5, 0.0025, -0.025)
  gamma[i] <- Gamma(FUN = dnt1, epsilon = 0.0001, S = x[i], K =
    1e6, U = 0.96, L = 0.92, sigma = 0.06, Time = 0.5, r = 0.02, b =
-0.02)
}


windows()
plot(x, vega, type = "l", xlab = "S",ylab = "", main = "Vega")
```

The following chart is the result of the preceding code:

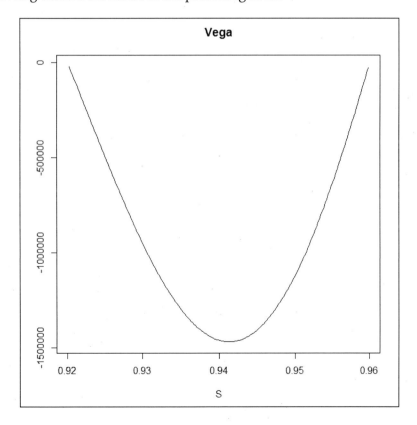

After having a look at the value chart, the delta of a DNT is also very close to intuitions; if we are coming close to the higher barrier, our delta gets negative, and if we are coming closer to the lower barrier, the delta gets positive as follows:

```
windows()
plot(x, delta, type = "l", xlab = "S",ylab = "", main = "Delta")
```

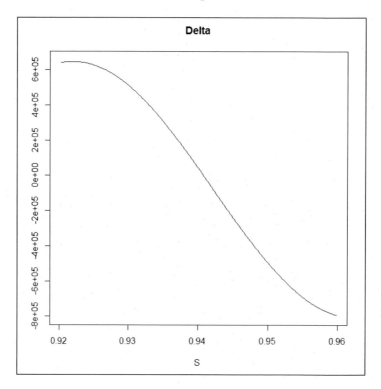

This is really a non-convex situation; if we would like to do a dynamic delta hedge, we will lose money for sure. If the spot price goes up, the delta of the DNT decreases, so we should buy some AUDUSD as a hedge. However, if the spot price goes down, we should sell some AUDUSD. Imagine a scenario where AUDUSD goes up 20 pips in the morning and then goes down 20 pips in the afternoon. For a dynamic hedger, this means buying some AUDUSD after the price moved up and selling this very same amount after the price comes down.

The changing of the delta can be described by the gamma as follows:

```
windows()
plot(x, gamma, type = "l", xlab = "S",ylab = "", main = "Gamma")
```

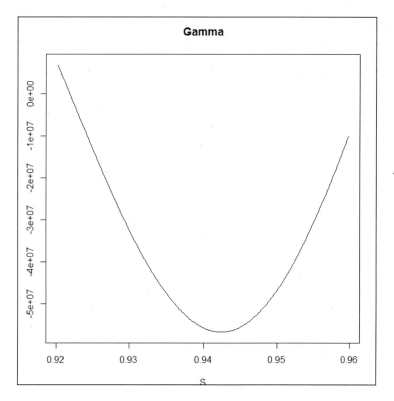

Negative gamma means that if the spot goes up, our delta is decreasing, but if the spot goes down, our delta is increasing. This doesn't sound great. For this inconvenient non-convex situation, there is some compensation, that is, the value of theta is positive. If nothing happens, but one day passes, the DNT will automatically worth more.

Here, we use theta as minus 1 times the partial derivative, since if (T-t) is the time left, we check how the value changes as t increases by one day:

```
windows()
plot(x, theta, type = "l", xlab = "S",ylab = "", main = "Theta")
```

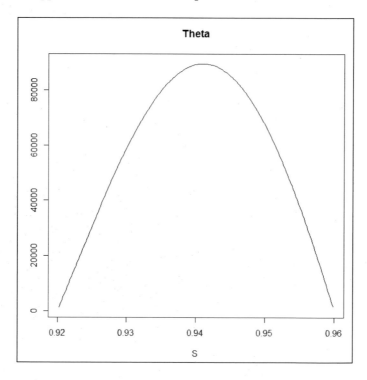

The more negative the gamma, the more positive our theta. This is how time compensates for the potential losses generated by the negative gamma.

Risk-neutral pricing also implicates that negative gamma should be compensated by a positive theta. This is the main message of the Black-Scholes framework for vanilla options, but this is also true for exotics. See *Taleb (1997)* and *Wilmott (2006)*.

We already introduced the Black-Scholes surface before; now, we can go into more detail. This surface is also a nice interpretation of how theta and delta work. It shows the price of an option for different spot prices and times to maturity, so the slope of this surface is the theta for one direction and delta for the other. The code for this is as follows:

```
BS_surf <- function(S, Time, FUN, ...) {
  n <- length(S)
```

```
  k <- length(Time)
  m <- matrix(0, n, k)
  for (i in 1:n) {
    for (j in 1:k) {
      l <- list(S = S[i], Time = Time[j], ...)
      m[i,j] <- do.call(FUN, l)
      }
  }
  persp3D(z = m, xlab = "underlying", ylab = "Time",
    zlab = "option price", phi = 30, theta = 30, bty = "b2")
}
BS_surf(seq(0.92,0.96,length = 200), seq(1/365, 1/48, length = 200),
  dnt1, K = 1000000, U = 0.96, L = 0.92, r = 0.0025, b = -0.0250,
    sigma = 0.2)
```

The preceding code gives the following output:

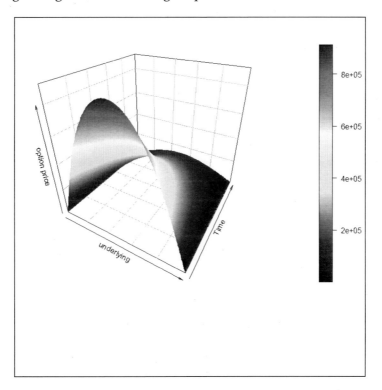

We can see what was already suspected; DNT likes when time is passing and the spot is moving to the middle of the (L,U) interval.

Another way to price the Double-no-touch option

Static replication is always the most elegant way of pricing. The no-arbitrage argument will let us say that if, at some time in the future, two portfolios have the same value for sure, then their price should be equal any time before this. We will show how double-knock-out (DKO) options could be used to build a DNT. We will need to use a trick; the strike price could be the same as one of the barriers. For a DKO call, the strike price should be lower than the upper barrier because if the strike price is not lower than the upper barrier, the DKO call would be knocked out before it could become in-the-money, so in this case, the option would be worthless as nobody can ever exercise it in-the-money. However, we can choose the strike price to be equal to the lower barrier. For a put, the strike price should be higher than the lower barrier, so why not make it equal to the upper barrier. This way, the DKO call and DKO put option will have a very convenient feature; if they are still alive, they will both expiry in-the-money.

Now, we are almost done. We just have to add the DKO prices, and we will get a DNT that has a payout of (U-L) dollars. Since DNT prices are linear in the payout, we only have to multiply the result by K*(U-L):

```
dnt2 <- function(S, K, U, L, sigma, T, r, b) {

    a <- DoubleBarrierOption("co", S, L, L, U, T, r, b, sigma, 0,
        0,title = NULL, description = NULL)
    z <- a@price

    b <- DoubleBarrierOption("po", S, U, L, U, T, r, b, sigma, 0,
        0,title = NULL, description = NULL)
    y <- b@price

    (z + y) / (U - L) * K
}
```

Now, we have two functions for which we can compare the results:

```
dnt1(0.9266, 1000000, 0.9600, 0.9200, 0.06, 0.25, 0.0025, -0.025)
[1] 48564.59


dnt2(0.9266, 1000000, 0.9600, 0.9200, 0.06, 0.25, 0.0025, -0.025)
[1] 48564.45
```

For a DNT with a USD 1 million contingent payout and an initial market value of over 48,000 dollars, it is very nice to see that the difference in the prices is only 14 cents. Technically, however, having a second pricing function is not a big help since low volatility is also an issue for `dnt2`.

We will use `dnt1` for the rest of the chapter.

The life of a Double-no-touch option – a simulation

How has the DNT price been evolving during the second quarter of 2014? We have the open-high-low-close type time series with five minute frequency for AUDUSD, so we know all the extreme prices:

```
d <- read.table("audusd.csv", colClasses = c("character",
rep("numeric",5)), sep = ";", header = TRUE)

underlying <- as.vector(t(d[, 2:5]))

t <- rep( d[,6], each = 4)

n <- length(t)

option_price <- rep(0, n)


for (i in 1:n) {
  option_price[i] <- dnt1(S = underlying[i], K = 1000000,
    U = 0.9600, L = 0.9200, sigma = 0.06, T = t[i]/(60*24*365),
      r = 0.0025, b = -0.0250)
}
a <- min(option_price)
b <- max(option_price)
option_price_transformed = (option_price - a) * 0.03 / (b - a) + 0.92


par(mar = c(6, 3, 3, 5))
matplot(cbind(underlying,option_price_transformed), type = "l",
    lty = 1, col = c("grey", "red"),
    main = "Price of underlying and DNT",
    xaxt = "n", yaxt = "n",  ylim = c(0.91,0.97),
    ylab = "", xlab = "Remaining time")
abline(h = c(0.92, 0.96), col = "green")
```

```
axis(side = 2, at = pretty(option_price_transformed),
    col.axis = "grey", col = "grey")
axis(side = 4, at = pretty(option_price_transformed),
    labels = round(seq(a/1000,1000,length = 7)), las = 2,
    col = "red", col.axis = "red")
axis(side = 1, at = seq(1,n, length=6),

    labels = round(t[round(seq(1,n, length=6))]/60/24))
```

The following is the output for the preceding code:

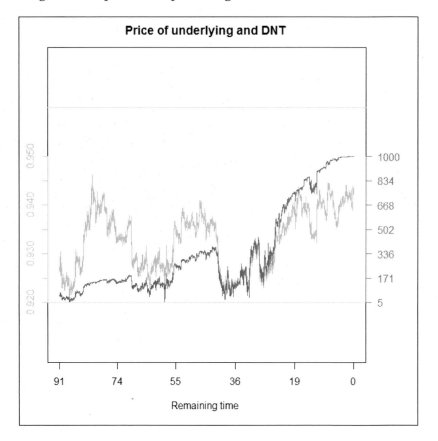

The price of a DNT is shown in red on the right axis (divided by 1000), and the actual AUDUSD price is shown in grey on the left axis. The green lines are the barriers of 0.9200 and 0.9600. The chart shows that in 2014 Q2, the AUDUSD currency pair was traded inside the (0.9200; 0.9600) interval; thus, the payout of the DNT would have been USD 1 million. This DNT looks like a very good investment; however, reality is just one trajectory out of an *a priori* almost infinite set. It could have happened differently. For example, on May 02, 2014, there were still 59 days left until expiry, and AUDUSD was traded at 0.9203, just three pips away from the lower barrier. At this point, the price of this DNT was only USD 5,302 dollars which is shown in the following code:

```
dnt1(0.9203, 1000000, 0.9600, 0.9200, 0.06, 59/365, 0.0025, -0.025)
[1] 5302.213
```

Compare this USD 5,302 to the initial USD 48,564 option price!

In the following simulation, we will show some different trajectories. All of them start from the same 0.9266 AUDUSD spot price as it was on the dawn of April 01, and we will see how many of them stayed inside the (0.9200; 0.9600) interval. To make it simple, we will simulate geometric Brown motions by using the same 6 percent volatility as we used to price the DNT:

```
library(matrixStats)
DNT_sim <- function(S0 = 0.9266, mu = 0, sigma = 0.06, U = 0.96,
  L = 0.92, N = 5) {
    dt <- 5 / (365 * 24 * 60)
    t <- seq(0, 0.25, by = dt)
    Time <- length(t)

    W <- matrix(rnorm((Time - 1) * N), Time - 1, N)
    W <- apply(W, 2, cumsum)
    W <- sqrt(dt) * rbind(rep(0, N), W)
    S <- S0 * exp((mu - sigma^2 / 2) * t + sigma * W )
    option_price <- matrix(0, Time, N)

    for (i in 1:N)
        for (j in 1:Time)
```

```
        option_price[j,i] <- dnt1(S[j,i], K = 1000000, U, L, sigma,
            0.25-t[j], r = 0.0025,
            b = -0.0250)*(min(S[1:j,i]) > L & max(S[1:j,i]) < U)


    survivals <- sum(option_price[Time,] > 0)
    dev.new(width = 19, height = 10)


    par(mfrow = c(1,2))
    matplot(t,S, type = "l", main = "Underlying price",
        xlab = paste("Survived", survivals, "from", N), ylab = "")
    abline( h = c(U,L), col = "blue")
    matplot(t, option_price, type = "l", main = "DNT price",
        xlab = "", ylab = "")}


set.seed(214)
system.time(DNT_sim())
```

The following is the output for the preceding code:

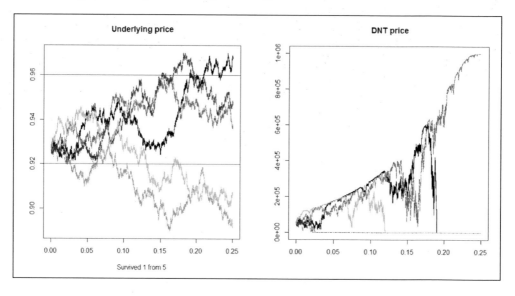

Here, the only surviving trajectory is the red one; in all other cases, the DNT hits either the higher or the lower barrier. The line `set.seed(214)` grants that this simulation will look the same anytime we run this. One out of five is still not that bad; it would suggest that for an end user or gambler who does no dynamic hedging, this option has an approximate value of 20 percent of the payout (especially since the interest rates are low, the time value of money is not important).

However, five trajectories are still too few to jump to such conclusions. We should check the DNT survivorship ratio for a much higher number of trajectories.

The ratio of the surviving trajectories could be a good estimator of the a priori real-world survivorship probability of this DNT; thus, the end user value of it. Before increasing N rapidly, we should keep in mind how much time this simulation took. For my computer, it took 50.75 seconds for N = 5, and 153.11 seconds for N = 15.

The following is the output for N = 15:

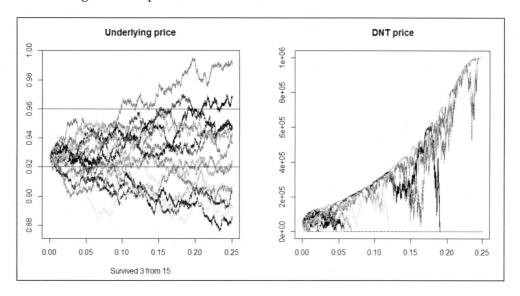

Now, 3 out of 15 survived, so the estimated survivorship ratio is still 3/15, which is equal to 20 percent. Looks like this is a very nice product; the price is around 5 percent of the payout, while 20 percent is the estimated survivorship ratio. Just out of curiosity, run the simulation for N equal to 200. This should take about 30 minutes.

The following is the output for N = 200:

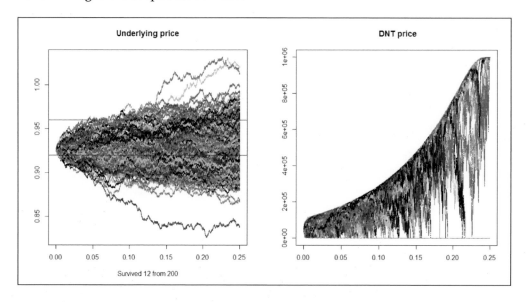

The results are shocking; now, only 12 out of 200 survive, and the ratio is only 6 percent! So to get a better picture, we should run the simulation for a larger N.

The movie *Whatever Works* by *Woody Allen* (starring Larry David) is 92 minutes long; in simulation time, that is N = 541. For this N = 541, there are only 38 surviving trajectories, resulting in a survivorship ratio of 7 percent.

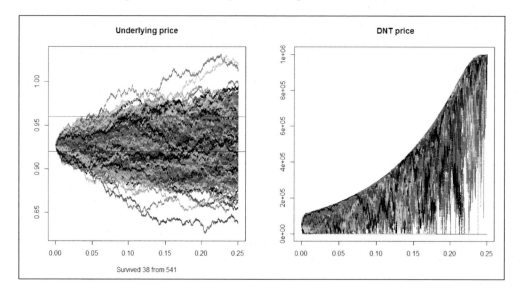

What is the real expected survivorship ratio? Is it 20 percent, 6 percent, or 7 percent? We simply don't know at this point. Mathematicians warn us that the law of large numbers requires large numbers, where large is much more than 541, so it would be advisable to run this simulation for as large an N as time allows. Of course, getting a better computer also helps to do more N during the same time. Anyway, from this point of view, *Hui's (1996)* relatively fast converging DNT pricing formula gets some respect.

So far, we have used the very same stochastic process for pricing that we used for the simulation. Common sense says that in some cases, market-implied volatility could be biased as either higher or lower than the expected volatility. Not surprisingly, running the simulation for these two conditions, N = 200 and sigma = 5.5 percent, results in more surviving trajectories, 15 for this seed. Running the simulation for N = 200 and sigma = 6.5 percent results in fewer surviving trajectories: nine for this seed. This again shows the high impact of vega in a very intuitive way. The number of surviving trajectories, which can be 9, 12, or 15, mostly depends on the volatility of the process. Survivorship rates are 4.5 percent, 6 percent, or 7.5 percent. This also raises a more philosophical question: what about risk premium? If the market needs vega, it could happen that we can purchase a DNT based on 6 percent volatility even if we expect 5.5 percent volatility. In some tense circumstances, the market could be really vega-thirsty. In these cases, risk premium is included.

Derivative pricing always assumes dynamic hedging because we are looking for the marginal cost of producing such an instrument then we use the no-arbitrage argument. Some market players are actually trying to play this strategy and become providers for the derivatives, like a factory. They are willing to take any side of a deal, since they will eliminate almost all of their risks by almost continuous dynamic hedging. They are the market makers. However, not all market players are derivative factories; there are many of them who deliberately seek sensitivities; thus, they are not hedging their derivative position. This second group is called the market takers or end users. Some of them are looking for sensitivities because they already have some and they want to decrease those (natural hedgers). Some others don't have any sensitivities at the beginning, but would like to make a financial bet (speculators).

Interestingly, there could be a significant difference between the price of the derivative and its value for the end user. By purchasing a DNT, an end-user can make a bet and eventually either get nothing, or win much more than the initial price. Is there any risk premium for this bet, or is it similar to a casino? Is the real-life expected value of a DNT higher than the risk-neutral expected value (which equals the price)? The value in use or the "user experience" could be different because the market maker will quote a price based on the implied volatilities. In the case of a tense market situation, the demand for vega could push its price (that is, the implied volatility) higher than the expected volatility.

In this case, anyone who can still sell volatility will get a premium. In the case of DNT, getting a premium means that its price will be lower than the real life expected value of its payout.

What about a **Double-one-touch (DOT)**? Since the Treasury Bill can be seen as the sum of a DNT and a DOT, if the DNT is too cheap, then the DOT must be too expensive. Thus, these exotic options are easy bets on volatilities; if a speculator thinks volatility will be significantly lower than the implied, purchasing a DNT is a straightforward bet. If the speculator expects higher volatility than the implied, a DOT is the proper bet.

In this sense, DNT is similar to a short straddle and DOT is to a long straddle; however, binary options are much easier to calibrate to the desired size. A long straddle is a long call and long put in the same size, strike price, and expiry. A short straddle is the mirror picture: short call and short put. A strangle is very similar to a straddle; the only difference is that the strike price of a call is not equal but higher than the strike price of the put. Compared to a short straddle or a short strangle, betting on volatility is much more convenient by purchasing a DNT, because holding a long DNT option position requires no further collateral adjustment. DNT is a highly-leveraged product; however, the total amount that can be lost is already paid upfront, so it fits to the menu of online trading platforms where the typical client is a small retail speculator.

Based on this logic, the risk premium goes only to players who are willing to take a position that is less favorable by other market players. If there is an extra demand for volatility, then DNTS will include risk premium, but if there is an extra supply for volatility then DOTs will include risk premium. It could also happen that the market is in a stable equilibrium and neither DNTs nor DOTs include any risk premium.

Exotic options embedded in structured products

Most of the time, exotic options are traded in camouflage; they are embedded in structured bonds or certificates. The exotic behavior is translated into a much more user-friendly language that is easier to understand by an everyday investor. For example, a binary payout can be calculated into a coupon yield; the investor gets a higher coupon if the circumstances let the binary option give its payout. A structure that includes a knock-out option could be called an airbag certificate, since as far as a long KO option is not knocked-out, it gives some protection against market losses, similar to an airbag that protects the driver in case of a less serious accident.

Another example is a turbo certificate, which, most of the time, is just a securitized form of a knock-out option with a deep in-the-money strike and a KO close to the strike. Lookback options can be found in capital guarantee products with coupons linked to the extreme values of stock indices.

As a numerical example, let's take a look at a three-month maturity certificate of deposit (CD) that either pays a 3 percent coupon or 0 percent, conditionally on the FX market behavior. This capital-guaranteed product can be seen as a portfolio of a T-Bill and a binary option. If the 3-month T-bill can be purchased at 99.75 percent, then there is 0.25 cent on each dollar that can be spent on a binary option. The capital at maturity will be granted by the T-Bill part, while the binary option will be responsible for the contingent 3 percent coupon.

At this point, any binary option would do the trick; purchasing a DNT would work too, but there are way too many parameters. Banks must fine-tune all the parameters to make the whole construction attractive. In the risk-neutral world from the market makers' point of view, a lower trigger of L=0.9200 with a 3-month maturity is almost the same as L=0.9195, with a bit more than a 3-month maturity:

```
dnt1(0.9266, 1000000, 0.9600, 0.9200, 0.06, 90/365, 0.0025, -0.025)
[1] 50241.58
dnt1(0.9266, 1000000, 0.9600, 0.9195, 0.06, 94/365, 0.0025, -0.025)
[1] 50811.61
```

This is a very common feature among options, including knock-out events; some extra time can most of the time compensate for pushing the barrier a bit further from the spot. In the risk-neutral world, the S/L distance is always divided by a factor of $\sigma\sqrt{(T-t)}$, so there is a trade-off; we can make L lower, but in return, we should increase the maturity. In the real world, the expectations of end users are driven by their subjective or perceived probabilities. Provided that we are not planning to dynamically hedge our DNT, we would prefer L = 0.9195 and T = 94 days over L = 0.9200 and T = 90 days.

That is why L, U, and T should be set in a way that helps the product look attractive to end users. Also, if the exotic option is embedded into a structure, the structure itself should be easy to sell. At the end, most of the structures will be cut into smaller, retail-sized pieces, like 1000 USD notional. Of course, each slice of the cake will be the same, so for the bank, it can be seen as one huge product.

Coming back to setting L, U, and T, it is easy to see that the price of a DNT is strictly a monotone function of L, U, and T (and also a monotone for volatility). Under certain market conditions (S, r, b, and volatility), we set, say, L = 0.9195 and T = 94 days. Now, we can ask the following inverse pricing question: for what U will the price of the DNT be 33 percent of the payout?

This will be the implied upper barrier, implied in a sense that the price is already given. Here comes a strange answer: it is not certain that such an implied U exists! This is because if we start increasing the upper barrier, the DNT price will converge to the price of a No-Touch (NT) option. If this NT is worth less than 33 percent, no U will make our DNT worth 33 percent. We use the `BinaryBarrierOption` function from the `fExoticOptions` package to price the No-Touch option which is depicted in the following code:

```
dnt1(0.9266, 1000000, 1.0600, 0.9200, 0.06, 94/365, 0.0025, -0.025)
```

```
[1] 144702
```

```
a <- BinaryBarrierOption(9, 0.9266, 0, 0.9200, 1000000, 94/365,
  0.0025, -0.025, 0.06, 1, 1, title = NULL, description = NULL)
```

```
(z <- a@price)
```

```
[1] 144705.3
```

In the risk-neutral world, if we push U 1000 pips higher, it will become almost completely irrelevant, so DNT behaves like an NT.

So, in this case, if we want the DNT to cost 33 percent, we should choose an L that is lower than 0.9195. Next, we set L = 0.9095 and find a U that makes the DNT worth 33 percent. At the end of this part, we will show a way to find an implied U by using the `implied_U_DNT` function which is shown in the following code. Now, suppose we use U = 0.9745 for other reasons.

```
dnt1(0.9266, 100, 0.9705, 0.9095, 0.06, 90/365, 0.0025, -0.025)
```

```
[1] 31.44338
```

This DNT costs only 31.44 percent of the payout, so there will still be some room for the bank to have some profit for all the hard work of structuring. Suppose the bank can sell a total of USD 100 million of this CD, then 3 months later, the bank has to pay to the clients either USD 100 million (0 percent per annum) or USD 100.75 million (approximately 3 percent per annum). This contingent promise can be hedged by purchasing T-Bills in 100 million USD notional and DNT options with 0.75 million USD payout. At the beginning, these instruments cost the bank *99.75%*100.000.000+31.44338%*750.000 = USD 99.985.825,35*; thus, the bank makes a profit of 14,174.65 USD.

In other cases, the implied time to maturity could be an interesting question. Under certain market conditions (where S, r, b, and volatility are given) for a given (L,U) pair, what is the T that makes the DNT cost, say, 50 percent? Even for a very tight (L-U) interval, we can find a T small enough to make the DNT price go up to 50 percent; this is also true the other way round; even a very wide (L,U) pair will make a DNT worth only 50 percent if there is enough time. See *implied_T_DNT* at the end of this section.

Unlike L, U, or T, we cannot choose the volatility parameter deliberately; however, calculating the implied volatility could be useful to price other derivatives. This is a key pricing concept; risk-neutral pricing is based on comparison. If we know the price (and all other parameters) of a DNT, we can find out what volatility was used for pricing. See *implied_vol_DNT* at the end of this section.

Next, we will show a lot of implied functions and finally draw the implied charts:

```
implied_DNT_image <- function(S = 0.9266, K = 1000000, U = 0.96,
  L = 0.92, sigma = 0.06, Time = 0.25, r = 0.0025, b = -0.0250) {
    S_  <- seq(L,U,length = 300)
    K_  <- seq(800000, 1200000, length = 300)
    U_  <- seq(L+0.01, L + .15, length = 300)
    L_  <- seq(0.8, U - 0.001, length = 300)
    sigma_  <- seq(0.005, 0.1, length = 300)
    T_  <- seq(1/365, 1, length = 300)
    r_  <- seq(-10, 10, length = 300)
    b_  <- seq(-0.5, 0.5, length = 300)

    p1 <- lapply(S_, dnt1, K = 1000000, U = 0.96, L = 0.92,
      sigma = 0.06, Time = 0.25, r = 0.0025, b = -0.0250)
    p2 <- lapply(K_, dnt1, S = 0.9266, U = 0.96, L = 0.92,
      sigma = 0.06, Time = 0.25, r = 0.0025, b = -0.0250)
    p3 <- lapply(U_, dnt1, S = 0.9266, K = 1000000, L = 0.92,
      sigma = 0.06, Time = 0.25, r = 0.0025, b = -0.0250)
    p4 <- lapply(L_, dnt1, S = 0.9266, K = 1000000, U = 0.96,
      sigma = 0.06, Time = 0.25, r = 0.0025, b = -0.0250)
    p5 <- lapply(sigma_, dnt1, S = 0.9266, K = 1000000, U = 0.96,
      L = 0.92, Time = 0.25, r = 0.0025, b = -0.0250)
    p6 <- lapply(T_, dnt1, S = 0.9266, K = 1000000, U = 0.96, L =
      0.92, sigma = 0.06, r = 0.0025, b = -0.0250)
    p7 <- lapply(r_, dnt1, S = 0.9266, K = 1000000, U = 0.96, L =
      0.92, sigma = 0.06, Time = 0.25,  b = -0.0250)
```

```
    p8 <- lapply(b_, dnt1, S = 0.9266, K = 1000000, U = 0.96, L =
      0.92, sigma = 0.06, Time = 0.25, r = 0.0025)
    dev.new(width = 20, height = 10)


    par(mfrow = c(2, 4), mar = c(2, 2, 2, 2))
    plot(S_, p1, type = "l", xlab = "", ylab = "", main = "S")
    plot(K_, p2, type = "l", xlab = "", ylab = "", main = "K")
    plot(U_, p3, type = "l", xlab = "", ylab = "", main = "U")
    plot(L_, p4, type = "l", xlab = "", ylab = "", main = "L")
    plot(sigma_, p5, type = "l", xlab = "", ylab = "", main =
      "sigma")
    plot(T_, p6, type = "l", xlab = "", ylab = "", main = "Time")
    plot(r_, p7, type = "l", xlab = "", ylab = "", main = "r")
    plot(b_, p8, type = "l", xlab = "", ylab = "", main = "b")
}


implied_vol_DNT <- function(S = 0.9266, K = 1000000, U = 0.96, L =
  0.92, Time = 0.25, r = 0.0025, b = -0.0250, price) {
    f <- function(sigma)
      dnt1(S, K, U, L, sigma, Time, r, b) - price
    uniroot(f, interval = c(0.001, 100))$root
}


implied_U_DNT <- function(S = 0.9266, K = 1000000, L = 0.92,
  sigma = 0.06, Time = 0.25, r = 0.0025, b = -0.0250, price = 4) {
    f <- function(U)
      dnt1(S, K, U, L, sigma, Time, r, b) - price
    uniroot(f, interval = c(L+0.01, L + 100))$root
}
```

```
implied_T_DNT <- function(S = 0.9266, K = 1000000, U = 0.96, L =
   0.92, sigma = 0.06, r = 0.0025, b = -0.0250, price = 4){
     f <- function(Time)
         dnt1(S, K, U, L, sigma, Time, r, b) - price
     uniroot(f, interval = c(1/365, 100))$root
}
library(rootSolve)
implied_DNT_image()
print(implied_vol_DNT(price = 6))
print(implied_U_DNT(price = 4))
print(implied_T_DNT(price = 30))
```

The following is the output for the preceding code:

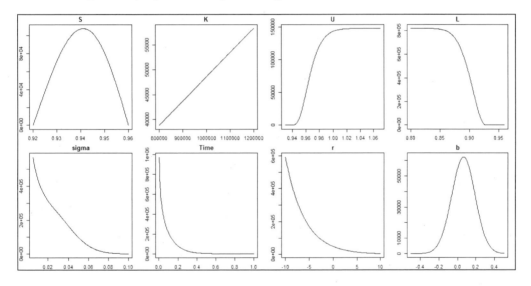

Summary

We started this chapter by introducing exotic options. In a brief theoretical summary, we explained how exotics and plain vanillas are linked together. There are many types of exotics. We showed one possible way of classification that is consistent with the fExoticOptions package. We showed how the Black-Scholes surface (a 3D chart that contains the price of a derivative dependent on time and the underlying price) can be constructed for any pricing function.

Pricing of exotic options is just the first step. Market makers keep thousands of different options in their trading books. This is possible only because each option can be decomposed into certain sensitivities, the so-called Greeks. Being partial derivatives, Greeks are additive; thus, the portfolio of derivatives has the sum of the Greeks of its elements. The next step was estimating Greeks for any derivative-pricing functions. Our numerical method can be calibrated to the real market conditions; for many parameters, we already know what the smallest possible change is. For example, the smallest change for an interbank AUDUSD fx rate is 0.0001. Even multiple partial derivatives such as gamma or vanna can be calculated with this numerical method.

In the second half of this chapter, we focused on one particular exotic option: the Double-No-Touch (DNT) binary option. The reason behind this focus is based on the popularity of DNT options and also because there are many tricks that can be shown on DNTs with conclusions relevant to many other exotic options. We showed two different ways to price DNT options. First, we implemented the *Hui (1996)* closed form solution, where the price is a result of an infinite sum. The speed of convergence is often very quick; however, this is not always the case. We showed a practical way of how convergence issues can be handled without wasting too much computing time. Another way to price a DNT is a static replication from one DKO call and one DKO put option. To price these DKO options, we used the fExoticOptions package. We found very little difference between the results of the two DNT pricing methods.

We showed how the DNT option behaves on real-life data by using 5 minutes frequency open-low-high-close type time series of AUDUSD fx rates from the second quarter of 2014. We estimated the survivorship probability of a DNT by simulation to show how risk premium can be included in DNTs or DOTs based on the supply-demand tensions for volatility. Finally, we showed some practical fine-tuning methods to find missing parameters for DNT with a certain price in the case of building a structured product by introducing functions to find implied parameters.

References

- **Black, F. and Scholes, M. [1973]**: *The Pricing of Options and Corporate Liabilities*, The Journal of Political Economy, 81(3), pp. 637-654

- **Carr, P., Ellis, K. and Gupta, V. [1998]**: *Static hedging of exotic options*, Journal of Finance, 53, 1165-1190

- **Derman, E., Ergener, D. and Kani, I. [1995]**: *Static Options Replication*, Journal of Derivatives, 2 (4), 78-95

- **DeRosa, D. F. [2011]**: *Options on Foreign Exchange*. Wiley Finance

- **Haug, E. G. [2007a]**: *The Complete Guide to Option Pricing Formulas*, 2nd edition. The McGraw-Hill Companies

- **Haug, E. G. [2007b]**: *Derivatives Models on Models*. John Wiley & Sons

- **Hui, C. H. [1996]**: One-touch Double Barrier Binary Option Values, Applied Financial Economics, 1996, 6, pp. 343-346

- **Merton, R. [1973]**: *Theory of Rational Option Pricing*, The Bell Journal of Economics and Management Science, 4(1), pp. 141-183

- **Taleb, N. N., [1997]**: *Dynamic Hedging*. John Wiley & Sons

- **Wilmott, P., [2006]**: *Quantitative Finance*, 2nd edition. John Wiley & Sons

8

Optimal Hedging

After discussing the theoretical background in the previous chapters, we will now focus on some practical problems of derivatives trading.

Derivatives pricing, as detailed in *Daróczi et al. (2013), Chapter 6, Derivatives Pricing,* is based on the availability of a replicating portfolio that consists of traded securities that offer the same cash flow as the derivative asset. In other words, the risk of a derivative can be perfectly hedged by holding a certain number of underlying assets and riskless bonds. Forward and futures contracts can be hedged statically, while the hedging of options needs a rebalancing of the portfolio from time to time. The perfect dynamic hedge presented by the **Black-Scholes-Merton (BSM)** model (*Black and Scholes, 1973, Merton, 1973*) has several limitations in reality.

In this chapter, we are going to go into the details of the hedging of derivatives in a static as well as a dynamic setting. The effects of discrete time trading and the presence of transaction costs are presented. As in the case of discrete time hedging, the cost of the synthetic reproduction of an option becomes stochastic; hence, there is a sharp trade-off between risk and transaction costs. The optimal hedging period is derived according to the different goals of the optimization and is affected not only by market factors, but investor-specific parameters such as risk aversion as well.

Hedging of derivatives

Hedging means to create a portfolio that offsets the risk of the original exposure. As risk is measured by the fluctuation of the future cash flow, the goal of hedging is usually the reduction of the variance of the total portfolio's value. The first chapter of *Daróczi et al. (2013)* presents the optimal hedging decision in the presence of the basis risk, when the hedging instrument and the position to be hedged are different. This often happens at the hedging of commodity exposure, because commodities are traded on exchanges, where only standardized (maturity, quantity, and quality) contracts are available.

The optimal hedge ratio is the proportion of the hedging instrument as a percentage of the exposure that minimizes the volatility of the whole position. In this chapter, we will deal with the hedging of derivative positions, assuming that the underlying is also traded in the OTC market; therefore, there will be no mismatch between the exposure and the hedging derivative, so no basis risk arises.

Market risk of derivatives

The value of a forward or futures contract depends on the spot price of the underlying asset, the time to maturity, the risk-free rate, and the strike price; in the case of plain vanilla options, the volatility of the underlying asset also has an effect on the option price. This statement holds only if the underlying asset provides no cash flow (no income and no cost) till the maturity of the derivative transaction; otherwise, this (both incoming and outgoing) cash flow also has an effect on the price. For the purpose of simplicity, here we will discuss derivatives pricing under the assumption of no cash flow (non-dividend-paying stocks), although an extension of the model to other underlying assets (like currencies and commodities) needs some modifications in the formulas, but it has no impact on the basic logic. As the strike price is stable during maturity, only changes to the other four factors can cause a change in the value of the derivative. The sensitivity of the derivative towards the mentioned variables is shown by the Greeks, the first partial derivatives according to the given variable, as presented in detail in *Daróczi et al. (2013) Chapter 6, Derivatives Pricing*.

The Black-Scholes-Merton model assumes that both the risk-free interest rate and the volatility of the underlying are constant, so as the change of time is deterministic, the only stochastic variable that affects the value of the derivative is the spot price of the underlying asset. The risk that is derived from the fluctuation of the spot price can be eliminated by holding the exact delta amount, which is the sensitivity of the derivative's price to the spot price (see Equation 1) of the underlying asset:

$$\Delta = \frac{\partial c}{\partial S}$$

Equation 1

Whether delta is stable or changes over time depends on the derivative, and leads to different (static or dynamic) hedging strategies (*Hull, 2009*) presented in the following section.

Static delta hedge

Hedging of a forward agreement is straightforward as it is a binding obligation for both parties. Being in a long-forward position, we are sure that we will buy at maturity, while a short position means a sale of the underlying asset with certainty. So we can perfectly hedge our forward position by selling (long forward) or buying (short forward) the underlying at the amount of the derivative. We can check the delta of the forward by differentiating the value of the long-forward position:

$$LF = S - PV\left(K\right)$$

Equation 2

Here, LF stands for the long forward, S denotes the spot price, and K is the strike price, which is the agreed forward price. The present value is denoted by PV.

So delta equals one, and it is independent of the actual market circumstances.

However, the value of a futures contract is the difference between the actual futures price (F) and the strike (S), because of the daily settlement of the position; hence, its delta is F/S and it changes with time. Consequently, a slight rebalancing of the position is needed, but in the absence of stochastic interest rates, the process of delta can be foreseen (*Hull, 2009*).

Dynamic delta hedge

In the case of options, the delivery of the underlying is uncertain. It depends on the decision of the party in a long position; this is the party that bought the option. Not surprisingly, the hedging of a contingent claim cannot be achieved by a static buy-and-hold strategy presented in the previous point. In the framework of the binomial model, an option position is always hedged for the next Δt period, while in the Black-Scholes-Merton model, Δt converges to zero; thus, the hedging position is to be rebalanced in every instant. However, in the real world, practice assets can only be traded at discrete points of time, so the hedging portfolio is adjusted also at discrete time points. Let's look at the consequences of this in the example of a plain vanilla **ATM (at-the-money)** call option written on a non-dividend paying stock.

R contains a package, `OptHedge`, for the estimation of the value of an option and hedging strategy of call and put options on a grid at discrete time intervals; however, our aim is to illustrate the effect of the length of the trading periods. Therefore, we will use our own functions for the calculations.

First, we install the package to be used:

```
install.packages("fOptions")
library(fOptions)
```

Then, we can check the BS price of the call by using the already known code on a chosen parameter set:

```
GBSOption(TypeFlag = "c", S = 100, X = 100, Time = 1/2, r = 0.05, b =
   0.05, sigma = 0.3)
```

We receive the given parameters and the price of the call option according to the Black-Scholes formula:

```
Parameters:
          Value:
 TypeFlag c
 S        100
 X        100
 Time     0.5
 r        0.05
 b        0.05
 sigma    0.3
Option Price:
 9.63487
```

Based on the BS model, the price of the call is 9.63487.

In practice, usually, the prices of the options are quoted in the standardized markets, and the implied volatility can be inferred from the Black-Scholes formula. A trader who expects lower volatility in the future than the implied volatility can make a profit by selling the option and simultaneously delta hedging it. In the following scenario, we present delta hedging of the short position in the preceding option on a stock following a **geometric Brownian motion (GBM)**. We assume that all assumptions of the BSM model, except for the continuous-time trading, hold. In order to hedge the short option, we have to have delta amount of the stock, and as delta changes, we have to rebalance our portfolio regularly, in the following case, weekly, which makes it 26 times during the lifetime of the option. The frequency of the rebalancing should adjust to the liquidity and volatility of the underlying asset.

Let's look at a possible future path of the stock price and the development of the delta. The `price_simulation` function generates the price process with the given parameters: initial stock price (S_0), drift (*mu*), and volatility (*sigma*) of the GBM process and the remaining parameters of the call option (*K, Time*) and the chosen rebalancing period (*Δt*). After simulating the spot price process, the function calculates the delta and the price of the option for every interim date, and also plots them. By using the `set.seed` function, we can create reproducible simulations:

```
set.seed(2014)

library(fOptions)

Price_simulation <- function(S0, mu, sigma, rf, K, Time,  dt, plots =
   FALSE) {

   t <- seq(0, Time, by = dt)

   N <- length(t)

   W <- c(0,cumsum(rnorm(N-1)))

   S <- S0*exp((mu-sigma^2/2)*t + sigma*sqrt(dt)*W)

   delta <- rep(0, N-1)

   call_ <- rep(0, N-1)

   for(i in 1:(N-1) ){

      delta[i] <- GBSGreeks("Delta", "c", S[i], K, Time-t[i], rf, rf,
         sigma)

      call_[i] <- GBSOption("c", S[i], K, Time-t[i], rf, rf,
         sigma)@price}

   if(plots){

      dev.new(width=30, height=10)

      par(mfrow = c(1,3))

      plot(t, S, type = "l", main = "Price of underlying")

      plot(t[-length(t)], delta, type = "l", main = "Delta", xlab =
         "t")

      plot(t[-length(t)], call_ , type = "l", main = "Price of option",
         xlab = "t")

   }

}
```

We then set the parameters of our function:

```
Price_simulation(100, 0.2, 0.3, 0.05, 100, 0.5, 1/250, plots = TRUE)
```

We will get a potential path of the stock price, the actual delta, and the corresponding option price:

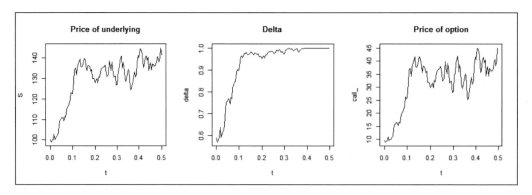

We can see a possible future scenario, according to which the spot price rises and quickly arrives at an in-the-money level, so the option is exercised at maturity. The delta of the call follows the stock price's fluctuations and converges to one. The probability of exercising the call option increases if the spot price moves up, and in order to replicate the call, we have to buy some more stock, while the falling stock price leads to a lower delta, indicating a sale. All in all, we buy if the stock is expensive, and sell if the price is low. The price of the option derives from this cost of the hedging. The shorter the rebalancing period, the less the price movement that we have to follow.

The cost of hedging is defined as the present value of the cumulative net costs of buying and selling the stock (see *Hull, 2009*) needed to hedge the position. The total cost will have two parts, the amount paid to buy shares and the interest of financing the position. Following the BSM model, we use the risk-free interest rate for compounding. We will see that the cost of hedging depends on the future price movements, and by simulating several stock price paths, we can draw the cost distribution. Higher stock price volatility causes higher volatility of the cost of hedging.

The Cost_simulation function calculates the cost of hedging for the written call:

```
cost_simulation = function(S0, mu, sigma, rf, K, Time,   dt){
t <- seq(0, Time, by = dt)
N <- length(t)
W <- c(0,cumsum(rnorm(N-1)))
S <- S0*exp((mu-sigma^2/2)*t + sigma*sqrt(dt)*W)
delta <- rep(0, N-1)
call_ <- rep(0, N-1)
```

```
for(i in 1:(N-1) ){
delta[i] <- GBSGreeks("Delta", "c", S[i], K, Time-t[i], rf, rf, sigma)
call_[i] <- GBSOption("c", S[i], K, Time-t[i], rf, rf, sigma)@price

}
```

In the following command, `share_cost` represents the cost of buying the underlying asset to maintain the hedge position, and `interest_cost` is the cost of financing the position:

```
share_cost <- rep(0,N-1)
interest_cost <- rep(0,N-1)
total_cost <- rep(0, N-1)
share_cost[1] <- S[1]*delta[1]
interest_cost[1] <- (exp(rf*dt)-1) * share_cost[1]
total_cost[1] <- share_cost[1] + interest_cost[1]
for(i in 2:(N-1)){
    share_cost[i] <- ( delta[i] - delta[i-1] ) * S[i]
    interest_cost[i] <- ( total_cost[i-1] + share_cost[i] ) *
(exp(rf*dt)-1)
    total_cost[i] <- total_cost[i-1] + interest_cost[i] + share_cost[i]
            }
c = max( S[N] - K , 0)
cost = c - delta[N-1]*S[N] + total_cost[N-1]
return(cost*exp(-Time*rf))
}
```

We can use the preceding defined function to generate different future price processes, based on which the cost of hedging can be calculated. Vector **A** collects several possible hedging costs and draws their histogram as a probability distribution. Next, we present hedging strategies, which rebalance weekly (A) and daily (B):

```
call_price = GBSOption("c", 100, 100, 0.5, 0.05, 0.05, 0.3)@price
A = rep(0, 1000)
for (i in 1:1000){A[i] = cost_simulation(100, .20, .30,.05, 100, 0.5,
1/52)}
B = rep(0, 1000)
for (i in 1:1000){B[i] = cost_simulation(100, .20, .30,.05, 100, 0.5,
1/250)}
```

```
dev.new(width=20, height=10)

par(mfrow=c(1,2))

hist(A, freq = F, main = paste("E = ",round(mean(A), 4) ," sd =
",round(sd(A), 4)), xlim = c(6,14), ylim = c(0,0.7))

curve(dnorm(x, mean=mean(A), sd=sd(A)), col="darkblue", lwd=2, add=TRUE,
yaxt="n")

hist(B, freq = F, main = paste("E = ",round(mean(B), 4) ," sd =
",round(sd(B), 4)), xlim = c(6,14), ylim = c(0,0.7))

curve(dnorm(x, mean=mean(B), sd=sd(B)), col="darkblue", lwd=2, add=TRUE,
yaxt="n")
```

The output is the histogram of the generated cost outcomes:

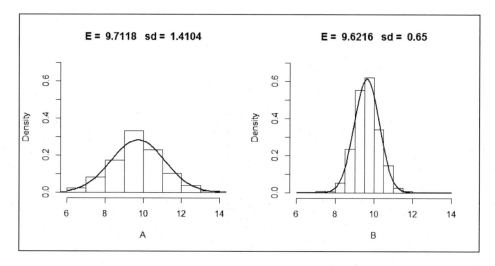

The histogram on the left side shows the cost distribution of the weekly strategy, while the histogram on the right side belongs to the daily rebalancing strategy.

As we can see, the standard deviation of the cost of hedging can be reduced by shortening Δt, which indicates more frequent rebalancing of the portfolio. It is worth noticing that it is not only the volatility of the hedging cost that decreases with the shorter period, but the expected value is also lower, approaching the BS price.

Comparing the performance of delta hedging

We can further investigate the effect of the rebalancing period by making a slight modification to the cost simulation function by which the same future paths will be selected. In this way, we can compare strategies with a different rebalancing period.

The performance measure of delta hedging is defined by *Hull (2009)* as the ratio of the standard deviation of the cost of writing the option and hedging it to the theoretical price of the option.

The `Cost_simulation` function needs to be modified so that we can calculate several rebalancing periods together:

```
library(fOptions)
cost_simulation = function(S0, mu, sigma, rf, K, Time, dt, periods){
t <- seq(0, Time, by = dt)
N <- length(t)
W = c(0,cumsum(rnorm(N-1)))
S <- S0*exp((mu-sigma^2/2)*t + sigma*sqrt(dt)*W)
SN = S[N]
delta <- rep(0, N-1)
call_ <- rep(0, N-1)
for(i in 1:(N-1) ){
delta[i] <- GBSGreeks("Delta", "c", S[i], K, Time-t[i], rf, rf, sigma)
call_[i] <- GBSOption("c", S[i], K, Time-t[i], rf, rf, sigma)@price
}
S = S[seq(1, N-1, by = periods)]
delta = delta[seq(1, N-1, by = periods)]
m = length(S)
share_cost <- rep(0,m)
interest_cost <- rep(0,m)
total_cost <- rep(0, m)
```

```
share_cost[1] <- S[1]*delta[1]

interest_cost[1] <- (exp(rf*dt*periods)-1) * share_cost[1]

total_cost[1] <- share_cost[1] + interest_cost[1]

for(i in 2:(m)){

    share_cost[i] <- ( delta[i] - delta[i-1] ) * S[i]

    interest_cost[i] <- ( total_cost[i-1] + share_cost[i] ) *
(exp(rf*dt*periods)-1)

    total_cost[i] <- total_cost[i-1] + interest_cost[i] + share_cost[i]

            }

c = max( SN - K , 0)

cost = c - delta[m]*SN + total_cost[m]

return(cost*exp(-Time*rf))

}
```

In the following command, the modified `cost_simulation` function is used for different rebalancing periods, and a table is generated that contains the expected value (*E*) with the lower and upper bound of the confidence level, the volatility of the cost of hedging (*v*), and the performance measure (*ratio*) ordered to the six rebalancing periods (0.5, 1, and 2 days, and 1, 2, and 4 weeks). We also receive two plots, the histograms of each strategy, and a chart that contains the normal curves fitted to the distributions:

```
dev.new(width=30,height=20)

par(mfrow = c(2,3))

i = 0

per = c(2,4,8,20,40,80)

call_price = GBSOption("c", 100, 100, 0.5, 0.05, 0.05, 0.3)@price

results = matrix(0, 6, 5)

rownames(results) = c("1/2 days", "1 day", "2 days", "1 week", "2
  weeks", "4 weeks")

colnames(results) = c("E", "lower", "upper", "v", "ratio")

for (j in per){

  i = i+1

  A = rep(0, 1000)

  set.seed(10125987)
```

```
for (h in 1:1000){A[h] = cost_simulation(100, .20, .30,.05, 100,
   0.5, 1/1000,j)}
E = mean(A)
v = sd(A)
results[i, 1] = E
results[i, 2] = E-1.96*v/sqrt(1000)
results[i, 3] = E+1.96*v/sqrt(1000)
results[i, 4] = v
results[i, 5] = v/call_price
hist(A, freq = F, main = "", xlab = "", xlim = c(4,16), ylim =
   c(0,0.8))
title(main = rownames(results)[i], sub = paste("E = ",round(E, 4)
   ," sd = ",round(v, 4)))
curve(dnorm(x, mean=mean(A), sd=sd(A)), col="darkblue", lwd=2,
   add=TRUE, yaxt="n")
}
print(results)
dev.new()
curve(dnorm(x,results[1,1], results[1,4]), 6,14, ylab = "", xlab =
   "cost")
for (l in 2:6) curve(dnorm(x, results[1,1], results[1,4]), add =
   TRUE, xlim = c(4,16), ylim = c(0,0.8), lty=l)
legend(legend=rownames(results), "topright", lty = 1:6)
```

In our simulation model, the output is as follows:

	E	lower	upper	v	ratio
1/2 days	9.645018	9.616637	9.673399	0.4579025	0.047526
1 day	9.638224	9.600381	9.676068	0.6105640	0,06337
2 days	9.610501	9.558314	9.662687	0.8419825	0,087389
1 week	9.647767	9.563375	9.732160	1.3616010	0,14132
2 weeks	9.764237	9.647037	9.881436	1.8909048	0,196256
4 weeks	9.919697	9.748393	10.091001	2.7638287	0,286857

The standard deviation of the cost of hedging becomes smaller as we rebalance the hedge position more often. The difference in the expected value is also significant at 95 percent significance level between the weekly and the monthly the rebalancing. Among the shorter periods, we did not find significant differences in the expected value:

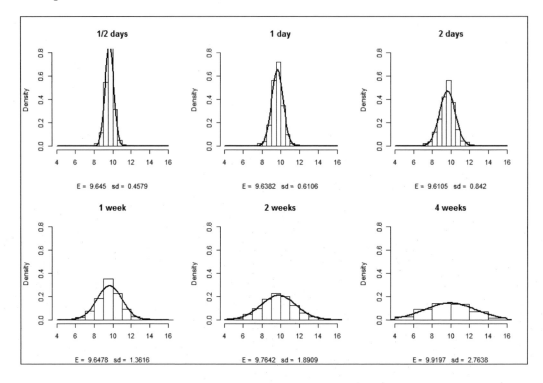

The charts shown in the preceding image are similar to the previous analysis (with weekly and daily rebalancing), but here, we have more rebalancing periods. The effect of rebalancing frequency is presented by the distribution of the cost of hedging.

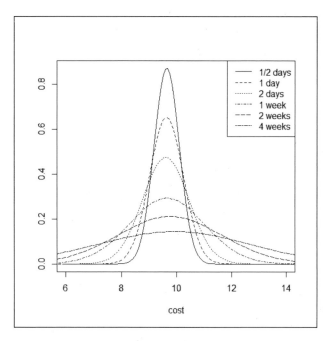

We can compare the cost distributions of the given rebalancing periods on a single chart, as illustrated in the preceding section.

The time consumption can be reduced by decreasing the number of simulations.

Hedging in the presence of transaction costs

As we shown earlier, increasing the number of portfolio adjustments leads to a decrease in the volatility of the hedging cost. As Δt approaches 0, the cost of hedging approximates the option price derived from the BS formula. Until now, we have disregarded the transaction costs, but here, we remove this assumption and analyze the effects of transaction costs on option hedging. As rebalancing becomes more frequent, transaction costs increase the cost of hedging, but at the same time, shorter rebalancing periods reduce the volatility of the hedging cost. Hence, it is worth examining this trade-off in more detail, and based on this, defining the optimal rebalancing strategy. An absolute (fixed for each transaction) or a relative (proportional to the transaction size) transaction cost can be added to the code by modifying the parameters when we define the function:

```
cost_simulation = function(S0, mu, sigma, rf, K, Time, dt, periods,
cost_per_trade)
```

Then, the cost calculation method for the absolute transaction cost can be programmed as follows:

```
share_cost[1] <- S[1]*delta[1] + cost_per_trade

interest_cost[1] <- (exp(rf*dt*periods)-1) * share_cost[1]

total_cost[1] <- share_cost[1] + interest_cost[1]

for(i in 2:m){
    share_cost[i] <- ( delta[i] - delta[i-1] ) * S[i] + cost_per_trade
    interest_cost[i] <- ( total_cost[i-1] + share_cost[i] ) *
(exp(rf*dt*periods)-1)
    total_cost[i] <- total_cost[i-1] + interest_cost[i] + share_cost[i]
        }
```

In the case of relative costs, the program code is as follows:

```
share_cost[1] <- S[1]*delta[1]*(1+trading_cost)
interest_cost[1] <- (exp(rf*dt*periods)-1) * share_cost[1]
total_cost[1] <- share_cost[1] + interest_cost[1]
for(i in 2:m){
    share_cost[i] <- (( delta[i] - delta[i-1] ) * S[i]) + abs(( delta[i]
- delta[i-1] ) * S[i]) * trading_cost
    interest_cost[i] <- ( total_cost[i-1] + share_cost[i] ) *
(exp(rf*dt*periods)-1)
    total_cost[i] <- total_cost[i-1] + interest_cost[i] + share_cost[i]
}
```

When referring to the `cost_simulation` function, the absolute or relative cost has to be given. Let's check the effect of an absolute cost of 0.02 per transaction (we suppose that the unit of the cost and the extent of the trade are the same). In order to shorten the time consumption, we used only 100 simulated paths here.

We have to change the parameters of the `cost_simulation` function in the cycle:

```
for (i in 1:100)
  A[i] = cost_simulation(100, .20, .30,.05, 100, 0.5, 1/1000,j,.02)
```

Then, we get the table shown as follows:

	E	lower	upper	v	ratio
1/2 days	12.083775	11.966137	12.20141	0.6001933	0.06229386
1 day	10.817594	10.643468	10.99172	0.8883994	0.09220668
2 days	10.244342	9.999395	10.48929	1.2497261	0.12970866
1 week	9.993442	9.612777	10.37411	1.9421682	0.20157700
2 weeks	10.305498	9.737017	10.87398	2.9004106	0.30103266
4 weeks	10.321880	9.603827	11.03993	3.6635388	0.38023748

Calculating with a fixed transaction cost of 0.02, the expected value of the hedging cost increases considerably. The shorter rebalancing periods are most affected as more trading enhances the costs. The standard deviation is also higher, mainly in cases of periods shorter than one week.

We can see the effect of the relative transaction cost of 1 percent by applying the following change in the code:

```
for (i in 1:100)
  A[i] = cost_simulation(100, .20, .30,.05, 100, 0.5, 1/1000,j, 0.01)
```

The expected hedging cost has increased further in the case of the shortest (daily or even more frequent) rebalancing periods, but we also found a more significant rise of the volatility (as shown in the following output table):

	E	lower	upper	v	ratio
1/2 days	13.56272	13.26897	13.85646	1.498715	0.1555512
1 day	12.53723	12.28596	12.78850	1.282005	0.1330589
2 days	11.89854	11.59787	12.19921	1.534010	0.1592144
1 week	11.37828	10.96775	11.78880	2.094506	0.2173881
2 weeks	11.55362	10.95111	12.15612	3.073993	0.3190487
4 weeks	11.43771	10.69504	12.18038	3.789128	0.3932724

The presence of transaction costs offsets the volatility reduction effect of the more frequent rebalancing, so the optimal rebalancing period is to be determined by weighting these effects relative to each other.

Optimization of the hedge

In order to find the optimal length of the rebalancing period, we have to define the optimization criterion and the measure that is to be maximized or minimized. The usual aim of hedging is the reduction of the risk, measured by the variance of the cost of the hedge. According to this, the optimal hedge minimizes the volatility of the cost of hedging. Another aim of the optimization can be the minimization of the expected value of the cost. As we have seen, in the absence of transaction costs, these goals can be achieved simultaneously by rebalancing the hedging portfolio more and more frequently. On the other hand, transaction costs boost not only the expected value of the cost but also the volatility, which can rise drastically when the readjustment is too frequent.

It is a widespread method in finance when trade-off between the expected value and volatility has to be considered in order to define a utility function and an optimum as the maximum utility. For example, in the portfolio theory, an individual utility function is assumed, which is positively affected by the expected value of the return and negatively affected by its variance. We can use the same technique by defining a utility function that contains the expected value of the cost of hedging and its variance. However, in our case, both factors have a negative impact on the utility of the trader; therefore, both parameters must have a positive sign, and the function is to be minimized. Accordingly, the objective function will be a utility function defined as follows:

$$U\left(x\right) = E\left(x\right) + \alpha\,Var\left(x\right)$$

Equation 3

Here, x is the cost of the hedge as a random variable, E denotes its expected value, Var stands for its variance, and a is the risk aversion parameter. A higher a indicates a more risk averse investor/trader.

An alternative solution to the mean-variance optimization can be setting the expected (cost) value minimization as the main goal with the boundary condition that keeps a chosen risk measure under a predefined value. Here, we chose Value-at-Risk as the control variable, which is a type of downside risk measure, defined as the maximal loss or worst outcome at a predefined probability and over a selected time horizon.

The following code calculates the cost distribution based on 1,000 simulations for different rebalancing periods from 1-80 Δt. The unit of Δt is a quarter of a day, so Δt of 1 means four readjustments a day; the longest Δt of 80 refers to a 20-day long period. The function collects the expected value, the standard deviation, and the 95 percentile of the distribution, and gives the result of the four different optimization scenarios in text format and also plots the results:

```
n_sim <- 1000

threshold <- 12

cost_Sim <- function(cost = 0.01, n = n_sim, per = 1){a <- replicate(n,
cost_simulation(100, .20, .30,.05, 100, 0.5, 1/1000,per,cost));

l <- list(mean(a), sd(a), quantile(a,0.95))}

A <- sapply(seq(1,80) ,function(per) {print(per); set.seed(2019759);
cost_Sim(per = per)})

e <- unlist(A[1,])

s <- unlist(A[2,])

q <- unlist(A[3,])

u <- e + s^2

A <- cbind(t(A), u)

z1 <- which.min(e)

z2 <- which.min(s)

z3 <- which.min(u)

    (paste("E min =", z1, "cost of hedge = ",e[z1]," sd = ", s[z1]))

    (paste("s min =", z2, "cost of hedge = ",e[z2]," sd = ", s[z2]))

    (paste("U min =", z3, "u = ",u[z3],"cost of hedge = ",e[z3]," sd = ",
s[z3]))

matplot(A, type = "l", lty = 1:4, xlab = "Δt", col = 1)

lab_for_leg = c("E", "Sd", "95% quantile","E + variance")

legend(legend = lab_for_leg, "bottomright", cex = 0.6, lty = 1:4)

abline( v = c(z1,z2,z3), lty = 6, col = "grey")

abline( h = threshold, lty = 1, col = "grey")

text(c(z1,z1,z2,z2,z3,z3,z3),c(e[z1],s[z1],s[z2],e[z2],e[z3],s[z3],u[z3]
),round(c(e[z1],s[z1],s[z2],e[z2],e[z3],s[z3],u[z3]),3), pos = 3, cex =
0.7)

e2 <- e

e2[q > threshold] <- max(e)

z4 <- which.min(e2)
```

```
z5 <- which.min(q)

if( q[z5] < threshold ){

print(paste(" min VaR = ", q[z4], "at", z4 ,"E(cost | VaR < threshold = "
,e[z4], " s = ", s[z4]))

 } else {

    print(paste("optimization failed, min VaR = ", q[z5], "at", z5 ,
"where cost = ", e[z5], " s = ", s[z5]))

             }
```

The last optimization searches for the minimal cost that can be achieved with the condition that Value-at-Risk at the q significance level (the q percentile) does not exceed the predetermined threshold. As it is not necessary that this minimum exists, if the optimization fails, the minimum of q-VaR is given as the result.

Optimal hedging in the case of absolute transaction costs

The task is to find the optimal length of the rebalancing period in the case of transaction costs and for a vanilla call option with the already investigated parameters. Let's suppose that the transaction cost is 0.01 per trade.

The output of the earlier function is a matrix **A** that contains the parameters of the distribution that belong to different rebalancing periods, and the optimum according to different criteria.

The first and last rows of the matrix **A** are shown next:

```
      [,1]       [,2]        [,3]        [,4]
 [1,] 14.568    0.3022379 15.05147 14.65935
 [2,] 12.10577 0.4471673 12.79622 12.30573

...

[79,] 10.00434 2.678289  14.51381 17.17757
[80,] 10.03162 2.674291  14.41796 17.18345
```

The number in the square brackets stands for the rebalancing period expressed in Δt. The next columns contain the expected value, the standard deviation, the 95 percent quantile, and the sum of the expected value and standard deviation. The results of the four optimization processes are summarized in the next output:

```
"E min = 50 cost of hedge =  9.79184040508574  sd =  2.21227796458088"
"s min = 1 cost of hedge =  14.5680033393436   sd =  0.302237879069942"
```

```
"U min = 8 u =  11.0296321604941 cost of hedge =  10.2898541853535  sd =
0.860103467694771"
```

```
" min VaR =  11.8082026178249 at 14 E(cost | VaR < threshold =
10.0172915117802  s =  1.12757856083913"
```

The following figure depicts the results in the function of the rebalancing periods (in Δt). The dashed line shows the standard deviation and the solid line is the expected cost, while the dot dash and dotted lines stand for the value of the utility function (Equation 3) with an alpha parameter of 1 and 95 percentile respectively.

Although the optimization depends on the parameters, the chart illustrates the trade-off between the expected cost and the volatility in the presence of transaction costs:

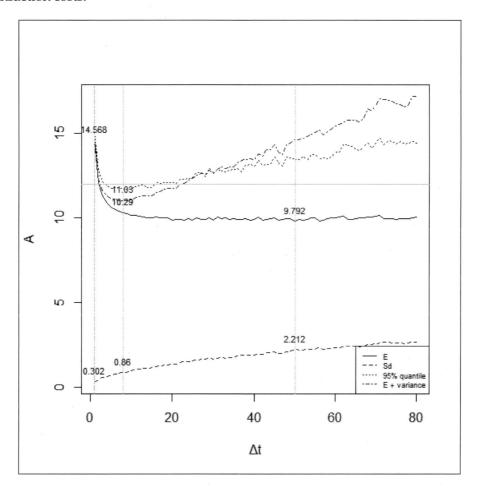

The minimum of the expected cost (9.79) is not far away from the BS price of 9.63. The optimal rebalancing period is then 50 Δt, that is, 12.5 days long. At the lowest expected cost, the standard deviation is 2.21.

The volatility minimization results in the most frequent rebalancing, which means rebalancing 4 times a day; then, the minimum of the standard deviation is 0.30, but the frequent trading increases the costs drastically. The expected cost is 14.57, which is about 50 percent higher than in the previous case.

The optimization model based on the utility function defined in Equation 3 considers both aspects of the hedge, and the earlier output shows 8 Δt long rebalancing periods as optimal, that is, exactly 2 days. We can achieve an expected value of 10.29, which only somewhat exceeds the minimum, and the standard deviation is 0.86.

The last row of the preceding output presents the results of the optimization using Value-at-Risk limits. We applied a 95% VaR and searched for the minimal expected cost at which, in 95% of the cases, the cost remains under a threshold of 12. According to this, the optimal length of the readjustment is 14 Δt, that is, 3.5 days. The expected value of the cost is slightly lower (10.02) than in the previous case, where the result is offset by a slightly higher standard deviation (1.13).

Optimal hedging in the case of relative transaction costs

In this section, the same optimization problem is solved as in the previous section, with the exception that now the transaction cost is 1 percent of the deal. All other parameters are the same.

The output contains the matrix **A** with the same data:

```
        [,1]      [,2]      [,3]      [,4]
 [1,]  16.80509 2.746488 21.37177 24.34829
 [2,]  14.87962 1.974883 18.20097 18.77978
...
[79,]  11.2743  2.770777 15.89386 18.9515
[80,]  11.31251 2.758069 16.0346  18.91945
```

Given that costs depend on the transaction size, we got a U-shape not only in the expected value, but also in the standard deviation. This indicates that too frequent trading is suboptimal also in regards to volatility minimization.

The other main difference compared to the previous optimization is that the threshold of VaR cannot be held (as shown in the following code):

```
"E min = 56 cost of hedge =  11.1495374978655  sd =  2.40795704676431"
"s min = 9 cost of hedge =  12.4747301348104  sd =  1.28919873150291"
"U min = 14 u =  13.9033123535802 cost of hedge =  12.0090095949856  sd =
1.37633671701175"
"optimization failed, min VaR =  14.2623891995575 at 21 where cost =
11.7028044352096  s =  1.518297863428"
```

The following screenshot gives the output of the preceding command:

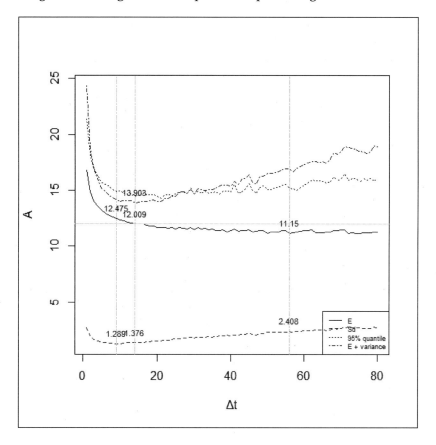

The lowest expected cost is 11.15 with a standard deviation of 2.41 at 56 Δt, indicating an optimal rebalancing period of 14 days.

The lowest volatility is 1.23 at Δt of 9, and the expected value is 12.47. The mean-variance optimization results in a rebalancing period of 14 Δt (3.5 days), the standard deviation is 1.38, and the expected value is 12.01.

As mentioned, the fourth optimization fails; the minimum of the 95% VaR is 14.26, which can be achieved at 21 Δt (5.25 days); the expected cost is 11.7, and the standard deviation is 1.52.

The optimization shows that in the presence of the transaction cost, the simple aim of volatility reduction causes a huge rise in the costs; therefore, an optimal hedging strategy has to take into consideration this effect as well.

Further extensions

The model can be further generalized by investigating other price processes. The returns of financial assets are usually not normally distributed as assumed in the BSM model, but their tails are fatter than predicted by the Gauss curve. This phenomenon can be described by the GARCH model (General Autoregressive Conditional Heteroscedasticity), where the variance is autocorrelated, which causes a clustering of volatility. Another way of catching the higher probability of extreme returns can be building random jumps into the process. Applying these processes in the model will make the hedging of the derivative even more expensive, thereby increasing the expected value and also the variance of the cost distribution.

We can see that changing the spot price causes the change of the delta that can be measured by the gamma, which is the second derivative of the option price with respect to the spot price. A gamma-neutral portfolio cannot be achieved by exclusively holding the option and the underlying asset, as the gamma of the latest is zero, but we have to buy options for the same underlying asset with any maturity or strike price.

Furthermore, if we disregard the assumption of constant volatility, the value of the derivative will be affected not only by the change of the underlying asset's spot price and the change of the remaining time to maturity, but also the change of the underlying asset's volatility. The effect of the changing volatility can be measured by the vega, the first derivative of the option price according to the volatility. A high value of vega causes a notable effect of the volatility on the option price (*Hull, 2009*). This can cause a situation where the price of the underlying asset is increasing, so the value of a call option should increase while the implied volatility has decreased, and the price of the option may decrease as well. In order to offset the effect of vega, either other options for the same underlying asset are to be bought, or we can hedge volatility with an index called the VIX index, which is a traded index that contains the implied volatilities of options.

This chapter was dedicated to analyzing delta hedging; detailing gamma and vega neutralization is beyond our focus.

Summary

In this chapter, we have shown some practical problems that arise in the hedging of derivatives. Although the Black-Scholes-Merton model assumes continuous time trading, resulting in continuous rebalancing of the hedging portfolio without transaction costs, in reality, trading occurs in discrete time, and it does have costs. Consequently, the cost of hedging depends on the future path of the spot price of the underlying asset; thus, it is not a single value presented by the analytical formula any more, but it is a stochastic variable that can be described by its probability distribution. In this chapter, we simulated different paths, calculated the cost of hedging, and presented the probability distribution assuming different rebalancing frequencies. We received that in the absence of transaction costs the volatility reduces with the shortening of the rebalancing period. On the other hand, transaction costs can boost not only the expected value of the cost of the hedge but also its variance. We presented several optimization algorithms to find the optimal hedging strategy.

We created several user-defined functions in R to simulate price movements and to generate the cost distribution. Finally, we applied numerical optimization according to the given optimization model.

References

- **Black, F. and Scholes, M. [1973]**: The Pricing of Options and Corporate Liabilities. *The Journal of Political Economy*, 81(3), pp. 637-654.

- **Hull, J. C. [2009]**: Option, Futures and other Derivatives. Pearson, Prentice Hall.

- **Merton, R. [1973]**: Theory of Rational Option Pricing. *The Bell Journal of Economics and Management Science*, 4(1), pp. 141-183.

- **Száz, J [2009]**: Devizaopciók és Részvényopciók Árazása, Jet Set, Budapest.

9
Fundamental Analysis

Now that the global financial crisis seems to come to an end, most of the investors are moving back to equity markets. By doing so, you face the problem of choosing the stocks that will outperform the other shares during the upcoming time period. To find the right investment asset to purchase, you have two basic options. On one hand, you may rely on any trends and patterns in the development of the historical prices. When developing an investment recommendation based on trends and patterns, you do a technical analysis. On the other hand, you may try to figure out which firms will exceed the market by analyzing their financial performance, strategic position, or future plans. This is called fundamental analysis.

This chapter provides you an aid on how to use R to identify successful fundamental trading strategies for equity investments. We will start by applying basic statistical methods and move on to advanced and more complex ones while we cover how to translate your fundamental investment ideas into statistically testable hypotheses.

The basics of fundamental analysis

When looking for possible investment assets, a wide range of choices is offered to you by the market. You may pick bonds, pieces of art, real estate, currencies, commodities, derivatives, or probably, the most well-known asset class, equity. Equities represent ownership right over a certain part of the given firm (issuer).

However, which shares shall we buy? When should we purchase and sell them? These decisions are of key importance as they will determine the return on your portfolio. There are two different views out there on these problems.

Technical analysis is built on historical price developments and believes that certain patterns may be identified that help predict the future movements of the quotes. Fundamental analysis, on the contrary, focuses on the firm and the value of the ownership right itself rather than on the market price of it. Here, we believe that sooner or later, market price has to reflect the fair value of the share that can be calculated from the future cash flows we collect when owning it, just like in the case of any other kind of investments.

While technical analysis focuses on how investors' behavior might push prices in the future based on historical patterns, fundamental analysis identifies the trends that prices should follow due to the predicted future performance of the firm. So, when performing fundamental analysis, we have to recall our corporate finance and accounting knowledge.

Even when checking for the fair price of just one given share, we may spend several days on modeling future performance and estimating sales growth, expenses, investments, changes in financing strategy, and cost of capital to get a valid discount rate for our cash-flow prediction. When developing a trading strategy, we need to review several thousands of potential investments, so there is no chance we could do such an in-depth analysis. Even trying it may be tricky. If you create large spreadsheet models for all equities, by the time you finish, your assumptions for the first firm could be outdated, and you have to restart the process without even considering your results from the first version of the model. So, instead of really predicting future financial statements, we have to build on historical experience to identify good investment patterns. We will try to connect previous fundamental ratios to historical price developments and expect that these connections will also hold in the future.

This is the key to understand that we do not want to find good companies to invest in; we rather have to find shares that are very likely to be mispriced. So, we want to find undervalued stocks to buy, or if shorting is allowed on the market, we want to find overvalued ones to sell. For the rest of this chapter, we will focus only on the upward potential, but you may use exactly the same techniques to identify shares to sell that have a huge downward potential. Finding the fundamental characteristics of firms for which we have seen the share price increase during the last 12 months may help us identify good investments for the next year based on the current financial statements.

So, when building a fundamental equity strategy, we need to follow these steps:

1. Collect financial statement data for possible equity investments.
2. Calculate fundamental ratios to standardize data.
3. Identify connections between ratios and future price development.
4. Follow the testing strategy that is, calculate results on another set of possible equities for the same period and/or same set of shares for a different period of time.

It is not enough to perform these steps once in a lifetime. Applying a strategy that would have performed well during the last year(s) assumes that there were no radical changes, neither within the firm nor in the economy that the company is active in. As markets tend to change, firm have to do so too. This means that what was the best practice last year may be just fine or average now. As a result of this, even if our investment strategy worked well for several years, we may see a gradual or even radical change in its effectiveness. So, a regular recheck and update is vital.

Collecting data

Building the required database could be one of the biggest challenges. Here, we do not only need dividend-adjusted price quotes but also financial statements data. *Chapter 4, Big Data – Advanced Analytics* described how to access some of the open data sources, but those rarely offer you all the required information in a package.

Another option might be to use professional financial data providers as a source. These platforms allow you to create tailor-made tables that can be exported to Microsoft Excel. For the sake of this chapter, we used a Bloomberg terminal. As a first step, we exported the data to Microsoft Excel.

Spreadsheets may be an excellent tool to build a database of data collected from different sources. No matter how you got your data ready on a spreadsheet, you need to notice that due to the changing output formats (xls, xlsx, xlsm, xlsb) and the advanced formatting features (for example, merging cells), this is not the best form to feed R with your data. Instead, you may be far better off with saving your data in a file in the comma-separated format or as CSVs. This can be easily read using the following commands:

```
d <- read.table("file_name", header = T, sep = ",")
```

Here, the = T header indicates that your database has a header row, and `sep = ","` indicates that your data is separated by commas. Note that some localized versions of Excel may use different separators, such as semicolons. In this case, use sep = ";". If your file is not located in your R working directory, you have to specify the whole path as part of `file_name`.

If you want to stick to your Excel file, the next method might work in most of the cases. Install the `gdata` package that extends the capabilities of R so that the software can read information form the `xls` or `xlsx` file:

```
install.packages("gdata")
library(gdata)
```

After that, you may read the Excel file as follows:

```
d <- read.xls("file_name", n)
```

Here, the second argument marked as n indicates the worksheet in the workbook from which you want to read.

To illustrate the process of building a fundamental trading strategy, we will use the NASDAQ Composite Index member firms. At the time of writing this chapter, 21,931 firms are included.

To create a solid base for our strategy, we should first clean our database. Extreme values may create a serious bias otherwise. For example, no one would be surprised if a firm with a P/E (Price/Earning per share) ratio of 150 a year ago showed a quick price increase during the last 12 months, but finding such a share now may be impossible, so our strategy might be worthless. The strategy should help us find what shares to invest in once the choice is not trivial (of course, you may also lose with high P/E shares), so we will only keep shares without extreme values. The following limitations were applied:

- P/E (Price/Earning per share) lower than 100
- The yearly Total Return to Shareholders (TRS), which is equal to price gain plus dividend yield, less than 100 percent
- Long Term Debt / Total Capital less than 100 percent (no negative shareholder capital)
- P/BV (Price per Book value) of equity for one piece of share bigger than 1, so the market value of equity is higher than the book value (no point in liquidating the firm)
- Operating income/sales less than 100 percent but bigger than 0 (historical performance can be held in the long run)

This way, only those firms remained that are not likely to be liquidated or go bankrupt, and they have shown performance that is clearly sustainable in the long run. After applying these filters, 7198 firms remained from all over the world.

The next step involves selecting the ratios we will potentially use when defining the strategy. Based on historical experience, we picked 15 ratios from the financial statements a year earlier, plus the name of the sectors the firms operate in and the total shareholder return for the last 12 months.

It may prove wise to check whether the remaining data is appropriate for our aims. A boxplot diagram would reveal whether, for example, most of our stocks show huge positive or negative return or whether there are heavy differences across industries due to which we would end up describing one given booming industry as not a good investment strategy. Luckily, here, we have no such issues: (*Figure 1*)

```
d <- read.csv2("data.csv", stringsAsFactors = F)
for (i in c(3:17,19)){d[,i] = as.numeric(d[,i])}
boxplot_data <- split( d$Total.Return.YTD..I., d$BICS.L1.Sect.Nm )
windows()
par(mar = c(10,4,4,4))
boxplot(boxplot_data, las = 2, col = "grey")
```

The following figure is the result of the preceding code:

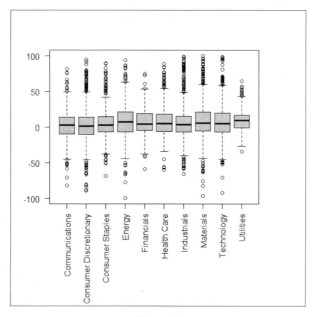

Figure 1

It could be also a good idea to check whether we should introduce new variables. One possible yet missing categorization could control for firm size, as many models assume higher required return for low capitalization stocks due to them being less liquid. To control this, we may apply a scatter diagram, the code and output for this is as follows:

```
model <- lm(" Total.Return.YTD..I. ~ Market.Cap.Y.1", data = d)

a <- model$coefficients[1]

b <- model$coefficients[2]

windows()

plot(d$Market.Cap.Y.1,d$Total.Return.YTD..I., xlim = c(0, 400000000000),
xlab = "Market Cap Y-1", ylab = "Total Return YTD (I).")

abline(a,b, col = "red")
```

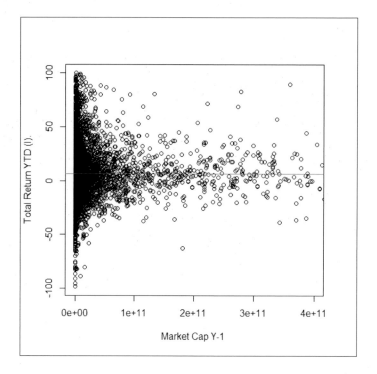

We cannot see a clear trend for capitalization and TRS. We may also try to fit a curve on the data and calculate R^2 for the goodness of the fit, but the figure does not support any strong connection. R square indicates the percentage of variance explained by your estimation, so any value above 0.8 is great, while values bellow 0.2 mean weak performance.

Revealing connections

To start our investigation for shares with huge upside potential, we have to check the connections between individual ratios quantified a year ago and the total return of the next year. For the sake of this chapter, we picked the following ratios. We took the values from 1 year earlier so that we can contrast these with last year's TRS:

- Cash/assets 1 year ago
- Net fixed assets/total number of assets 1 year ago
- Assets/1000 employees 1 year ago
- Price/cash flow average of last 5 years 1 year ago
- Price/cash flow 1 year ago
- Operating income/net sales 1 year ago
- Dividend payout ratio 1 year ago
- Asset turnover 1 year ago
- P/BV 1 year ago
- Operating income/net sales 1 year ago
- Revenue growth in the last 1 year 1 year ago
- Long-term debt/capital 1 year ago
- Debt/EBITDA 1 year ago
- Market capitalization 1 year ago
- P/E 1 year ago

Calculating Pearson's correlation coefficients may be a good start:

```
d_filt <- na.omit(d)[,setdiff(1:19, c(1,2,18))]
cor_mtx <- cor(d_filt)
round(cor_mtx, 3)
```

When looking at the correlation table, there are two important conclusions to draw. They are as follows:

- There are only four financial ratios that show a significant correlation with TRS, but even there, the connections are very weak; that is, they remain in the range between -0.08 and +0.08. This means there is no clear linear connection between any of our ratios and the TRS.

- The financial ratios chosen are quite independent. Out of the 105 (15*14/2) potential connections, only 15 are significant. Even all those fit into the interval of -0.439 and +0.425, and only eight of them have a bigger absolute value than 0.2.

So, we see that it is not easy to set up a good strategy. Just relying on one single ratio would lead us nowhere. We shall go for more complex methods.

Including multiple variables

One method to build a performance-prediction model could be using multiple variable regression models. A linear estimation should only include variables with minimal linear connection among them. As we have just seen, our explanatory variables are more or less independent of each other, which is great. It is bad news, though, that these variables individually also have low correlation with the dependent variable, TRS.

To get the best linear estimation, we may choose from several methods. One option is to first include all variables and ask R to drop step by step the one with the lowest significance (step-wise method). Under another widely used method, R could start with one variable only and enter stepwise the next one with the highest explanatory power (the backward method). Here, we picked the latter, as the first method could not end with a significant model:

```
library(MASS)
vars <- colnames(d_filt)
m <- length(vars)
lin_formula <- paste(vars[m], paste(vars[-m], collapse = " + "), sep = "
~ ")
fit <- lm(formula = lin_formula, data = d_filt)
fit <- stepAIC(object = fit, direction = "backward", k = 4)
summary(fit)


Coefficients:
```

	Estimate	Std. Error	t value	Pr(>|t|)
(Intercept) ***	6.77884	1.11533	6.078	1.4e-09
Cash.Assets.Y.1 **	-0.08757	0.03186	-2.749	0.006022

```
Net.Fixed.Assets.to.Tot.Assets.Y.1  0.07153    0.01997    3.583 0.000346
***

R.D.Net.Sales.Y.1                    0.30689    0.07888    3.891 0.000102
***

P.E.Y.1                             -0.09746    0.02944   -3.311 0.000943
***

---

Signif. codes:  0 '***' 0.001 '**' 0.01 '*' 0.05 '.' 0.1 ' ' 1


Residual standard error: 19.63 on 2591 degrees of freedom
Multiple R-squared:  0.01598,    Adjusted R-squared:  0.01446
F-statistic: 10.52 on 4 and 2591 DF,  p-value: 1.879e-08
```

The backward method ended up with an R squared of 1.6 percent, only meaning that the regression cannot explain more than 1.6 percent of the total variance of the TRS. In other words, the model's performance is extremely bad. Notice that the poor performance is due to the weak (linear) connection between explanatory variables and TRS. Should you have some variables with stronger connection, your linear regressions will show better results. With an R squared above 50 percent, you are very likely to build a great stock-selection strategy by buying shares that have high values for significant explanatory variables with a positive sign in the model, while they have low values for variables with a negative sign in the model. As we cannot use this method here, we have to follow a different logic.

Separating investment targets

An alternative method to build an investment strategy could be to separate good investment targets and check what is common between them. A good way to find similarities among stocks that performed well could be to create groups based on the TRS values and compare low- and high-performer clusters. The first step to this should be to analyze the following code:

```
library(stats)
library(matrixStats)
h_clust <- hclust(dist(d[,19]))
plot(h_clust, labels = F, xlab = "")
```

The following dendogram is the output for the preceding code:

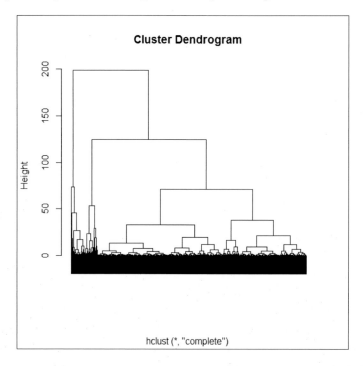

Based on the dendrogram, three clusters separate very well, but to cut the biggest of them into two subgroups, we may need to increase the number of clusters up until seven. To keep the overview, we should try to keep the number of cluster to the lowest possible, so first, we will try to create three clusters only using the k-means method:

```
k_clust <- kmeans(d[,19], 3)
K_means_results <- cbind(k_clust$centers, k_clust$size)
colnames(K_means_results) = c("Cluster center", "Cluster size")
K_means_results
```

Our results are pretty encouraging. Our three clusters have 1000 to 4000 elements, and we can very clearly identify the overperformers, underperformers, and, mid-range performers:

```
  Cluster center Cluster size
1       9.405869         3972
2      48.067540          962
3     -16.627188         2264
```

Next, we have to check whether there are significant differences regarding the average ratio values among these three groups. For this, we will use the Anova table. This statistical tool would compare the deviation across group averages and the standard deviation within the individual groups. Once the classification is valid, you would find huge differences among group averages but lesser differences when comparing firms within the same clusters:

```
for(i in c(3,4,6,10,12,14,16,17)) { print(colnames(d)[i]); print(summary(
aov(d[,i]~k_clust$cluster  , d))) }
```

Output:

```
[1] "Cash.Assets.Y.1"
                 Df  Sum Sq Mean Sq F value Pr(>F)
k_clust$cluster    1    7491    7491   41.94 1e-10 ***
Residuals       7195 1285207     179
---
Signif. codes:  0 '***' 0.001 '**' 0.01 '*' 0.05 '.' 0.1 ' ' 1
1 observation deleted due to missingness
[1] "Net.Fixed.Assets.to.Tot.Assets.Y.1"
                 Df  Sum Sq Mean Sq F value   Pr(>F)
k_clust$cluster    1   19994   19994   40.26 2.36e-10 ***
Residuals       7106 3529208     497
---
Signif. codes:  0 '***' 0.001 '**' 0.01 '*' 0.05 '.' 0.1 ' ' 1
90 observations deleted due to missingness
[1] "P.CF.5Yr.Avg.Y.1"
                 Df  Sum Sq Mean Sq F value Pr(>F)
k_clust$cluster    1   24236   24236     1.2  0.273
Residuals       4741 95772378   20201
2455 observations deleted due to missingness
[1] "Asset.Turnover.Y.1"
                 Df Sum Sq Mean Sq F value  Pr(>F)
k_clust$cluster    1      7   6.759   11.64 0.00065 ***
Residuals       7115   4133   0.581
---
Signif. codes:  0 '***' 0.001 '**' 0.01 '*' 0.05 '.' 0.1 ' ' 1
```

```
81 observations deleted due to missingness
[1] "OI...Net.Sales.Y.1"
                 Df  Sum Sq Mean Sq F value  Pr(>F)
k_clust$cluster    1    1461  1461.4   10.12 0.00147 **
Residuals       7196 1038800   144.4
---
Signif. codes:  0 '***' 0.001 '**' 0.01 '*' 0.05 '.' 0.1 ' ' 1
[1] "LTD.Capital.Y.1"
                 Df  Sum Sq Mean Sq F value Pr(>F)
k_clust$cluster    1    1575  1574.6   4.134 0.0421 *
Residuals       7196 2740845   380.9
---
Signif. codes:  0 '***' 0.001 '**' 0.01 '*' 0.05 '.' 0.1 ' ' 1
[1] "Market.Cap.Y.1"
                 Df   Sum Sq   Mean Sq F value Pr(>F)
k_clust$cluster    1 1.386e+08 138616578   2.543  0.111
Residuals       7196 3.922e+11  54501888
[1] "P.E.Y.1"
                 Df  Sum Sq Mean Sq F value  Pr(>F)
k_clust$cluster    1    1735  1735.3   8.665 0.00325 **
Residuals       7196 1441046   200.3
---
Signif. codes:  0 '***' 0.001 '**' 0.01 '*' 0.05 '.' 0.1 ' ' 1
```

In the output, R marks significance with an asterisk (*) after the F test probabilities (Pr). So, you learned from the previous table that six of the variables show significant differences across clusters. To see the average values per cluster, you need to type the following code:

```
f <- function(x) c(mean = mean(x, na.rm = T), N =
  length(x[!is.na(x)]), sd = sd(x, na.rm = T))
output <- aggregate(d[c(19,3,4,6,10,12,14,16,17)],
  list(k_clust$cluster), f)
rownames(output) = output[,1]; output[,1] <- NULL
output <- t(output)
output <- output[,order(output[1,])]
output <- cbind(output, as.vector(apply(d[c(19,3,4,6,10,12,14,16,17)], 2,
  f)))
```

```
colnames(output) <- c("Underperformers", "Midrange",
  "Overperformers", "Total")
options(scipen=999)
print(round(output,3))
```

Our output was as follows. As you see, each variable has three rows (mean, number of elements, and standard deviation). That is why, the table is so long.

	Underperformers	Midrange	Overperformers	Total
Total.Return. YTD..I..mean	-16.627	9.406	48.068	6.385
Total.Return. YTD..I..N	2264.000	3972.000	962.000	7198.000
Total.Return. YTD..I..sd	12.588	8.499	17.154	23.083
Cash.Assets. Y.1.mean	15.580	13.112	12.978	13.870
Cash.Assets. Y.1.N	2263.000	3972.000	962.000	7197.000
Cash.Assets. Y.1.sd	14.092	12.874	13.522	13.403
Net.Fixed. Assets .to.Tot.Assets. Y.1.mean	26.932	29.756	31.971	29.160
Net.Fixed. Assets.to. Tot.Assets. Y.1.N	2252.000	3899.000	957.000	7108.000
Net.Fixed. Assets.to. Tot.Assets. Y.1.sd	21.561	22.469	23.204	22.347
P.CF.5Yr.Avg. Y.1.mean	18.754	19.460	28.723	20.274

	Underperformers	Midrange	Overperformers	Total
P.CF.5Yr.Avg. Y.1.N	1366.000	2856.000	521.000	4743.000
P.CF.5Yr.Avg. Y.1.sd	57.309	132.399	281.563	142.133
Asset.Turnover. Y.1.mean	1.132	1.063	1.052	1.083
Asset.Turnover. Y.1.N	2237.000	3941.000	939.000	7117.000
Asset.Turnover. Y.1.sd	0.758	0.783	0.679	0.763
OI...Net.Sales. Y.1.mean	13.774	14.704	15.018	14.453
OI...Net.Sales. Y.1.N	2264.000	3972.000	962.000	7198.000
OI...Net.Sales. Y.1.sd	11.385	12.211	12.626	12.023
LTD.Capital. Y.1.mean	17.287	20.399	17.209	18.994
LTD.Capital. Y.1.N	2264.000	3972.000	962.000	7198.000
LTD.Capital. Y.1.sd	18.860	19.785	19.504	19.521
P.E. Y.1.mean	20.806	19.793	19.455	20.067
P.E. Y.1.N	2264.000	3972.000	962.000	7198.000
P.E. Y.1.sd	14.646	13.702	14.782	14.159

As we have seen in our preceding Anova table, in the case of six out of eight financial ratios, we find significant differences among the three groups. This method helps to find even nonlinear connections (in contrast to correlation ratios). A good example of this is Cash.Assets; Overperformers and mid-range shows very similar values, but underperformers have a significantly higher amount of (probably unused) cash. This means that being below a certain level, cash/asset gives us the hint that the given share is not a good investment. We will find the same pattern with the asset turnover.

The 5-year average of **Price/Cash flow (P/CF)** is another good example of how we may discover connections that remain hidden when only checking correlations. This ratio shows the J form, that is, the lowest value is with the mid-range group, and the highest with the overperformers.

Based on these results, the best investment targets may have, at the same time, lower cash ratio and financial leverage (LT debt / capital) but higher fixed asset rate and P/CF ratio, while P/E and asset turnover are just average. In short, the best firms use their current capital efficiently; they average the asset turnover with not too much free cash. They have further room to increase their leverage and have a good cash flow growth outlook reflected by the higher P/CF rate. Before testing this selection method, we shall check whether we may refine this by either adding more exact rules to separate potential investment or by simplifying it by removing some of these criteria.

Setting classification rules

Let's follow a different logic to develop decision rules so that we can contrast the two results later. Let's select which shares offered the best returns. Decision or classification trees are great for this purpose. Here, R will pick from the given list of variables those that can create the most effective decision rules. Instead of building joint rules, like we did previously, first, it selects the variable using which we may create subgroups of the shares regarding their TRS. Then, for each of these subgroups, it will choose the second most effective variable and so on. The output is a kind of decision tree:

```
d_tree <- d[,c(3:17,19)]
vars <- colnames(d_tree)
m <- length(vars)
tree_formula <- paste(vars[m], paste(vars[-m], collapse = " + "), sep = " ~ ")
library(rpart)
tree <- rpart(formula = tree_formula, data = d_tree, maxdepth = 5 ,cp = 0.001)
```

```
tree <- prune(tree, cp = 0.003)
par(xpd = T)
plot(tree)
text(tree, cex = .5, use.n = T, all = T)
```

In our case, the resulting tree has five levels, as you can see in the next figure. In each node, we get the indication of the average TRS for the created subgroups. The decision rule is also indicated: if the logical statement is true, go down on the branch to the left; if it is false, you will follow the right branch. As seen here, we will focus only on high return possibilities. We have to check the bottom of the tree to see what subgroups were created and which of them would show a particularly high TRS:

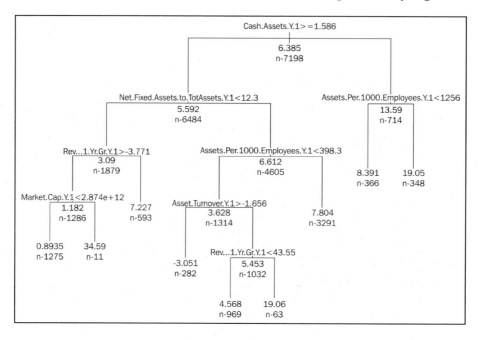

Our database ended up with three subgroups with particularly high-average TRS. Based on the tree, we have to check the Cash/Assets ratio first.

Firms with a ratio higher than (or equal to) 1.6 percent should be divided further based on the net fixed assets / total assets. If the ratio is above 12.3 percent and the asset/employee rate is below 398, plus the asset turnover is lower than 1.66, we only need to be sure that the 1 year growth of the revenue for the previous year was above 43.5 percent to get a subgroup of 63 firms with an average TRS of 19 percent.

If the Cash/Assets is above (or equal to) 1.6 percent and the net fixed assets / total assets ratio is below 12.3 percent, we need to look for the yearly growth of the revenue for the previous year. For the 11 companies where that ratio is above 3.77 percent and the market capitalization exceeds 2874 billion dollars, we will find an average TRS of 34.6 percent.

There is also a third group of overperformers. The 348 firms with a cash ratio lower than 1.6 and the companies with an asset/employee rate higher than 2156 generated an average TRS of 19 percent.

Considering the number of elements in these three groups compared to the total number of firms being analyzed, the first and the last one may offer us a realistic investment strategy. The group with 11 companies only represents 0.15 percent of the total, and so, it may be the result of random or unexpected events.

So, to sum this up, a high cash ratio (over 1.6) should go hand in hand with higher than 12.3 percent fixed asset ratio, an asset/employee value below 398, an asset turnover below 1.66, and a yearly revenue growth for the previous year exceeding 43.5 percent. If your cash ratio is lower than 1.6, asset/employee should be higher than 2156 to pick shares from our portfolio.

Notice that here, only five variables are included in our investment decision program, while previously, a constellation of eight variables was set up. Also, note that there are only three ratios (Cash/Assets, fixed assets ratio, and asset turnover), which are used in both of these decision processes. Our next step may be comparing the efficiency of the two methods.

Backtesting

The word "backtesting" refers to calculating the results of a trading strategy on a historical dataset. In our case, we will use the same dataset because of which we will overestimate the effectiveness, as our statistical models were optimized on exactly the same data. In the real life, we might go for a different time period or a different group of equities (or both) to measure efficiency more objectively.

No matter how we got the best performers separated, testing the investment idea follows the same logic. You translate the result into rules, pick the firms (normally from a different sample) that fulfill the requirements and place them into one cluster, and then create another cluster to contain all the other companies. Finally, compare the mean and/or median performance of the two groups.

To test the selection rules of the decision tree, we have to create a subset of firms that fulfil the requirements of having a cash ratio above 1.6, fixed asset ratio exceeding 12.3 percent, an asset/employee rate below 398, and 1 year growth of the revenue for the previous year at least 43.5 percent. Then, we have to add the firms with a cash ratio below 1.6 and an asset/employee above 2156:

```
d$condition1 <- (d[,3]  >   1.6)
d$condition2 <- (d[,4]  >  12.3)
d$condition3 <- (d[,5]  <   398)
d$condition4 <- (d[,10] <  1.66)
d$condition5 <- (d[,13] >  43.5)
d$selected1 <- d$condition1 & d$condition2 & d$condition3 & d$condition4
& d$condition5
d$condition6 <- (d[,3]  <   1.6)
d$condition7 <- (d[,5]  >  2156)
d$selected2  <- d$condition6 & d$condition7
d$tree <- d$selected1 | d$selected2
```

To do this, we will create two new variables (one for both subsets) that are equal to 1 if requirements are fulfilled; otherwise, they will be equal to 0. Next, we will calculate a third variable that is the sum of the previous two. This way, we will end up with two clusters: 1 for firms qualifying for investment and 0 for all others:

```
f <- function(x) c(mean(x), length(x), sd(x), median(x))
report <- aggregate( x = d[,19], by = list(d$tree), FUN = f )$x
colnames(report) = c("mean","N","standard deviation","median")
report <- rbind(report, f(d[,19]))
rownames(report) <- c("Not selected","Selected","Total")
print(report)
```

Once we are ready with the reclustering, an ANOVA table will help us compare the performance of the firms selected and not selected. To assure that it is not due to outliers that we have significantly different averages, it is always wise to compare medians too. In our case, the categorization seems to work just fine, as even among the medians, we have a huge difference:

	mean	N	standard deviation	median
Not selected	5.490854	6588	22.21786	3.601526
Selected	19.620651	260	24.98839	15.412807
Total	6.384709	7198	23.08327	4.245684

Testing the cluster-based investment idea is slightly more complicated. Here, we only see that the cluster of the better firms is different in average in some respect from the other two groups. It is important to notice that these were not the differences that we used to create the clusters; it is simply us turning the logic over and saying that criteria on the financial ratios may result is separating the better performers.

We need to go through all the eight variables that showed significant differences and create a range of acceptance. Using very narrow ranges may lead to a very small number of shares to pick; applying a range far too wide will make the difference between groups in TRS disappear. Once again, checking medians may help.

To get the means and medians for the three clusters that we identified previously, we will use the following code. To save space when printing the table instead of using the original names, we numbered the three groups as follows:

1. Underperformers
2. Mid-range performers
3. Overperformers.

Here is the code:

```
d$cluster = k_clust$cluster
z <- round(cbind(t(aggregate(d[,c(19,3,4,6,10,12,14,16,17)],
list(d$selected) ,function(x) mean(x, na.rm = T))),
t(aggregate(d[,c(19,3,4,6,10,12,14,16,17)], list(d$selected) ,function(x)
median(x, na.rm = T))))[-1,], 2)
> colnames(z) = c("1-mean","2-mean","3-mean","1-median", "2-median",
"3-median")

> z
```

	1-mean	2-mean	3-mean	1-median	2-median	3-median
Total.Return.YTD..I.	-16.62	9.41	48.07	-13.45	8.25	42.28
Cash.Assets.Y.1	15.58	13.11	12.98	11.49	9.07	8.95
Net.Fixed.Assets.to.Tot.Assets.Y.1	26.93	29.76	31.97	21.87	24.73	26.78
P.CF.5Yr.Avg.Y.1	18.75	19.46	28.72	11.19	10.09	10.08
Asset.Turnover.Y.1	1.13	1.06	1.05	0.96	0.89	0.91

```
OI...Net.Sales.Y.1             13.77  14.71  15.02    10.59    11.23
11.49
LTD.Capital.Y.1                17.28  20.41  17.21    11.95    16.55
10.59
Market.Cap.Y.1                278.06 659.94 603.10     3.27     4.97
4.43
P.E.Y.1                        20.81  19.79  19.46    16.87    15.93
14.80
```

The following table shows our rules developed based on the Anova table for the clusters. Due to the small differences or overlapping ranges, we dropped three variables from the criteria rules. Remember that your main task is to separate overperformers from underperformers, so an overlap with the mid-range is more acceptable (set wider ranges of acceptance where mid-range is really in the middle) than any with the underperformers.

	Cash/ Assets	Net Fixed Assets to Total Assets	P/CF 5Yr Average	Asset Turnover	OI/ Net Sales	LTD/ Capital	Market Cap (M)	P/E
Min	none	23	dropped	none	11	dropped	dropped	none
Max	14	none	dropped	1,7	none	dropped	dropped	20

Table 1

With the following code, we will first arrange all the requirements into one variable. Then, a final comparison table is created:

```
d$selected <- (d[,3] <= 14) & (d[,4] >= 23) & (d[,10] <= 1.7) & (d[,12]
>= 11) & (d[17] <= 20)
d$selected[is.na(d$selected)] <- FALSE
h <- function(x) c(mean(x, na.rm = T), length(x[!is.na(x)]), sd(x, na.rm
= T), median(x, na.rm = T))
backtest <- aggregate(d[,19], list(d$selected), h)
backtest <- backtest$x
backtest <- rbind(backtest, h(d[,19]))
colnames(backtest) = c("mean", "N", "Stdev", "Median")
rownames(backtest) = c("Not selected", "Selected", "Total")
print(backtest)
                 mean     N    Stdev    Median
Not selected 5.887845 6255 23.08020 3.710650
Selected     9.680451  943 22.84361 7.644033
Total        6.384709 7198 23.08327 4.245684
```

As you can see, our selected firms have an average return of 9.68 percent, while the median amounted to 7.6 percent. Here, we may draw the conclusion that the strategy developed based on the decision tree performed better with respect to both the mean (19.05 percent) and median (14.98 percent). To check the overlap, we will calculate a crosstab:

```
d$tree <- tree$where %in% c(13,17)
crosstable <- table(d$selected, d$tree)
rownames(crosstable) = c("cluster-0","cluser-1")
colnames(crosstable) = c("tree-0","tree-1")
crosstable <- addmargins(crosstable)
crosstable
```

	tree-0	tree-1	Sum
cluster-0	5970	285	6255
cluser-1	817	126	943
Sum	6787	411	7198

Here, we see that the two strategies are pretty different: only 126 firms got selected under both strategies. But are they something extraordinary? Indeed. These shares achieved an average TRS of 19.9 percent with a median of 14.4, which is calculated as follows:

```
mean(d[d$selected & d$tree,19])
[1] 19.90455
median(d[d$selected & d$tree,19])
[1] 14.43585
```

Industry-specific investment

Until this point, we considered the entire sample as one. It could be a logical decision to focus only on some industries. Note that choosing the right industry to invest should not be based on past performance pattern; we rather have to analyze comovements with global economic trends over a number of years, and then, based on our prediction for the coming periods, we should pick the one with the best outlook. This method helps you to determine the right weights of the industries in your portfolio, but then, you still need to select individual shares that may overperform the others.

Of course, once one given industry is selected, we may end up with different investment rules than those on the whole sample. So, we may further improve our investment performance by performing the previously shown steps for each industry separately.

At the same time, recall that the more specific you are in data selection (time period, industry, and firm size), the less likely will the strategy created show good performance on other samples or in the future. By increasing the degree of freedom of your strategy building (rerunning all statistical tests for subsamples), you make recommendations fit nearly perfectly to the given sample that may reflect the effects of a number of random events. As these random effects never occur again, adding more and more flexibility after a certain limit will actually worsen the end result.

For the sake of the example, we picked Communications. If we apply the decision-tree technique here, we would end up with the following figure. After that, we have to invest into firms that have seen their revenue growing by less than 21 percent but more than 1.31 percent during the last year, while the net fixed assets ratio was at least 8.06 percent:

```
d_comm <- d[d[,18] == "Communications",c(3:17,19)]

vars <- colnames(d_comm)

m <- length(vars)

tree_formula <- paste(vars[m], paste(vars[-m], collapse = " + "), sep = "
~ ")

library(rpart)

tree <- rpart(formula = tree_formula, data = d_comm, maxdepth = 5 ,cp =
0.01, control = rpart.control(minsplit = 100))

tree <- prune(tree, cp = 0.006)

par(xpd = T)

plot(tree)

text(tree, cex = .5, use.n = T, all = T)

print(tree)
```

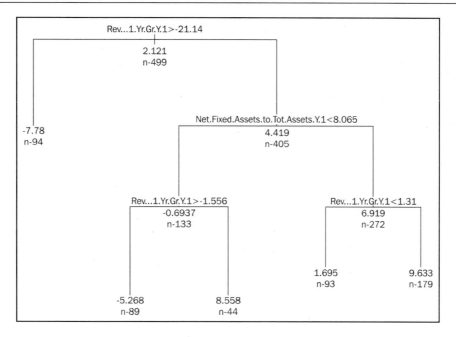

At the same time, building a strategy based on a general sample of a given period may end up overweighting certain industries that show great performance during the given year(s), while, of course, there is no guarantee that the coming years will also prefer the same sectors. So, after building our strategy, we should crosscheck whether there is a serious industry dependency behind that strategy.

A cross-table controlling for the connection of the industry and decision-tree-based investment strategy reveals that we heavily overweighted the Energy and Utilities sectors. The cluster-based strategy, at the same time, gives an extra weight to materials. The code for the latter is shown here:

```
cross <- table(d[,18], d$selected)
colnames(cross) <- c("not selected", "selected")
cross
```

	not selected	selected
Communications	488	11
Consumer Discretionary	1476	44
Consumer Staples	675	36
Energy	449	32

Financials	116	1
Health Care	535	37
Industrials	1179	53
Materials	762	99
Technology	894	7
Utilities	287	17

```
prop.table(cross)
```

	not selected	selected
Communications	0.0677966102	0.0015282023
Consumer Discretionary	0.2050569603	0.0061128091
Consumer Staples	0.0937760489	0.0050013893
Energy	0.0623784385	0.0044456794
Financials	0.0161155877	0.0001389275
Health Care	0.0743262017	0.0051403168
Industrials	0.1637954987	0.0073631564
Materials	0.1058627396	0.0137538205
Technology	0.1242011670	0.0009724924
Utilities	0.0398721867	0.0023617672

We may also be interested in how good our strategy performs across industries. For this, we should see the average TRS of firms chosen and not chosen for all the individual sectors. To create a table like this, we need to use the following command. The output illustrates how the decision-tree-based strategy performs (0 not selected, 1 selected):

```
t1 <- aggregate(d[ d$tree,19], list(d[ d$tree,18]), function(x)
c(mean(x), median(x)))

t2 <- aggregate(d[!d$tree,19], list(d[!d$tree,18]), function(x)
c(mean(x), median(x)))

industry_crosstab <- round(cbind(t1$x, t2$x),4)

colnames(industry_crosstab) <- c("mean-1","median-1","mean-0","median-0")

rownames(industry_crosstab) <- t1[,1]

industry_crosstab
```

	mean-1	median-1	mean-0	median-0
Communications	10.4402	11.5531	1.8810	2.8154
Consumer Discretionary	15.9422	10.7034	2.7963	1.3154
Consumer Staples	14.2748	6.5512	4.5523	3.1839
Energy	17.8265	16.7273	5.6107	5.0800
Financials	33.3632	33.9155	5.4558	3.5193
Health Care	26.6268	21.8815	7.5387	4.6022
Industrials	29.2173	17.6756	6.5487	3.7119
Materials	22.9989	21.3155	8.4270	5.6327
Technology	43.9722	46.8772	7.4596	5.3433
Utilities	11.6620	11.1069	8.6993	7.7672

As shown in the preceding output, our strategy performs pretty well in all sectors; though in `Consumer Staples`, the median of the selected firms is somewhat near to that of not selected. In other cases, we may end up seeing that in some sectors, we do not get very good results, and the TRS of the chosen firms may even be lower than that of the other group. In this case, we would build a separate stock-selection model for those sectors where our model performed weaker.

Summary

In this chapter, we investigated how to use R to build an investment strategy on fundamental bases. After building and loading our database to R, we first checked whether some of our variables show a strong connection with TRS. Then, we checked whether some linear combinations of them would perform well and controlled them.

As neither method led to an acceptable result, we turned the logic upside down. We created clusters of firms based on TRS performance; then, we checked what is typical for overperformers. We also used decision trees to look for the best way to separate the firms with the highest TRS. Then, based on the results, we described stock-selection rules and performed backtesting.

Our example showed that even if individual explanatory variables show no strong linear connection to performance, it is possible to build an effective fundamental stock-selection strategy. When applying these techniques, recall the limitations: too much flexibility may hurt. A model with a nearly perfect fit for a historical dataset may perform very badly in the future if you achieved the good fit by providing too much freedom to your model.

References

- **Brealey, Richard – Myers, Stewart – Marcus, Alan (2011)**: Fundamentals of Corporate Finance, McGraw-Hill/Irwin; 7th edition

- **Ross, Stephen – Westerfield, Randolph – Jordan, Bradford D. (2009)**: Fundamentals of Corporate Finance Standard Edition McGraw-Hill/Irwin; 9th edition

- **Koller, Tim – Goedhart, Marc – Wessels, David (2010)**: Valuation, Measuring and managing the value of companies, 5th edition, John Wiley & Sons, New York

- **Damodaran, Aswath (2002)**: Investment Valuation, Tools and Techniques for Determining the Value of Any Asset, John Wiley & Sons, Inc., New York

10

Technical Analysis, Neural Networks, and Logoptimal Portfolios

In this chapter we give a brief introduction to different methods that may help to improve the performance of your portfolio: technical analysis, neural networks and log-optimal portfolios. The common idea behind these methods is that past price movements may help in forecasting future trends. In other words, we implicitly assume that prices do not follow a Markov process (for example random walk), but they have some kind of long lasting memory, hence patterns from the past may reoccur also in the future, all in all markets are not efficient.

In the first part we introduce the most common tools of technical analysis and present some indicative examples of how to program them in the R environment. In the second part we outline the concept of neural networks and their design by R's built-in function. Technical analysis and neural network are applied on the bitcoin database, thus we focus on a single asset and investigate for reliable signals of buying and selling. Finally, in the third part we discuss the so called log-optimal portfolio strategies that enable us to optimize our portfolio of several assets (in our example some NYSE stocks) for the long run.

The main goal of this chapter is just to give a helicopter view on the concepts, the most common tools that are used and to provide some examples of their programming. Therefore we would like to underline here that, by need of being concise, we only intend to give you some insight into the field and to entice you to check the references, learn more and try further tools yourself.

Market efficiency

Markets are efficient to the extent that all information is built into the current prices. The weak form of market efficiency requires that the latest price already incorporates all the information which can be obtained from the chart of past prices and trading volumes. Clearly, if markets were efficient at least in this weak sense, returns would be totally independent over time and strategies based on technical analysis, neural networks and the logoptimal portfolio theory would be completely worthless, see *Hull (2009), Model of the behavior of stock prices.*

However, the efficiency of a given market is purely an empirical question. You can never be sure that asset returns in the real world are really completely independent in time. Therefore, you should not take market efficiency as a fact but you are encouraged to test it on your own by inventing and implementing new technically inspired strategies. If your strategy calibrated on past trading data proves to be robust enough and works well in the future, then the market will generously honor your efforts by enhancing the risk/return profile of your portfolio, and, as a result, you will earn an extra profit. Studies have shown that emerging currency markets, for instance, are less efficient due to illiquidity and to central bank interventions, see *Tajaddini-Crack (2012);* whereas most technicist strategies do not hold on the more developed American stock market *Bajgrowicz-Scaillet (2012), Zapranis-Prodromos (2012).* Furthermore, the same studies indicate that when technical trading is successful, its combination with fundamental analysis is even more so. *Zwart et al. (2009).*

Despite being sort of an apocrypha still today, technical analysis is widely used even among fundamental investors. This is mainly due to its self-fulfilling nature: as market players know that more and more of their peers are using the TA tools they keep an eye on them, too. If, for instance, a 200-day moving average is breached on a main index chart, it is likely to make the headlines and cause a selling wave.

Technical analysis

Technical analysis (**TA**) can help you achieve better results if you do not overestimate its predictive power. Technical analysis is especially good at predicting short-term trends and at indicating market sentiment. Fundamental investors (and one of the writers of this chapter) use them to choose their buy-in and sell-out point: given their fundamentally backed view on the direction of the market technical analysis is a valuable help in choosing the short-term optimum. It can also eliminate such common trading flaws as badly chosen position size (indication on the strength of the trend), shaky hands (only sell when there is a sign) and inability to press the button (but when there is a sign, do sell).

Three golden rules to remember before we jump to technicalities:

1. **Each market has its own mix of tools that work**: For example head-and-shoulders mostly appear on stock charts whereas support-resistance levels temper the trading on forex markets, and within the markets each asset can be specific. Therefore, as a rule of thumb, use tailor-made sets of indicators and neural networks specific to the actual asset you are looking at.

2. **No pain, no gain**: Keep in mind that there is no holy grail, if one achieves to sustain winning on 60% of the trades then she has found a viable and well-rewarding trading strategy.

3. **Avoid impulsive trading**: Maybe this is the most important above all. It might hurt that you lost on your last trade but do not let it influence your future decisions. Trade only when there is a sign. If you consider opening a live trade account read extensively on money management (handling risk and position size, leverage) and on psychology of trading (greed, fear, hope, regret).

The TA toolkit

Technical analysis abounds of tools but most of them can be categorized into four main groups. We advise you to use the old ones as these are more followed by professionals and are more likely to trigger price movements themselves (being self-fulfilling) besides being usually more user-friendly.

1. **Support-resistance and price channels**: Price levels often influence trading: strategic levels may act either as support, keeping price levels from falling below, or as resistance, an obstacle to further rises. Parallel lines applied to the primary conditions of a trend (bottoms for an increasing trend, tops for a decreasing trend) define price channels - they are tools of the top-bottom analysis, just like the next category, the chart patterns. As these are usually harder to program we do not deal with them in detail.

2. **Chart patterns – Head-and-shoulders, saucers**: sound familiar? Perhaps, due to their easily recognizable nature, chart patterns are the most widely known tools of technical analysis. They have three categories: trend makers (mast, flag), trend breakers (double tops) and decision point signals (triangles). These, too, are rather intuitive, hardly programmable, and thus fall out of the scope of this chapter.

3. **Candle patterns**: As candlestick charts are the most widespread technicists started to spot signals on these and have given those names like morning star, three white soldiers or the famous key reversal. More than any other TA tool, they are significant only if combined with other signals, in most cases strategic price levels. They can be a combination of two-five candles.

4. **Indicators –**: This is the type we will deal with the most in the following pages. Easy to program, technical indicators serve as basis of **high frequency trading (HFT)**, a strategy based on algorithmic decisions and rapid market orders. These indicators have four categories: momentum-based, trend follower, money flow (based on volume) and volatility-based.

In this chapter we are going to present a strategy that combines elements from types (3) and (4), we will be looking for potential trend changes by the help of indicators and signal key reversals there.

Markets

Although everyone should explore by her own the TA tools that best work on the respective markets some general observations can be formulated.

1. **Stocks** usually form nice chart patterns and are sensitive to candle patterns and to strategic moving average crossings, too. Asymmetric information is an important issue, although less than in the case of commodities, for instance, and unpredictable spikes can alter the course of the prices at news releases.

2. **FX** is traded continuously around the globe and is strongly decentralized which implies two things. First, no overall volume data is available, so one should have a general idea about the liquidity of the markets to weigh the importance of price changes – for example in summer liquidity is lower, therefore even a smaller buy-in can generate volatility. Second, different people trade at different times and each of them has different habits. In EURJPY, for instance, during the US and European trading hours the tens and round numbers tend to be psychological supports, whereas there is a switch to the 8s during the Asian trading (8 being a lucky number). From a TA toolkit perspective: no characteristic chart patterns besides triangles and masts, important support-resistance levels and price channels, zone-thinking, stuck-launch dynamics and Fibonacci proportions are mostly used.

Plotting charts - bitcoin

Charting programs, if not provided by brokerages in the trading program, can get expensive and not always provide sophisticated TA tools. To circumvent this problem you can use R to trace your charts and can program all the indicators you like – if they are not yet built in.

Let's look at an example now: plotting charts for bitcoin. Bitcoin is a crypto currency that got popular in the summer of 2014 where its price was up to $1162 from below $1 and is traded on many freshly founded and therefore rudimentary exchanges. This posed a problem to many small investors: how to trace the chart? And, even if they were okay with BitStamp's uneasy platform, granular data was only available in spreadsheet format and is still today.

You can source data from `http://bitcoincharts.com/`. Herein we included a code that draws in live data and thus acts as if it was a live charting tool. With this useful trick you can avoid paying hundreds of dollars for a professional software. We plot candlestick charts (also called OHLC), the commonly used type. Before we start here is a graphic that explains how they work.

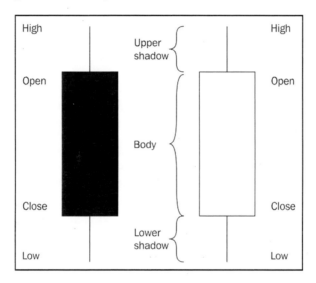

Here we provide the program code of the live data fetcher that draws OHLC chart.

We will use the RCurl package to get data from the Internet. First let's have a look at the following function:

```
library(RCurl)
```

```
get_price <- function(){
```

First we use the getURL function from the RCurl package to read the whole website as a string:

```
a <- getURL("https://www.bitcoinwisdom.com/markets/bitstamp/btcusd",
  ssl.verifypeer=0L, followlocation=1L)
```

If we have a look at the HTML code we can easily find the bitcoin price we are looking for. The function returns it as a numeric value.

```
n <- as.numeric(regexpr("id=market_bitstampbtcusd>", a))
a <- substr(a, n, n + 100)
n <- as.numeric(regexpr(">", a))
m <- as.numeric(regexpr("</span>", a))
a <- substr(a, n + 1, m - 1)
as.numeric(a)
}
```

Or we can grab the exact same information with the help of the XML package, which was created to parse HTML and XML files and to extract information:

```
library(XML)
as.numeric(xpathApply(htmlTreeParse(a, useInternalNodes = TRUE),
    '//span[@id="market_bitstampbtcusd"]', xmlValue)[[1]])
```

This practice of getting price data is of course only for demonstration purposes. Live price data should be provided by our broker (for which we can still use R). Now let's see, how to draw a live candle chart:

```
DrawChart <- function(time_frame_in_minutes,
  number_of_candles = 25, l = 315.5, u = 316.5) {

  OHLC <- matrix(NA, 4, number_of_candles)
  OHLC[, number_of_candles] <- get_price()
  dev.new(width = 30, height = 15)
  par(bg = rgb(.9, .9, .9))
  plot(x = NULL, y = NULL, xlim = c(1, number_of_candles + 1),
    ylim = c(l, u), xlab = "", ylab = "", xaxt = "n", yaxt = "n")
  abline(h = axTicks(2), v = axTicks(1), col = rgb(.5, .5, .5), lty = 3)
  axis(1, at = axTicks(1), las = 1, cex.axis = 0.6,
    labels = Sys.time() - (5:0) * time_frame_in_minutes)
  axis(2, at = axTicks(2), las = 1, cex.axis = 0.6)
  box()
  allpars = par(no.readonly = TRUE)
  while(TRUE) {
    start_ <- Sys.time()
    while(as.numeric(difftime(Sys.time(), start_, units = "mins")) <
      time_frame_in_minutes) {
      OHLC[4,number_of_candles] <- get_price()
```

```
    OHLC[2,number_of_candles] <- max(OHLC[2,number_of_candles],
      OHLC[4,number_of_candles])
OHLC[3,number_of_candles] <- min(OHLC[3,number_of_candles],
    OHLC[4,number_of_candles])
    frame()
    par(allpars)
    abline(h = axTicks(2), v=axTicks(1), col = rgb(.5,.5,.5),
      lty = 3)
    axis(1, at = axTicks(1), las = 1, cex.axis = 0.6,
      labels = Sys.time()-(5:0)*time_frame_in_minutes)
    axis(2, at = axTicks(2), las = 1, cex.axis = 0.6)
    box()
    for(i in 1:number_of_candles) {
      polygon(c(i, i + 1, i + 1, i),
        c(OHLC[1, i], OHLC[1, i], OHLC[4, i], OHLC[4, i]),
          col = ifelse(OHLC[1,i] <= OHLC[4,i],
            rgb(0,0.8,0), rgb(0.8,0,0)))
      lines(c(i+1/2, i+1/2), c(OHLC[2,i], max(OHLC[1,i],
        OHLC[4,i])))
      lines(c(i+1/2, i+1/2), c(OHLC[3,i], min(OHLC[1,i],
        OHLC[4,i])))
    }
    abline(h = OHLC[4, number_of_candles], col = "green",
      lty = "dashed")
  }
  OHLC <- OHLC[, 2:number_of_candles]
  OHLC <- cbind(OHLC, NA)
  OHLC[1,number_of_candles] <- OHLC[4,number_of_candles-1]
  }
}
```

To fully understand this code some time and some programming experience is probably needed. To summarize the algorithm does the following: in an infinite loop, reads price data and stores it in a matrix with four rows as OHLC. Every time the last column of this matrix is recalculated to assure that H is the highest and L is the lowest price observed in that time interval. When the time determined by the `time_frame_in_minutes` variable is reached matrix columns roll, the oldest observations (first column) are dropped, and each column is replaced by the next one. The first column is then filled with NAs except the O (open) price, which is considered as the close price of the previous column, so the chart is continuous.

The remaining code is only for drawing the candles with the "polygon" method. (We can do it with built-in functions as well, as we will see later.)

Let's call this function and see what happens:

```
DrawChart(30,50)
```

See more on data manipulation in *Chapter 4, Big Data – Advanced Analytics*.

Built-in indicators

R has many built-in indicators, such as the **simple moving average (SMA)**, the **exponential moving average (EMA)**, the **relative strength indicator (RSI)**, and the famous MACD. These constitute an integral part of technical analysis, their main goal is to visualize a relative benchmark so that you could get an idea whether your asset is overbought, relatively well-performing or at a strategic level compared to some reference period. Here you find a brief explanation to what each of them does, and how you can put them on your chart.

SMA and EMA

Moving averages are the simplest among all indicators: they show the average price level for you on a rolling basis. For example, if you trace the 15-candle SMA, it will give you the average price level of the 15 preceding candles. Obviously, if your current candle's time is up and a new candle starts, the SMA will calculate a new average leaving out the previously first candle and taking in the newest one instead. The difference between SMA and EMA is that SMA weighs all candles equally whereas EMA gives exponential weights – hence the name: it overweighs current candles to previous ones. This is a good approach if you want a benchmark that is more tied to current price levels and that reacts more quickly where there are shifts in price levels. These are overlay indicators that are directly plotted on the chart.

RSI

The relative strength index is a band-indicator: its value can vary between 0 and 100 with three bands within this range. With an RSI between 0 to 30 the asset is oversold, between 70 to 100 it is overbought. RSI endeavors to judge upon price variations' intensity by using the relative strength ratio: average price of up closes divided by the average price of down closes (aka green candles' average close per red candles' average close). The average's summing period may vary, 70 is the most used.

$$RSI = 100 - \frac{100}{(1+RS)}; \; where \, RS = \frac{average\,of\,upcloses}{average\,of\,downcloses}$$

As the formula suggests this indicator often gives signals, mostly in strong trends. As prices might remain at overbought or oversold levels use this indicator carefully, always in combination with some other type of indicator, or chart pattern like a trend breaker, also called failure swing. You might also consider diminishing your position size or looking for warning signs if, for instance, it shows that the asset you are long on is overbought.

Here you can see how to trace this indicator and a moving average:

```
library(quantmod)
bitcoin <- read.table("Bitcoin.csv", header = T, sep = ";", row.names =
1)
bitcoin <- tail(bitcoin, 150)
bitcoin <- as.xts(bitcoin)
dev.new(width = 20, height = 10)
chartSeries(bitcoin, dn.col = "red", TA="addRSI(10);addEMA(10)")
```

By looking at the above chart we can conclude that during this period the market became rather oversold as the RSI tended to remain at low territories and it has hit the extreme levels several times.

MACD

MACD (Mac Dee) stands for **Moving Average Convergence-Divergence**. It is a combination of a slow (26-candles) and a quick (12 candles) exponential moving average, a trend follower indicator: it gives signals rarely, but these tend to be more accurate. MACD gives signals when the quick EMA crosses the slow one. This is a buy if the quick crosses from below and a sell if it crosses from above (the 12-canlde average price being lower than the 26-candle, long-term average). The position of the EMA(12) marks the general direction of the trend – for example if it is above the EMA(26) the market is bullish. Important restriction: MACD gives false alarms in ranges, use only in strong trends. Some use the direction of the changes of the distance between the two lines, too, plotted in red or green histograms: once there are four bars in the same color, the strength of the trend is confirmed.

For technical analysis, you can use different R-packages: `quantmod`, `ftrading`, `TTR`, and so on. We mostly rely on `quantmod`. Here you can see how to trace the MACD on a previously saved dataset, named `Bitcoin.csv`:

```
library(quantmod)
bitcoin <- read.table("Bitcoin.csv", header = T, sep = ";", row.names = 1)
bitcoin <- tail(bitcoin, 150)
bitcoin <- as.xts(bitcoin)
dev.new(width = 20, height = 10)
chartSeries(bitcoin, dn.col = "red", TA="addMACD();addSMA(10)")
```

You can see the MACD under the chart, in the strong downwards trend it gives valid signals.

Candle patterns: key reversal

Now that you got a general grasp of R's TA features let us program a rather easy strategy. The following script recognizes key reversals, a candlestick pattern, at strategic price levels.

To do this, we applied the following dual rationale: first, we gave a discretional definition to what a strategic price level is. For instance, we recognized as mature increasing trend the price movement whose bottoms are monotonously increasing (bottom being the candle body's lowest point) and whose current MA(25) level is higher than the MA(25) measured 25 candles before. We underline here that this does not constitute part of the standard TA tools and that its parameters have been chosen to best fit the actual chart we deal with, that of bitcoin. If you would like to apply it to other assets we advise you to adjust it to provide the best fit. This is not a trend recognition algorithm on itself: it only serves as part of our signal system.

If this algorithm recognized a strategic price level in a mature trend that would be likely to break down if a candle pattern appeared, we started to look for key reversals. The key reversal is a trend breaker candlestick pattern, it occurs when the previous trend's last candle that points to the same direction as the trend itself (it is green for a rising trend, red for a falling one), but suddenly prices turn and the next candle points in the opposite direction of the trend with a bigger candle body than the previous one. The trend breaker candle should start at least as high as the previous one, or, if the quotes are not continuous, a bit above the close for a rising trend, and a bit below for a falling one. See our graphic below for a key reversal in a rising trend:

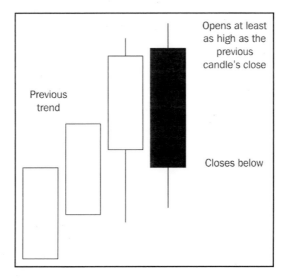

Here you find the code of the function that recognizes this pattern:

Earlier in the bitcoin section we used the polygon method to create candle charts manually. Here we are using the quantmod package and the `chartSeries` function to do the same more easily wrapped in the OHLC function to make it more flexible.

```
library(quantmod)
OHLC <- function(d) {
  windows(20,10)
  chartSeries(d, dn.col = "red")
}
```

The following function takes the time series and two indices (*i* and *j*) as arguments, and decides, weather it is an increasing trend from i to j or not:

```
is.trend <- function(ohlc,i,j){
```

First: if the MA(25) is not increasing then it is not an increasing trend so we return FALSE.

```
avg1 = mean(ohlc[(i-25):i,4])
avg2 = mean(ohlc[(j-25):j,4])
if(avg1 >= avg2) return(FALSE)
```

In this simple algorithm a candle is called a **valley**, if the bottom of the candle body is lower than the previous one and the next one. If the valleys make a monotonous non-decreasing series we have an increasing trend.

```
ohlc <- ohlc[i:j, ]
  n <- nrow(ohlc)
  candle_l <- pmin(ohlc[, 1], ohlc[, 4])
  valley <- rep(FALSE, n)
  for (k in 2:(n - 1))
    valley[k] <- ((candle_l[k-1] >= candle_l[k]) &
      (candle_l[k+1] >= candle_l[k]))
  z <- candle_l[valley]
  if (all(z == cummax(z))) return(TRUE)
  FALSE
}
```

This was the trend recognition. Let's see the trend reversal. First we use the previous function to check the conditions of the increasing trend. Then we check the last two candles for the reversal pattern. That's it.

```
is.trend.rev <- function(ohlc, i, j) {
  if (is.trend(ohlc, i, j) == FALSE) return(FALSE)
  last_candle <- ohlc[j + 1, ]

  reverse_candle <- ohlc[j + 2, ]
  ohlc <- ohlc[i:j, ]
  if (last_candle[4] < last_candle[1]) return(FALSE)
  if (last_candle[4] < max(ohlc[,c(1,4)])) return(FALSE)
  if (reverse_candle[1] < last_candle[4] |
      reverse_candle[4] >= last_candle[1]) return(FALSE)
  TRUE
}
```

We are out of the woods. Now we can use this in real data. We simply read the bitcoin data and run the trend reversal recognition on it. If there is a reversed trend with at least 10 candles we plot it.

```
bitcoin <- read.table("Bitcoin.csv", header = T, sep = ";", row.names =
1)
n <- nrow(bitcoin)
result <- c(0,0)
for (a in 26:726) {
  for (b in (a + 3):min(n - 3, a + 100)) {
    if (is.trend.rev(bitcoin, a,b) & b - a > 10 )
      result <- rbind(result, c(a,b))
    if (b == n)
      break
  }
}

z <- aggregate(result, by = list(result[, 2]), FUN = min)[-1, 2:3]
for (h in 1:nrow(z)) {
  OHLC(bitcoin[z[h, 1]:z[h, 2] + 2,])
  title(main = z[h, ])
}
```

Evaluating the signals and managing the position

Our code successfully recognizes four key reversals, including the historical turning point in the bitcoin price giving us a nice short selling signal. We can conclude that the signaling was successful, the only thing left to do is to use them wisely.

Aware of the fundamentals of bitcoin (its acceptance as money undermined, ousting from such previously core markets as China), one could have made a nice profit whilst following the signal (the last candle on the chart) which is as follows:

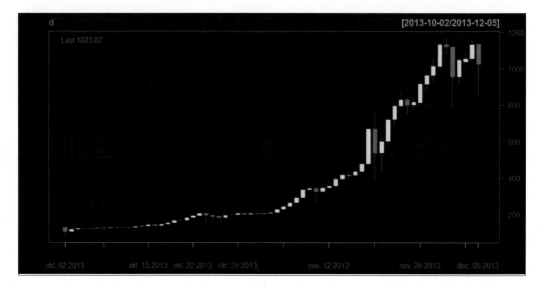

TA is useful while setting take profits and stop losses, in other words managing your position. If you chose to sell at the signal, you could have set these as follows.

The system signals that you might want to sell at $1023,9 on December 5, 2013, in the last candle of the above chart, highlighted with an arrow on the next chart. You decide to proceed and open a position. Since bitcoin prices fluctuate quite much, especially after an exponentially increasing previous trend, you decide to put your stop loss to the historical high, to 1163, because you don't want false spikes to close you out of the position.

On the next chart, here below, you can see that this approach is justified, after the fall in prices volatility increases significantly and shadows grow.

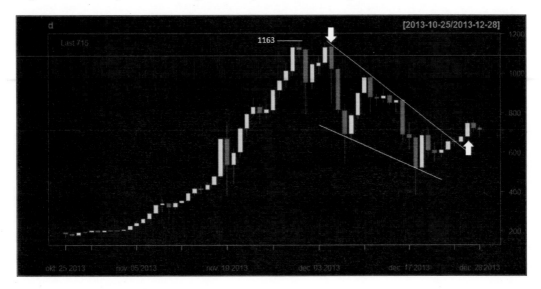

By the end of 2013 a supposed trend line can be traced if you connect the tops of the candles bodies (in white, drawn manually). This seems to hold and a lower trendline forms on the bottoms, with a lower slope, giving a triangle. We say that a triangle is valid on a chart if the price leaves it before it reaches 3/4 of its length.

This is what happens: on December 26, 2013 the daily chart breaks the line upwards with a big green candle (pointed at by an arrow). The MACD crosses, giving a strong bullish signal, and we close the position on the top of the body, at 747.0 – if not before. So, we earned $276.9, or a 27% return on the trade.

A word on money management

Let's look at the risk profile of this trade to show how technical analysis can be used to manage your exposure. The best way to do so is to calculate your risk-reward ratio, given by the below formula:

$$Risk - reward\ ratio = \frac{Expected\ gain}{Units\ at\ risk}$$

The denominator is easy to define, this is the possible loss on the position, (1163.0-1023.9) = $139.1 in the case of the activation of the stop loss. The numerator, the possible gain can be approximated by a Fibonacci retracement, a tool that uses the golden section to predict possible price reversals, particularly useful in this exponential trend. You can see it below on a graph from `https://bitcoinwisdom.com/`:

If you take the height of the trend as 100%, you can expect prices to touch Fibonacci levels when the trend breaks. Since a key reversal is a strong sign, let's take the 38.2%, which equals $747.13, so we expect prices to go down there. So the numerator of the risk-reward ratio is (1023.9-747.1) = $276.8, giving a final result of 276.8 /139.1 = 1.99, meaning that there is an ex-ante profit potential of $1.99 per one dollar at risk. This is a just fine potential, the trade should be approved.

Whenever you consider entering into a position, calculate how much you risk compared to how much you expect to gain. If it is below 3/2, the position is not the best, if below 1, you should forget the trade altogether. The possible ways to improve your risk/reward ratio are a tighter stop loss or the choice of a stronger sign. Technical analysis provides you with useful risk management tactics if you wish to be successful at trading, do not forget about them.

Wraping up

Technical analysis, and particularly the presented chartist approach, is a highly intuitive, graphical way of analyzing financial assets. It uses support-resistance levels, chart- and candle patterns and indicators to predict future price movements. R enabled us to fetch live data for free and plot it as an OHLC chart, plot indicators on it and receive automated signs for key reversals, a candlestick pattern. We used one of these to show how a real position could have been managed manually and have shown that the appeal of TA is that it not only tells you when to open a position but also when to close it and calculate the strength of the signal by using risk management practices.

Neural networks

After remaining a long time in academic circles due to their advanced mathematical background, **neural networks (NN)** rapidly grew in popularity as more practically usable formats are available – like the built-in function of R. NNs are artificial intelligence adaptive software that can detect complex patterns in data: it is just like an old trader who has a good market intuition but cannot always explain to you why he is convinced you should go short on the **Dow Jones Industrial Average index (DIJA)**.

The network architecture consists of a number of nodes connected by links. Networks usually have 3 or 4 layers: input, hidden and output layers, and in each layer several neurons can be found. The number of first layer's nodes corresponds to the number of the model's explanatory variables, while the last layer's equals to the number of the response variables (usually 2 neurons in case of binary target variable or 1 neuron in case of continuous target variable). The model's complexity and forecast ability is determined by the number of nodes in the hidden layer(s). Normally, each node of one layer has connections to all the other nodes of the next layer, and these edges (see the figure) represent weights. Every neuron receives inputs from the previous layer and, by the use of a non-linear function, it transforms to the next layer's input.

A feed-forward NN with one hidden layer can be useful almost in case of any kind of complex problems *(Chauvin-Rumelhart, 1995)*, that is why it often used by researchers. *(Sermpinis et al., 2012; Dai et al, 2012)* *Atsalakis-Valavanis (2009)* pointed out, that the **multi-layer precepton (MLP)** model that belongs to the family of **feed-forward neural networks (FFNN)** can be the most effective to forecast financial time series. The next graph depicts the structure of a 3 layer MLP neural network, according to *(Dai et al, 2012)*.

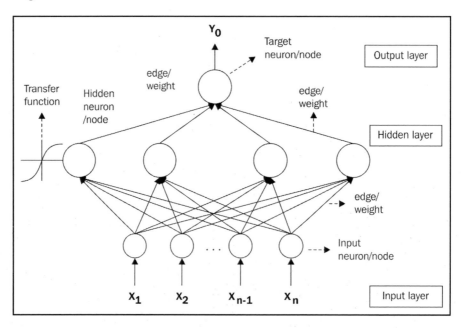

The connection weights (the values of the edges) are assigned initial values first. The error between the predicted and actual output values is back-propagated via the network for updating the weights. The supervised learning procedure then attempts to minimize the error (usually MSE, RMSE or MAPE) between the desired and forecasted outputs. Since the network with certain number of neurons in the hidden layer can learn any relationship on the learning data (even the outliers and noise), by halting the learning algorithm early the prevention of the over-learning is possible. The learning process of the network stops when the test segment has reached its minimum. Then, with the given parameter the network has to be run on the validation segment, see (Wang et al., 2012).

There are many practical problems to solve when you create and perform your own neural network, for example, the selection of appropriate network topology, the selection and the transformation of input variables, the reduction of output variance and most importantly the mitigation of over fitting which refers to the situation when the error on the training set is very small, but when we fit the network on new data the error is large. It means that the network has just memorized the training examples but was not successful in understanding the general structure of the relationships. In order to avoid overfitting, we need to split the data into three subsets: train, validation, test. The training set usually accounting for the 60-70% of the total data is used for learning and fitting the network parameters. The validation data set (10-20%) is used for minimizing the overfitting effect and tuning the parameters, for example to choose the number of hidden nodes in a NN. The test data (10-20%) set is used only for testing the final solution in order to confirm the predictive power of the network.

Forecasting bitcoin prices

Let us see how it works in practice. This example applies trading strategies based on the forecasting of the closing prices of Bitcoin. The period between 3 August 2013 and 8 May 2014 were selected for analysis. There were totally 270 data points in the dataset and the first 240 data points was used as the training sample while the remaining 30 points was used as the testing sample (the forecasting models were tested on the last one months of this time series of 9 months).

First we load the dataset from `Bitcoin.csv` which can be found on the website of the book.

```
data <- read.csv("Bitcoin.csv", header = TRUE, sep = ",")
data2 <- data[order(as.Date(data$Date, format = "%Y-%m-%d")), ]
price <- data2$Close
HLC <- matrix(c(data2$High, data2$Low, data2$Close),
  nrow = length(data2$High))
```

In the second step we calculate the log returns and install the TTR library in order to generate technical indicators.

```
bitcoin.lr <- diff(log(price))
install.packages("TTR")
library(TTR)
```

The six technical indicators selected for modeling have been widely and successfully used by researchers and professional traders as well.

```
rsi    <- RSI(price)
MACD   <- MACD(price)
macd   <- MACD[, 1]
will   <- williamsAD(HLC)
cci    <- CCI(HLC)
STOCH  <- stoch(HLC)
stochK <- STOCH[, 1]
stochD <- STOCH[, 1]
```

We create the Input and Target matrix for training and validation dataset. The training and validation dataset include the closing prices and technical indicators between August 3, 2013 (700) and April 8, 2014 (940).

```
Input <- matrix(c(rsi[700:939], cci[700:939], macd[700:939],
  will[700:939], stochK[700:939], stochD[700:939]), nrow = 240)
Target <- matrix(c(bitcoin.lr[701:940]), nrow = 240)
trainingdata <- cbind(Input, Target)
colnames(trainingdata) <- c("RSI", "CCI", "MACD", "WILL",
  "STOCHK", "STOCHD", "Return")
```

Now, we install and load the `caret` package order to split our learning dataset.

```
install.packages("caret")
library(caret)
```

We split the learning dataset in 90-10% (train-validation) ratio.

```
trainIndex <- createDataPartition(bitcoin.lr[701:940],
  p = .9, list = FALSE)
bitcoin.train <- trainingdata[trainIndex, ]
bitcoin.test <- trainingdata[-trainIndex, ]
```

We install and load the `nnet` package.

```
install.packages("nnet")
library(nnet)
```

The appropriate parameters (number of neurons in hidden layer, learning rate) are selected by means of the grid search process. The network's input layer comprise six neurons (in accordance with the number of explanatory variables), whereas networks of 5, 12, ..., 15 neurons were tested in the hidden layer. The network has one output: the daily yield of the bitcoin. The models were tested at low learning rates (0.01, 0.02, 0.03) in the learning process. The convergence criterion used was a rule that the learning process would be halted if the 1000th iteration has been reached. The network topology with the lowest RMSE in the test set was chosen as optimal.

```
best.network <- matrix(c(5, 0.5))

best.rmse <- 1

for (i in 5:15)

  for (j in 1:3) {

    bitcoin.fit <- nnet(Return ~ RSI + CCI + MACD + WILL + STOCHK +
      STOCHD, data = bitcoin.train, maxit = 1000, size = i,
        decay = 0.01 * j, linout = 1)

    bitcoin.predict <- predict(bitcoin.fit, newdata = bitcoin.test)

    bitcoin.rmse <- sqrt(mean
      ((bitcoin.predict - bitcoin.lr[917:940])^2))

    if (bitcoin.rmse<best.rmse) {

      best.network[1, 1] <- i

      best.network[2, 1] <- j

      best.rmse <- bitcoin.rmse

    }

  }
```

In this step, we create the Input and Target matrix for the test dataset. The test dataset include the closing prices and technical indicators between April 8, 2013 (940) and May 8, 2014 (969).

```
InputTest <- matrix(c(rsi[940:969], cci[940:969],
  macd[940:969], will[940:969], stochK[940:969],
    stochD[940:969]), nrow = 30)

TargetTest <- matrix(c(bitcoin.lr[941:970]), nrow = 30)
  Testdata <- cbind(InputTest,TargetTest)

colnames(Testdata) <- c("RSI", "CCI", "MACD", "WILL",
  "STOCHK", "STOCHD", "Return")
```

Finally, we fit the best neural network model on test data.

```
bitcoin.fit <- nnet(Return ~ RSI + CCI + MACD + WILL +
  STOCHK + STOCHD, data = trainingdata, maxit = 1000,
    size = best.network[1, 1], decay = 0.1 * best.network[2, 1],
      linout = 1)

bitcoin.predict1 <- predict(bitcoin.fit, newdata = Testdata)
```

We repeat and average the model 20 times in order to eliminate the outlier networks.

```
for (i in 1:20) {
  bitcoin.fit <- nnet(Return ~ RSI + CCI + MACD + WILL + STOCHK +
  STOCHD, data = trainingdata, maxit = 1000,
    size = best.network[1, 1], decay = 0.1 * best.network[2, 1],
      linout = 1)
  bitcoin.predict <- predict(bitcoin.fit, newdata = Testdata)
  bitcoin.predict1 <- (bitcoin.predict1 + bitcoin.predict) / 2
}
```

We calculate the result of the buy-and-hold benchmark strategy and neural network on the test dataset.

```
money <- money2 <- matrix(0,31)
money[1,1] <- money2[1,1] <- 100
for (i in 2:31) {
  direction1 <- ifelse(bitcoin.predict1[i - 1] < 0, -1, 1)
  direction2 <- ifelse(TargetTest[i - 1] < 0, -1, 1)
  money[i, 1] <- ifelse((direction1 - direction2) == 0,
    money[i-1,1]*(1+abs(TargetTest[i - 1])),
      money[i-1,1]*(1-abs(TargetTest[i - 1])))
  money2[i, 1] <- 100 * (price[940 + I - 1] / price[940])
}
```

We plot the investment value according to the benchmark and the neural network strategy on the test dataset (1 month).

```
x <- 1:31
matplot(cbind(money, money2), type = "l", xaxt = "n",
  ylab = "", col = c("black", "grey"), lty = 1)
legend("topleft", legend = c("Neural network", "Benchmark"),
  pch = 19, col = c("black", "grey"))
axis(1, at = c(1, 10, 20, 30),
```

```
  lab = c("2014-04-08", "2014-04-17", "2014-04-27", "2014-05-07"))
box()
mtext(side = 1, "Test dataset", line = 2)
mtext(side = 2, "Investment value", line = 2)
```

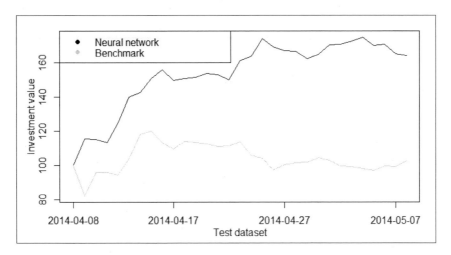

Evaluation of the strategy

We note that in this illustrative example NN strategy has outperformed the "buy-and-hold" strategy in terms of the realized return. With neural network we achieved a return of 20% in a month, while with the passive buy and hold strategy it was only 3%. However, we didn't take into account the transaction costs, the bid-ask spreads and the price impacts and these factors may reduce the neural network's profit significantly.

Logoptimal portfolios

Contrary to the previous points, let us suppose that there are a finite number of risky assets available on the market. These assets are traded continuously without any transaction costs. The investor analyses historical market data and based on this, can reset her portfolio at the end of each day. How can she maximize her wealth in the long run? If returns are independent in time, then markets are efficient in the weak sense and the time series of returns have no memory. If returns are also identically distributed (i.i.d), the optimal strategy is to set portfolio weights for example, according to the Markowitz model (see *Daróczi et al. 2013*) and to keep portfolio weights fixed over the whole time horizon. In this setting, any rearrangements would have negative effects on the portfolio value in the long run.

Now, let us suspend the assumption of longitudinal independency, hence let us allow for hidden patterns in the asset returns, therefore markets are not efficient and it is worth analyzing historical price movements. The only assumption we keep is that asset returns are generated by a stationary and ergodic process. It can be shown that the best choice is the so called **logoptimal portfolio**, see *Algoet-Cover (1988)*. More precisely, there are no other investment strategies which have asymptotically higher expected return than the logoptimal portfolio. The problem is that in order to determine logoptimal portfolios one should know the generating process.

But, what can we do in a more realistic setting when we know nothing about the nature of the underlying stochastic process? A strategy is called **universally consistent** if it ensures that asymptotically the average growth rate approximates that of the logoptimal strategy for any (!) generating process being stationary and ergodic. It is surprising, but universally consistent strategies exist, see *Algoet-Cover (1988)*. Thus, the basic idea is to search for patterns in the past that are similar to the most recently observed pattern, and building on this, to forecast the future returns and to optimize the portfolio relative to this forecast. The concept of similarity can be defined in different ways, therefore we can use different approaches, for example partitioning estimator, core function based estimator and nearest neighbor estimator. For illustration purposes, in the next point we present a simple universally consistent strategy which is based on the core function approach according to *Györfi et al. (2006)*.

A universally consistent, non-parametric investment strategy

Let us suppose that there are d different stocks traded on the market. Vector b containing portfolio weights can be rearranged every day. We suppose that portfolio weights are nonnegative (short selling is not allowed) and the sum of the weights is always 1 (the portfolio must be self-financing). Vector x contains price relatives $\left(\frac{P_{i+1}}{P_i}\right)$ where P stands for the closing price on the ith day. The investor's initial wealth is S_0, hence her wealth at the end of the nth period is as follows:

$$S_n = S_0 \prod_{j=1}^{d} b^{(j)} x^{(j)} = S_0 \langle b, x \rangle = S_0 e^{nW_n(B)}$$

where $\langle b, x \rangle$ is the scalar product of the two vectors, n is the number of the days we followed the investment strategy, W_n is the average log return over the n days and B represents all the b vectors applied. Therefore, the task is to determine a reallocation rule in a way that W_n be maximal in the long run. Here we present a simple universally consistent strategy which disposes this attractive property. Let J_n denote the set of days which are similar to the most recently observed day in terms of the Euclidean distance. It is determined by the formula

$$ J_n = \left\{ i \leq n \,\middle|\, \left\| x_{i-1} - x_{n-1} \right\| \leq r_l \right\} $$

where r_l is the maximum allowed distance (radium) selected by the lth expert. The logoptimal portfolio according to the lth expert on day n can be expressed in the following way:

$$ h^{(1)} = \arg \max_b \sum_{i \in J_n} ln\langle b, x \rangle $$

In order to get a well-balanced and robust strategy we define different experts (portfolio managers) with different radium, and we allocate our wealth to different experts according to a weight vector q. Weights can be equal; or can depend on the previous performance of the experts or on other characteristics. This way we combine the opinion of several experts and our wealth on the nth day is

$$ S_n(B) = \sum_l q_l S_n\left(h^{(1)}\right) $$

Let us suppose that we are an expert and we follow the above strategy between 1997 and 2006 on the market of four NYSE stocks (aph, alcoa, amerb, and coke) plus a U.S. treasury bond and we use a moving time-window of one year. Data can be collected for example from here: http://www.cs.bme.hu/~oti/portfolio/data.html. Let us first read the data in.

```
all_files <- list.files("data")
d <- read.table(file.path("data", all_files[[1]]),
        sep = ",", header = FALSE)
colnames(d) = c("date", substr(all_files[[1]], 1,
  nchar(all_files[[1]]) - 4))
for (i in 2:length(all_files)) {
```

```
  d2 <- read.table(file.path("data", all_files[[i]]),
    sep = ",", header = FALSE)
  colnames(d2) = c("date", substr(all_files[[i]], 1,
    nchar(all_files[[i]])-4))
  d <- merge(d, d2, sort = FALSE)
}
```

This function calculates the expected value of the portfolio in line with the portfolio weights depending on the radium (*r*) we set in advance.

```
log_opt <- function(x, d, r = NA) {
  x <- c(x, 1 - sum(x))
  n <- ncol(d) - 1
  d["distance"] <- c(1, dist(d[2:ncol(d)])[1:(nrow(d) - 1)])
  if (is.na(r)) r <- quantile(d$distance, 0.05)
  d["similarity"] <- d$distance <= r
  d["similarity"] <- c(d[2:nrow(d), "similarity"], 0)
  d <- d[d["similarity"] == 1, ]
  log_return <- log(as.matrix(d[, 2:(n + 1)]) %*% x)
  sum(log_return)
}
```

This function calculates the optimal portfolio weights for a particular day.

```
log_optimization <- function(d, r = NA) {
  today <- d[1, 1]
  m <- ncol(d)
  constr_mtx <- rbind(diag(m - 2), rep(-1, m - 2))
  b <- c(rep(0, m - 2), -1)
  opt <- constrOptim(rep(1 / (m - 1), m - 2),
    function(x) -1 * log_opt(x, d), NULL, constr_mtx, b)
  result <- rbind(opt$par)
  rownames(result) <- today
  result
}
```

Now we optimize the portfolio weight for all the days we found similar. At the same time we also calculate the actual value of our investment portfolio for each day.

```
simulation <- function(d) {
  a <- Position( function(x) substr(x, 1, 2) == "96", d[, 1])
  b <- Position( function(x) substr(x, 1, 2) == "97", d[, 1])
  result <- log_optimization(d[b:a,])
  result <- cbind(result, 1 - sum(result))
  result <- cbind(result, sum(result * d[b + 1, 2:6]),
    sum(rep(1 / 5, 5) * d[b + 1, 2:6]))
  colnames(result) = c("w1", "w2", "w3", "w4", "w5",
    "Total return", "Benchmark")
  for (i in 1:2490) {
    print(i)
    h <- log_optimization(d[b:a + i, ])
    h <- cbind(h, 1 - sum(h))
    h <- cbind(h, sum(h * d[b + 1 + i, 2:6]),
      sum(rep(1/5,5) * d[b + 1 + i, 2:6]))
    result <- rbind(result,h)
  }
  result
}
A <- simulation(d)
```

Finally, let us plot the investment value in time.

```
matplot(cbind(cumprod(A[, 6]), cumprod(A[, 7])), type = "l",
  xaxt = "n", ylab = "", col = c("black","grey"), lty = 1)
legend("topright", pch = 19, col = c("black", "grey"),
  legend = c("Logoptimal portfolio", "Benchmark"))
axis(1, at = c(0, 800, 1600, 2400),
  lab = c("1997-01-02", "2001-03-03", "2003-05-13", "2006-07-17"))
```

We got the following graph:

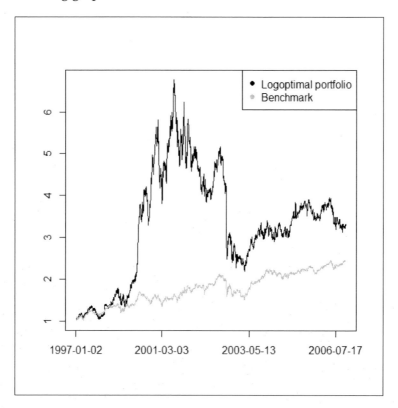

Evaluation of the strategy

We can see on the above graph that our log-optimal strategy outperformed the passive benchmark of keeping portfolio weights equal and fixed over time. However, it is notable that not only the average return, but also the volatility of the investment value is much higher in the former case.

It is mathematically proven that there exist non-parametric investment strategies which are able to effectively reveal hidden patterns in the realized returns and to exploit them in order to achieve an "almost" optimal growth rate in the investor's wealth. For this, we do not have to know the underlying process; the only assumption is that the process is stationary and ergodic. However, we cannot be sure that this assumption holds in reality. It is also important to emphasize that these strategies are optimal only in the asymptotic sense, but we know little about the short run characteristics of the potential paths.

Summary

In this chapter we overviewed not only technical analysis but also some corresponding strategies, like neural networks and log-optimal portfolios. These methods are similar in the sense that when applying them, we implicitly suppose that past situations may reappear in the future; therefore we took the courage to challenge the concept of market efficiency and to build up an active trading strategy. In this setting, we discussed the problems of forecasting the price of a single asset (bitcoin), optimizing the timing of our trading, and also optimizing our portfolio of several risky assets (NYSE stocks) in a dynamic manner. We demonstrated that some simple algorithms based on the toolkit available in R can produce significant extra profit relative to the passive strategy of buying-and-holding. We also note however, that a comprehensive performance analysis focuses not only on the average returns, but also on the corresponding risks. Therefore, we suggest that when optimizing your strategy take care of the downturns, the volatility and other risk measures as well. And, of course, you must be aware of the limitations of the presented methods: you cannot be sure to know the return generating process; if you trade frequently, you have to pay a lot of transaction costs; and the more you get rich, the more you suffer from the adverse price impact and so on. However, we do hope you got new inspirations and useful hints to develop your own sophisticated trading strategy.

References

- Algoet, P.; Cover, T. (1988) Asymptotic optimality, asymptotic equipartition properties of logoptimal investments, Annals of Probability, 16, pp. 876-898

- Atsalakis, G. S. Valavanis, K. P. (2009) Surveying stock market forecasting techniques-Part II. Soft computing methods. Expert Systems with Applications, 36(3), pp. 5932-5941

- Bajgrowicz, P; Scaillet, O. (2012) Technical trading revisited: False discoveries, persistence tests, and transaction costs, Journal of Financial Economics, Vol. 106, pp. 473-491

- Chauvin, Y.; Rumelhart, D. E. (1995) Back propagation: Theory, architectures, and applications. New Jersey: Lawrence Erlbaum associates.

- Dai, W.; Wu, J-Y.; Lu, C-J. (2012) Combining nonlinear independent component analysis and neural network for the prediction of Asian stock market indexes. Expert Systems with Application, 39(4), pp. 4444-4452

- Daróczi, G. et al. (2013) Introduction to R for Quantitative Finance, Packt

- Györfi, L.; Lugosy, G.; Udina, F. (2006) Non-parametric Kernel-based sequential investment strategies, International Journal of Theoretical and Applied Finance, 10, pp. 505-516

- Sermpinis, G.; Dunis, C.; Laws, J.; Stasinakis, C. (2012) Forecasting and trading the EUR/USD exchange rate with stochastic Neural Network combination and time-varying leverage. Decision Support Systems, 54(1), pp. 316-329

- Tajaddini, R.; Falcon Crack, T. (2012) Do momentum-based trading strategies work in emerging currency markets?, Journal of International Financial Markets, Institutions & Money, Vol. 22, pp. 521-537

- Wang, J. J.; Wang, J. Z.; Zhang, Z. G.; Guo, S. P. (2012) Stock index forecasting based on a hybrid model. Omega, 40(6), pp. 758-766

- Zapranis, A.; T. E. Prodromos (2012) A novel, rule-based technical pattern identification mechanism: Identifying and evaluating saucers and resistant levels in the US stock market, Expert Systems with Applications, Vol. 39, pp. 6301-6308

- Zwart, G.; Markwat, T.; Swinkels, L.; van Dijk, D. (2009) The economic value of fundamental and technical information in emerging currency markets, Journal of International Money and Finance, Vol. 28. pp. 581-604

11
Asset and Liability Management

This chapter introduces the usage of R for commercial bank **asset and liability management (ALM)** purposes. The ALM function in a bank is traditionally associated with interest rate risk and liquidity risk management of banking book positions. Both of the interest rate positioning and liquidity risk management require the modeling of banking products. Nowadays, professional ALM units use complex **Enterprise Risk Management (ERM)** frameworks, which are able to incorporate the management of all risk types and provide an adequate tool for ALM to steer the balance sheet. Our general objective is to set up a simplified framework of ALM to illustrate the use of R for certain ALM tasks. These tasks are based on the interest rate and liquidity risk management and the modeling of non-maturing accounts.

This chapter is structured as follows. We start with the data-preparation process of ALM analysis. The process of planning and measurement needs special information about the banking book, market conditions, and the business strategy. This part establishes a data-management tool that consists of the major input datasets, and extracts data into the form that we use in the rest of this chapter.

Next, we will be dealing with the measurement of the interest rate risk. There are two common approaches in the banking industry to quantify interest rate risk in the banking book. Simpler techniques use repricing gap table analysis to manage the interest rate risk exposure and calculate parallel yield curve shocks to forecast the **net interest income (NII)** and calculate the **market value of equity (MVoE)**. More advanced methods use dynamic simulation of balance sheets and stochastic simulation of interest rate development. Choosing which tool to use depends on the targets and the balance sheet structure.

For example, a savings bank (with client term deposits on the liability side and fix bond investments on the asset side) focuses on its market value of equity risk, while a corporate bank (with floating interest position) concentrates on the net interest income risk. We illustrate how to efficiently provide a repricing gap table and net interest income forecasts with R.

Our third topic is related to the liquidity risk. We define three types of liquidity risks: structural, funding, and contingency risks. Structural liquidity risks arise from the different contractual maturities on the asset and liability side. Commercial banks usually collect short-term client deposits and place the acquired funding into long-term client loans. As a result, the bank is exposed to a roll-over risk on the liability side as it is uncertain how much of the maturing short term client funding will be rolled over, which endangers the solvency of the bank. Funding liquidity risks occur during the roll-overs; it refers to the uncertainty of the cost of renewed funding. In ordinary course of business, even though a bank can roll over its maturing interbank deposits, the cost of the deals highly depends on the available liquidity on the market. Contingency risk refers to the behavior of the clients in unforeseen scenarios. For example, a contingency risk appears as sudden withdrawals of term deposits or premature repayments among the client loans. While ALM appropriately handles the structural and funding liquidity risks by regulating bank positions, contingency liquidity risks can only be hedged by buffering liquid assets. We show how to build up liquidity gap tables and forecast net financing needs.

In the last section of this chapter, we will concentrate on the modeling of non-maturing products. Client products can be classified by their maturity structure and interest rate behavior. Examples of typical non-maturing liability products are on-demand deposits and savings accounts without any notice period of withdrawal. The clients can withdraw their money at any time, while the bank has the right to modify the offered interest rate. On the asset side, overdrafts and credit cards show quite similar characteristics. The complex models of non-maturing products make the work of ALM quite challenging. Practically, the modeling of non-maturing products means the mapping of the cash-flow profiles, estimating the interest rate elasticity of the demand, and analyzing the liquidity-related costs in the internal **funds transfer pricing (FTP)** system. Here, we demonstrate how to measure the interest sensitivity of the non-maturing deposits.

Data preparation

Complex ERM software are essential tools in the banking industry to quantify the net interest income and the market value of equity risks, and to prepare reports particularly on the asset and liability portfolio, the re-pricing gaps, and the liquidity positions. We set up a simplified simulation and reporting environment using R, which reproduces the key features of the commercially used ALM software solutions.

Typical ALM data processes follow the so-called **extract, transform, and load (ETL)** logic.

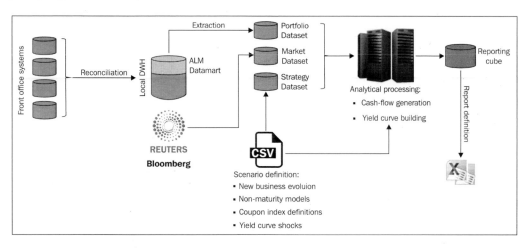

Extraction, which is the first phase, means that the bank has already collected the deal-level and account-based source data from the local **data warehouse (DWH)**, the mid-office, the controlling or the accounting systems. The source data of the total balance sheet (here called a portfolio) is also extracted in order to save calculation time, memory and storage space. Moreover, single deal-level data is aggregated by the given dimensions (for example, by currency denomination, interest behavior, amortization structure, and so on). Market data (such as yield curves, market prices, and volatility surfaces) is also prepared in a raw dataset. The next step is to set the simulation parameters (for example, yield curve shocks and volume increments of the renewed business), in which we call strategy. For the sake of simplicity, here we reduce this strategy to keep the existing portfolio therefore the balance sheet remains the same forecasted period.

At the stage of transformation, the portfolio, market, and strategy datasets are combined and used for further analysis, and are transformed into new structures. In our terms, this means that the cash-flow table is generated by using the portfolio and market descriptors, and it is converted into a narrow data form.

At the time of loading, the results are written into a reporting table. Usually, users can define what dimensions of the portfolio and values of risk measures should be loaded into the result database. We will show how liquidity risk and interest rate risk can be measured and documented in the following sections.

Data source at first glance

We call the data source that lists the balance sheet items "portfolios". Market data (such as yield curves, market prices, and volatility surfaces) is also prepared in a raw dataset. Let's import our initial datasets into R. First of all, we need to download the datasets and the functions to be used in this chapter from the link of Packt Publishing. Now, let's import the sample portfolio and market datasets that are stored in standard csv format in a local folder that is used in the code as follows:

```
portfolio <- read.csv("portfolio.csv")

market <- read.csv("market.csv")
```

The selected datasets contain dates that have to be converted into the appropriate format. We transform the date formats with the as.Date function:

```
portfolio$issue <- as.Date(portfolio$issue, format = "%m/%d/%Y")

portfolio$maturity <- as.Date(portfolio$maturity, format =
  "%m/%d/%Y")

market$date <- as.Date(market$date, format = "%m/%d/%Y")
```

Print the first few rows of the imported portfolio dataset with the head(portfolio) command. It results the following output:

```
head(portfolio)
  id account                  account_name volume
1  1    cb_1 Cash and balances with central bank    930
2  2   mmp_1         Money market placements   1404
3  3   mmp_1         Money market placements    996
4  4    cl_1                 Corporate loans    515
5  5    cl_1                 Corporate loans    655
6  6    cl_1                 Corporate loans    560
  ir_binding reprice_freq spread      issue   maturity
1        FIX           NA      5 2014-09-30 2014-10-01
2        FIX           NA      7 2014-08-30 2014-11-30
3        FIX           NA     10 2014-06-15 2014-12-15
4      LIBOR            3    301 2014-05-15 2016-04-15
5      LIBOR            6    414 2014-04-15 2016-04-15
6      LIBOR            3    345 2014-03-15 2018-02-15
  repayment payment_freq yieldcurve
1    BULLET            1      EUR01
```

2	BULLET	1	EUR01
3	BULLET	1	EUR01
4	LINEAR	3	EUR01
5	LINEAR	6	EUR01
6	LINEAR	3	EUR01

The columns of this data frame refer to the identification number (the number of the row), the account type, and the product characteristics. The first three columns represent the product identifier, the account identifier (or the short name), and the long name of the account. Using the `levels` function, we can easily list the type of accounts that are related to the typical commercial bank products or balance sheet items:

```
levels(portfolio$account_name)
 [1] "Available for sale portfolio"
 [2] "Cash and balances with central bank"
 [3] "Corporate loans"
 [4] "Corporate sight deposit"
 [5] "Corporate term deposit"
 [6] "Money market placements"
 [7] "Other non-interest bearing assets"
 [8] "Other non-interest bearing liabilities"
 [9] "Own issues"
[10] "Repurchase agreements"
[11] "Retail overdrafts"
[12] "Retail residential mortgage"
[13] "Retail sight deposit"
[14] "Retail term deposit"
[15] "Unsecured money market funding"
```

The `portfolio` dataset also contains the notional volume in EUR, the type of the interest binding (FIX or LIBOR), the repricing frequency of the account in the number of months (if the interest binding is LIBOR), and the spread component of the interest rate in basis points. Furthermore, other columns describe the cash-flow structure of the products. The columns are issue date (this is the first repricing day), maturity date, the type of principal repayment structure (bullet, linear, or annuity), and the repayment frequency in number of months. The last column stores the identifier of the interest rate curve, what we use for the calculation of future floating rate payments.

Actual interest rates are stored in the `market` dataset. Let's list some of the first few rows to check the content:

```
head(market)
    type        date        rate  comment
1 EUR01 2014-09-01   0.3000000      1M
2 EUR01 2014-12-01   0.3362558      3M
3 EUR01 2015-03-01  -2.3536463      6M
4 EUR01 2015-09-01  -5.6918763      1Y
5 EUR01 2016-09-01  -5.6541774      2Y
6 EUR01 2017-09-01   1.0159576      3Y
```

The first column indicates the yield curve type (for example, yields are from the bond market or the interbank market). The `type` column has to be the same as in `portfolio` to connect the two datasets. The `date` column shows the maturity of the current rate, and `rate` indicates the value of the rate in basis points. As you can see, the yield curve is very unusual at this time as there are negative yield curve points for certain tenors. The last column stores the label of the yield curve tenor.

The datasets reflect the current state of the bank portfolio and the current market environment. The actual date is September 30, 2014 in our analysis. Let's declare it as a date variable called NOW:

```
NOW <- as.Date("09/30/2014", format = "%m/%d/%Y")
```

Now, we finished the preparation of our source data. This is a sample dataset created by the authors for illustrative purposes, and demonstrates the simplified version of a hypothetical commercial bank balance sheet structure.

Cash-flow generator functions

After we import the static data of our balance sheet and the current yield curve, we use this information to generate the total cash-flow of the bank. First, we calculate the floating interest rates using the forward yield curve; after that, we can generate separately the principal and interest cash-flows. For this purpose, we predefine the basic functions to calculate principal cash-flows based on payment frequencies and to extract floating interest rates for variable interest rate products. This script is also available on the link provided by Packt Publishing.

Copy it into the local folder and run the script of the predefined functions from the working directory.

```
source("bankALM.R")
```

This source file loads the xts, zoo, YieldCurve, reshape, and car packages, and if necessary, it installs these required packages. Let's take a look at the most important functions we use from this script file. The cf function generates a predefined cash-flow structure. For example, generating a bullet payment structure loan with the nominal value of EUR 100, a maturity of three years, and a fixed interest rate of 10 percent looks like this:

```
cf(rate = 0.10, maturity = 3, volume = 100, type = "BULLET")
$cashflow
[1]   10   10 110
$interest
[1] 10 10 10
$capital
[1]   0   0 100
$remaining
[1] 100 100   0
```

The function provides the entire cash-flow, the interest and capital repayment structure, and the value of the remaining capital in each period. The get.yieldcurve.spot function provides a fitted spot yield curve on a certain sequence of dates. This function uses the YieldCurve package, what we have already loaded before. Let's define a test variable of dates, as follows:

```
test.date <- seq(from = as.Date("09/30/2015", format = "%m/%d/%Y"),
  to = as.Date("09/30/2035", format = "%m/%d/%Y") , by = "1 year")
```

Get and plot the fitted spot yields on the specified dates using the market data:

```
get.yieldcurve.spot(market, test.date, type = "EUR01", now = NOW,
  showplot = TRUE)
```

The following screenshot is the result of the preceding command:

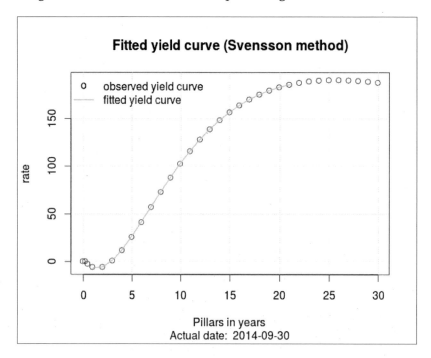

The preceding graph draws the observed yield curve (points) and the fitted yield curve (line). Looking at the get.yieldcurve.forward and get.floating functions, we see that both of them use the repricing date of the balance sheet product. The following example generates a sequence of repricing dates for a period of 20 timepoints.

```
test.reprice.date <- test.date[seq(from = 1,to = 20, by = 2)]
```

Extract the forward yield curve using the market data:

```
test.forward <- get.yieldcurve.forward(market, test.reprice.date,
   type = "EUR01", now = NOW)
```

Now, let's generate the floating rates and illustrate the difference between the forward curve and the test.floating variable by setting the showplot option to TRUE.

```
test.floating<-get.floating(test.date, test.reprice.date, market,
   type = "EUR01", now = NOW, shoplot = TRUE)
```

The following screenshot gives the output for the preceding command:

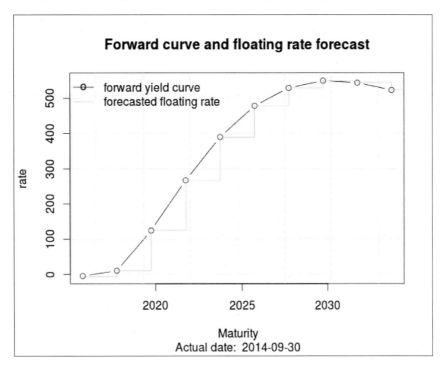

As you can see, the floating rate forecast consists of a step-wise function. For pricing purposes, the floating rate is substituted by the actual forward rate; however, the floating rate is only updated at the time of repricing.

Preparing the cash-flow

In the next steps, we will demonstrate the cash-flow table that we produce from our `portfolio` and `market` datasets. The `cf.table` function calls the functions detailed earlier and provides a cash-flow of the exact product, which has the `id` identification number. In the `portfolio` dataset, identification numbers have to be integers, and they have to be in an increasing order. Practically, each of them should be the line number of the given row. Let's generate the cash-flow of all products:

```
cashflow.table <- do.call(rbind, lapply(1:NROW(portfolio),
    function(i) cf.table(portfolio, market, now = NOW, id = i)))
```

As the `portfolio` dataset contains 147 products, the running of this code might take a few (10-60) seconds. When we are ready, let's check the result that shows the first few lines:

```
head(cashflow.table)
   id account        date        cf interest capital remaining
1  1     cb_1 2014-10-01  930.0388  0.03875     930         0
2  2    mmp_1 2014-10-30    0.0819  0.08190       0      1404
3  2    mmp_1 2014-11-30 1404.0819  0.08190    1404         0
4  3    mmp_1 2014-10-15    0.0830  0.08300       0       996
5  3    mmp_1 2014-11-15    0.0830  0.08300       0       996
6  3    mmp_1 2014-12-15  996.0830  0.08300     996         0
```

Now we are done with the creation of the cash-flow table. We can also calculate the present value of the products and, the market value of the equity of the bank. Let's run the `pv.table` function in the following loop:

```
presentvalue.table <- do.call(rbind, lapply(1:NROW(portfolio),
   function (i) pv.table(cashflow.table[cashflow.table$id ==
     portfolio$id[i],], market, now = NOW)))
```

Print the initial rows of the table to check the results:

```
head(presentvalue.table)
   id account        date presentvalue
1  1     cb_1 2014-09-30     930.0384
2  2    mmp_1 2014-09-30    1404.1830
3  3    mmp_1 2014-09-30     996.2754
4  4     cl_1 2014-09-30     530.7143
5  5     cl_1 2014-09-30     689.1311
6  6     cl_1 2014-09-30     596.3629
```

The results might differ slightly because the `Svensson` method may produce different outputs. To get the market value of equity, we need to add the present values.

```
sum(presentvalue.table$presentvalue)
[1] 14021.19
```

The cash-flow table handles liabilities as negative assets; hence, adding up all the items provides us with the appropriate results.

Interest rate risk measurement

Managing interest rate risk is one of the most important components of asset and liability management. Variation of the interest rate could affect both the interest earnings and the market value of equity. Interest rate management focuses on the sensitivity of net interest income. Net interest income (NII) equals the difference between interest revenues and interest expenses:

$$NII = (SA + NSA)i_A - (SL + NSL)i_L$$

Here, SA and SL denote the interest sensitive assets and liabilities, and NSA and NSL refer to the non-sensitive ones. Interest rate of assets and liabilities are noted with i_A and i_L. The traditional approach of interest rate risk positioning of the balance sheet is based on gap models. Interest rate gap refers to the net asset position for a certain time period between interest-bearing assets and liabilities, which are repriced at the same time. The interest rate gap (G) equals:

$$G = SA - SL$$

The re-pricing gap table shows these interest-bearing items in the balance sheet grouped by the time of repricing and the basis of repricing (that is, 3 months EURIBOR or 6 months EURIBOR). Interest earnings variation can be characterized as the risk-bearing items multiplied by the change of interest rate (Δi), shown as follows:

$$\Delta NII = (SA - SL)\Delta i = G\Delta i$$

The sign of the gap is crucial from an interest rate risk point of view. A positive gap indicates increasing earnings when interest rates rise, and indicates decreasing earnings when interest rates decline. The repricing gap table can also capture the basis risk by aggregating the interest-bearing assets and liabilities based on their reference interest rate (that is 3 months or 6 months EURIBOR). Interest rate gap tables can be sufficient tools to determine the risk exposure from the earnings perspective. However, gap models cannot be used as a single risk measure to quantify rather the net interest income risk of the total balance sheet. Interest rate gaps are management tools, which provide guidance on interest rate risk positioning.

Here, we show how to build up net interest income and repricing gap tables and how to create figures about the net interest income term structure. Let's construct the interest rate gap table from the `cashflow.table` data. Continuing from the previous section, we use the predefined `nii.table` function to produce the desired data form:

```
nii <- nii.table(cashflow.table, now = NOW)
```

Considering the net interest income table for the next 7 years, we get the following table:

```
round(nii[,1:7], 2)
```

	2014	2015	2016	2017	2018	2019	2020
afs_1	6.99	3.42	0.00	0.00	0.00	0.00	0.00
cb_1	0.04	0.00	0.00	0.00	0.00	0.00	0.00
cl_1	134.50	210.04	88.14	29.38	0.89	0.00	0.00
cor_sd_1	-3.20	-11.16	-8.56	-5.96	-3.36	-0.81	0.00
cor_td_1	-5.60	-1.99	0.00	0.00	0.00	0.00	0.00
is_1	-26.17	-80.54	-65.76	-48.61	-22.05	-1.98	0.00
mmp_1	0.41	0.00	0.00	0.00	0.00	0.00	0.00
mmt_1	-0.80	-1.60	0.00	0.00	0.00	0.00	0.00
oth_a_1	0.00	0.00	0.00	0.00	0.00	0.00	0.00
oth_l_1	0.00	0.00	0.00	0.00	0.00	0.00	0.00
rep_1	-0.05	0.00	0.00	0.00	0.00	0.00	0.00
ret_sd_1	-8.18	-30.66	-27.36	-24.06	-20.76	-17.46	-14.16
ret_td_1	-10.07	-13.27	0.00	0.00	0.00	0.00	0.00
rm_1	407.66	1532.32	1364.32	1213.17	1062.75	908.25	751.16
ro_1	137.50	187.50	0.00	0.00	0.00	0.00	0.00
total	633.04	1794.05	1350.78	1163.92	1017.46	888.00	736.99

It is easy to read what account brings interest revenues or costs for the bank. The net interest rate table can be plotted as follows:

```
barplot(nii, density = 5*(1:(NROW(nii)-1)), xlab = "Maturity",
  cex.names = 0.8, Ylab = "EUR", cex.axis = 0.8,
    args.legend = list(x = "right"))
title(main = "Net interest income table", cex = 0.8,
  sub = paste("Actual date: ",as.character(as.Date(NOW))) )
    par(fig = c(0, 1, 0, 1), oma = c(0, 0, 0, 0),mar = c(0, 0, 0, 0),
      new = TRUE)
plot(0, 0, type = "n", bty = "n", xaxt = "n", yaxt = "n")
legend("right", legend = row.names(nii[1:(NROW(nii)-1),]),
  density = 5*(1:(NROW(nii)-1)), bty = "n", cex = 1)
```

The result is shown in the following graph:

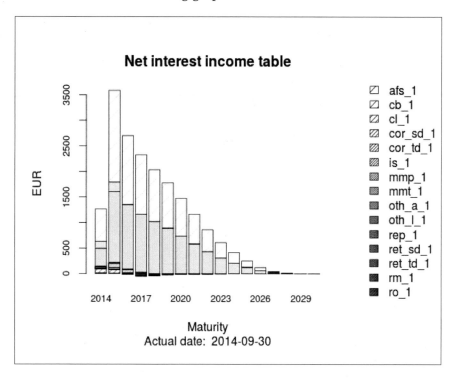

Now, we can explore the re-pricing gaps by composing the re-pricing gap table. Let's use the predefined `repricing.gap.table` function and get the monthly gaps, and then plot the results with `barplot`.

```
(repgap <- repricing.gap.table(portfolio, now = NOW))
          1M   2M   3M   4M   5M   6M   7M   8M   9M  10M  11M  12M
volume 6100 9283  725 1787 7115 6031 2450 5919 2009 8649 6855 2730
barplot(repgap, col = "gray", xlab = "Months", ylab = "EUR")
title(main = "Repricing gap table", cex = 0.8,
  sub = paste("Actual date: ",as.character(as.Date(NOW))))
```

With the preceding code, we can illustrate the marginal gaps for the next 12 months:

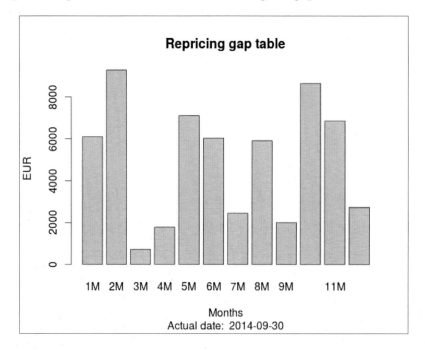

We have to mention that there are more sophisticated tools for interest rate risk management. In practice, simulation models are applied for risk management purposes. However, the banking book risks are not explicitly subjected to capital charge under Pillar 1 of the Basel II regulations; Pillar 2 covers the interest rate risk in the banking book. Regulators lay particular emphasis also on the risk assessment regarding the market value of equity. Risk limits are based on specific stress scenarios, which could be either deterministic interest rate shocks or historical volatility-based earnings at risk concepts. Therefore, risk measurement techniques stand for scenario-based or stochastic simulation approaches, focusing on the interest earnings or the market value of equity. Net interest income simulation is rather a dynamic, forward-looking approach, while calculation of the market value of equity provides a static result. Equity duration is also a widely used measure for interest rate risk of the banking book. Duration of the assets and liabilities are calculated to quantify the duration of equity. ALM professionals often use effective duration, which incorporates embedded options (caps, floors, and so on) in the interest rate sensitivity calculation.

Liquidity risk measurement

Traditional liquidity risk measurement tools are the so-called static and dynamic liquidity gap tables. A liquidity gap table gives a cash-flow view of the balance sheet, and organizes the balance sheet items according to their contractual cash-inflows and cash-outflows into maturity buckets. The net cash-flow gap in each bucket shows the bank structural liquidity position. The static view assumes a rundown balance sheet while the dynamic liquidity table also takes into account the cash-flows from rollovers and new businesses. For the sake of simplicity, we demonstrate here only the static view of the liquidity positions.

Starting with the preparation of daily cash-flow positions. Sometimes, we need to know what the forecasted liquidity position is on a given date. It is easy to aggregate the `cashflow.table` by date.

```
head(aggregate(.  ~ date, FUN = sum,
   data = subset(cashflow.table,select = -c(id, account))))
        date             cf      interest       capital remaining
1 2014-10-01    930.0387500    0.0387500    930.0000       0.00
2 2014-10-14      0.6246667    0.6246667      0.0000    3748.00
3 2014-10-15   2604.2058990  127.5986646   2476.6072   13411.39
4 2014-10-28    390.7256834  124.6891519    266.0365   23444.96
5 2014-10-30  -3954.2638670   52.6149502  -4006.8788  -33058.12
6 2014-10-31     -0.1470690   -0.1470690      0.0000   -2322.00
```

Secondly, let's prepare a liquidity gap table and create a chart. We can also use a predefined function (`lq.table`) and check the resulting table.

```
lq <- lq.table(cashflow.table, now = NOW)
round(lq[,1:5],2)
               1M      2-3M      3-6M      6-12M      1-2Y
afs_1         2.48  3068.51  14939.42      0.00      0.00
cb_1        930.04     0.00      0.00      0.00      0.00
cl_1       3111.11     0.00    649.51   2219.41   2828.59
cor_sd_1   -217.75  -217.73   -653.09  -1305.69  -2609.42
cor_td_1     -1.90  -439.66  -6566.03      0.00      0.00
is_1         -8.69   -17.48  -2405.31   -319.80   -589.04
mmp_1         0.16  2400.25      0.00      0.00      0.00
mmt_1        -0.12    -0.54     -0.80  -1201.94      0.00
oth_a_1       0.00     0.00      0.00      0.00      0.00
oth_l_1       0.00     0.00      0.00      0.00      0.00
rep_1      -500.05     0.00      0.00      0.00      0.00
```

```
ret_sd_1   -186.08 -186.06   -558.04 -1115.47 -2228.46
ret_td_1 -4038.96    -5.34 -5358.13 -3382.91     0.00
rm_1       414.40  808.27  1243.86  2093.42  4970.14
ro_1       466.67  462.50  1362.50  2612.50   420.83
total      -28.69 5872.72  2653.89  -400.48  2792.63
```

To plot the liquidity gap figure, we can use the `barplot` function, which is as follows:

```r
plot.new()

par.backup <- par()

par(oma = c(1, 1, 1, 6), new = TRUE)

barplot(nii, density=5*(1:(NROW(nii)-1)), xlab="Maturity",
  cex.names=0.8, ylab = "EUR", cex.axis = 0.8,
    args.legend = list(x = "right"))

title(main = "Net interest income table", cex = 0.8,
  sub = paste("Actual date: ",as.character(as.Date(NOW))) )

par(fig = c(0, 1, 0, 1), oma = c(0, 0, 0, 0),mar = c(0, 0, 0, 0),
  new = TRUE)

plot(0, 0, type = "n", bty = "n", xaxt = "n", yaxt = "n")

legend("right", legend = row.names(nii[1:(NROW(nii)-1),]),
  density = 5*(1:(NROW(nii)-1)), bty = "n", cex = 1)

par(par.backup)
```

The output of the `barplot` function is as follows:

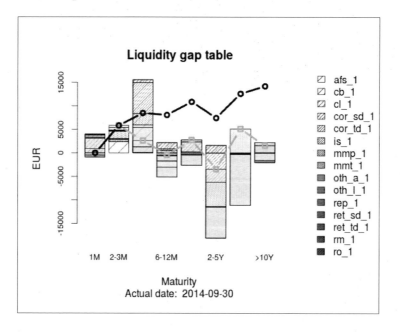

The bars on the plot show the liquidity gap in each time bucket. The dashed line with squares represents the net liquidity position (financial need), while the solid black line shows the cumulative liquidity gap.

Modeling non-maturity deposits

The importance of **non-maturity deposits (NMD)** in banking is substantially high as the large part of commercial banks' balance sheets consist of client products with non-contractual cash-flow features. Non-maturity deposits are special financial instruments as the bank has an option to change the paid interest on the deposit account at any time, and the client has the option to withdraw any amount from the account without a period of notice. The liquidity and interest rate risk management of these products are a crucial part of ALM analysis; therefore, modeling of non-maturity deposits needs special attention. The uncertain maturity and interest rate profile generates a high level of complexity in their hedging, internal transfer pricing, and risk modeling.

A Model of deposit interest rate development

In the following code, we use Austrian non-maturity deposit time series data that we queried from the ECB Statistical Database, which is publicly available. We have monthly deposit interest rates (cpn), end-of-month balances (bal), and the 1 month EURIBOR fixing (eur1m) in our dataset. The time series are stored in a csv file in the local folder. The command for that is ads follows:

```
nmd <- read.csv("ecb_nmd_data.csv")
nmd$date <- as.Date(nmd$date, format = "%m/%d/%Y")
```

First, we plot the 1 month EURIBOR rate and the deposit interest rate development by using the following command:

```
library(car)
plot(nmd$eur1m ~ nmd$date, type = "l", xlab="Time", ylab="Interest rate")
lines(nmd$cpn~ nmd$date, type = "l", lty = 2)
title(main = "Deposit coupon vs 1-month Euribor", cex = 0.8 )
legend("topright", legend = c("Coupon","EUR 1M"),
   bty = "n", cex = 1, lty = c(2, 1))
```

The following screenshot displays the graph of **Deposit Coupon vs 1-month EURIBOR**:

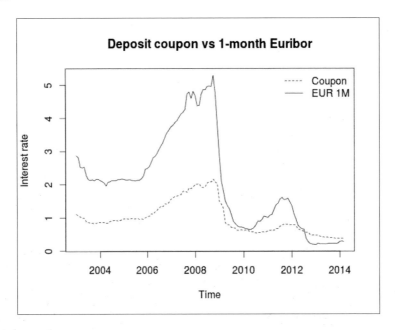

Our first goal is to estimate an error correction model (ECM) to describe the long-term explanatory power of 1 month EURIBOR rate on the non-maturity deposit interest rate. Measuring the pass-through effect of market rates into deposit interest rates has gained high importance in recent years from the regulatory point of view as well. ECB required euro-zone banks to estimate the pass-through effect in certain stress-test scenarios. We use the Engle-Granger two-step method to estimate the ECM model. In the first step, we estimate the cointegrating vector with a regression model. We take the residuals, and in the second step, we estimate the long-term and short-term effects of EURIBOR on deposit rates using the error-correction mechanism. Before the first step, we have to test whether both time series are integrated in the same order. Therefore, we run Augmented Dickey-Fuller (ADF) and the KPSS tests from the `urca` package on the original and the differentiated time series. The script is as follows:

```
library(urca)
attach(nmd)
#Unit root test (ADF)
cpn.ur <- ur.df(cpn, type = "none", lags = 2)
dcpn.ur <- ur.df(diff(cpn), type = "none", lags = 1)
```

```
eur1m.ur <- ur.df(eur1m, type = "none", lags = 2)
deur1m.ur <- ur.df(diff(eur1m), type = "none", lags = 1)
sumtbl <- matrix(cbind(cpn.ur@teststat, cpn.ur@cval,
                       dcpn.ur@teststat, dcpn.ur@cval,
                       eur1m.ur@teststat, eur1m.ur@cval,
                       deur1m.ur@teststat, deur1m.ur@cval), nrow=4)
colnames(sumtbl) <- c("cpn", "diff(cpn)", "eur1m", "diff(eur1m)")
rownames(sumtbl) <- c("Test stat", "1pct CV", "5pct CV", "10pct CV")
#Stationarty test (KPSS)
cpn.kpss <- ur.kpss(cpn, type = "mu")
eur1m.kpss <- ur.kpss(eur1m, type = "mu")
sumtbl <- matrix(cbind( cpn.kpss@teststat, cpn.kpss@cval,
   eur1m.kpss@teststat, eur1m.kpss@cval), nrow = 5)
colnames(sumtbl) <- c("cpn", "eur1m")
rownames(sumtbl) <- c("Test stat", "10pct CV", "5pct CV", "2.5pct
   CV", 1pct CV")
print(cpn.ur@test.name)
print(sumtbl)
print(cpn.kpss@test.name)
print(sumtbl)
```

As a result, we get the following summary tables:

```
Augmented Dickey-Fuller Test
```

	cpn	diff(cpn)	eur1m	diff(eur1m)
Test stat	-0.9001186	-5.304858	-1.045604	-5.08421
1pct CV	-2.5800000	-2.580000	-2.580000	-2.58000
5pct CV	-1.9500000	-1.950000	-1.950000	-1.95000
10pct CV	-1.6200000	-1.620000	-1.620000	-1.62000

```
KPSS
```

	cpn	eur1m
Test stat	0.8982425	1.197022
10pct CV	0.3470000	0.347000
5pct CV	0.4630000	0.463000
2.5pct CV	0.5740000	0.574000
1pct CV	0.7390000	0.739000

The null-hypothesis of the ADF test cannot be refused for the original time series, but the test results show that the first difference of the deposit rate and 1 month EURIBOR time series does not contain the unit root. This means that both series are integrated at the first order, and they are I(1) processes. The KPSS test has a similar result. The next step is to test the cointegration of the two I(1) series by testing the residuals of the simple regression equation, where we regress the deposit interest rates on the 1 month EURIBOR rate. Estimate the cointegrating equation:

```
lr <- lm(cpn ~ eurlm)
res <- resid(lr)
lr$coefficients
(Intercept)          eurlm
  0.3016268      0.3346139
```

Do the unit root test of residuals as follows:

```
res.ur <- ur.df(res, type = "none", lags = 1)
summary(res.ur)
###############################################
# Augmented Dickey-Fuller Test Unit Root Test #
###############################################


Test regression none


Call:
lm(formula = z.diff ~ z.lag.1 - 1 + z.diff.lag)


Residuals:
      Min        1Q     Median        3Q        Max
-0.286780 -0.017483 -0.002932  0.019516   0.305720


Coefficients:
          Estimate Std. Error t value Pr(>|t|)
z.lag.1    -0.14598    0.04662  -3.131  0.00215 **
z.diff.lag -0.06351    0.08637  -0.735  0.46344
---
Signif. codes:  0 '***' 0.001 '**' 0.01 '*' 0.05 '.' 0.1 ' ' 1
```

```
Residual standard error: 0.05952 on 131 degrees of freedom
Multiple R-squared:  0.08618,   Adjusted R-squared:  0.07223
F-statistic: 6.177 on 2 and 131 DF,  p-value: 0.002731


Value of test-statistic is: -3.1312


Critical values for test statistics:
      1pct  5pct  10pct
tau1 -2.58 -1.95 -1.62
```

The test statistic of the ADF test is lower than the 1 percent critical value, so we can conclude that the residuals are stationary. This means that the deposit coupon and 1 month EURIBOR are cointegrated, as the linear combination of the two $I(1)$ time series gives us a stationary process. The existence of cointegration is important because it is a prerequisite for the error-correction model estimation. The basic structure of an ECM equation is as follows:

$$\Delta Y_t = \alpha + \beta_1 \Delta X_{t-1} + \beta_2 EC_{t-1} + \varepsilon_t$$

We estimate the long-term and short-term effect of X on Y; the lagged residuals from the cointegration equation represent the error-correction mechanism. The β_1 coefficient measures the short-term correction part, while β_2 is the coefficient of the long-term equilibrium relationship, which captures the correction of deviations from the equilibrium of X. Now, we estimate the ECM model using the dynlm package, which is suitable to estimate dynamic linear models with lags:

```
install.packages('dynlm')
library(dynlm)
res <- resid(lr)[2:length(cpn)]
dy <- diff(cpn)
dx <- diff(eurlm)
detach(nmd)
ecmdata <- c(dy, dx, res)
ecm <- dynlm(dy ~ L(dx, 1) + L(res, 1), data = ecmdata)
summary(ecm)
```

```
Time series regression with "numeric" data:
Start = 1, End = 134


Call:
dynlm(formula = dy ~ L(dx, 1) + L(res, 1), data = ecmdata)


Residuals:
     Min       1Q    Median       3Q       Max
-0.36721 -0.01546  0.00227  0.02196  0.16999


Coefficients:
              Estimate Std. Error t value Pr(>|t|)
(Intercept) -0.0005722  0.0051367  -0.111    0.911
L(dx, 1)     0.2570385  0.0337574   7.614 4.66e-12 ***
L(res, 1)    0.0715194  0.0534729   1.337    0.183
---
Signif. codes:  0 '***' 0.001 '**' 0.01 '*' 0.05 '.' 0.1 ' ' 1


Residual standard error: 0.05903 on 131 degrees of freedom
Multiple R-squared:  0.347,      Adjusted R-squared:  0.337
F-statistic:  34.8 on 2 and 131 DF,   p-value: 7.564e-13
```

The lagged changes in 1 month EURIBOR are corrected in the deposit interest rates by 25.7 percent ($\beta_1 = 0.2570385$) on the short run. We cannot conclude that deviations from the long-term equilibrium are not corrected as beta$_2$ is not significant and has a positive sign, meaning that the errors are not corrected but boosted by 7 percent. The economic interpretation of the results is that we cannot identify a long-term relationship between NMD coupons and 1 month EURIBOR rate, but deviations in the EURIBOR are reflected in the coupons by 25.7 percent in the short term.

Static replication of non-maturity deposits

A possible method to hedge interest-rate-related risks of non-maturity deposits is to construct a replicating portfolio of zero-coupon instruments to mimic the interest payment of non-maturity deposits, and earn a margin on the higher-yielding replicating instruments over the low interest on deposit accounts.

Let's assume that we include 1-month and 3-month EUR money market placements and 1Y, 5Y, and 10Y government benchmark bonds in our replicating portfolio. We queried the historical time series of the yields from ECB Statistical Data Warehouse and stored the data in a csv file in the local folder. We will call the csv file using the following command:

```
ecb.yc <- read.csv("ecb_yc_data.csv")
ecb.yc$date <- as.Date(ecb.yc$date, format = "%d/%m/%Y")
```

Plot the results:

```
matplot(ecb.yc$date, ecb.yc[,2:6], type = "l", lty = (1:5), lwd = 2,
    col = 1, xlab = "Time", ylab = "Yield", ylim = c(0,6), xaxt = "n")
legend("topright", cex = 0.8, bty = "n", lty = c(1:5), lwd = 2,
    legend = colnames(ecb.yc[,2:6]))
title(main = "ECB yield curve", cex = 0.8)
axis.Date(1,ecb.yc$date)
```

The following screenshot shows the ECB yield curve:

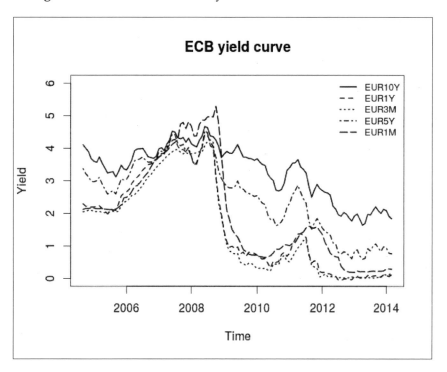

Our goal is to calculate those portfolio weights of the five hedging instruments in the replicating portfolio, which ensures that the minimum volatility of the margin compared to the deposit coupon (cpn) in the given time horizon. In other words, we would like to minimize the tracking error of the interest earning of our replicating portfolio. The problem can be formulated in the following least squares minimization formula:

$$min \left\| Ax - b \right\|^2$$

This is subject to:

$$\sum x = 1$$

$$x \geq 0$$

$$x'm = l$$

Here, A is the $(t \times 5)$ matrix's historical rates, b is the vector of the deposit coupons, and x is the vector of portfolio weights. The function to be minimized is the squared difference between the vector b and the linear combination of x with the columns of matrix A. The first condition is that the portfolio weights have to be non-negative and summed up to 1. We introduce an additional condition on the average maturity of the portfolio, which should be equal to the l constant. The vector m contains the maturity in months of the five hedging instruments. The rationale behind this constraint is that banks usually assume that the core base of non-maturity deposit volume stays in the bank for a longer term. The tenor of this long-term part is usually derived from a volume model, which could be the ARIMA model or a dynamic model with dependency on market rates and the deposit coupon.

To solve the optimization problem, we use the `solve.QP` function from the `quadprog` package. This function is suitable to solve quadratic optimization problems with equality and inequality constraints. We reformulate the least squares minimization problem in order to derive the proper parameter matrix $(A'A)$ and parameter vector $(b'A)$ of the `solve.QP` function.

We also set $l = 60$, assuming 5 year final maturity for the replicating portfolio, which mimics the liquidity characteristics of the core part of the NMD portfolio through the following command:

```
library(quadprog)

b <- nmd$cpn[21:135]

A <- cbind(ecb.yc$EUR1M, ecb.yc$EUR3M,
    ecb.yc$EUR1Y, ecb.yc$EUR5Y, ecb.yc$EUR10Y)

m <- c(1, 3, 12, 60, 120)

l <- 60

stat.opt <- solve.QP( t(A) %*% A, t(b) %*% A,
            cbind( matrix(1, nr = 5, nc = 1),
                   matrix(m, nr = 5, nc = 1),
                   diag(5)),
            c(1, 1, 0,0,0,0,0),
            meq=2 )

sumtbl <- matrix(round(stat.opt$solution*100, digits = 1), nr = 1)

colnames(sumtbl) <- c("1M", "3M", "1Y", "5Y", "10Y")

cat("Portfolio weights in %")

Portfolio weights in % > print(sumtbl)
      1M    3M 1Y 5Y   10Y
[1,]   0  51.3  0  0  48.7
```

Our result suggests that based on historical calibration, we should keep 51 percent in 3 month money market placement and 49 percent in a 10 year government bond instrument in our replicating portfolio to replicate the coupon development of NMDs with the smallest tracking error. With these portfolio weights, the income on our replicating portfolio and the expense on deposit accounts are calculated by the following code:

```
mrg <- nmd$cpn[21:135] - stat.opt$solution[2]*ecb.yc$EUR3M +
    stat.opt$solution[5]*ecb.yc$EUR10Y

plot(mrg ~ ecb.yc$date, type = "l", col = "black", xlab="Time", ylab="%")

title(main = "Margin of static replication", cex = 0.8 )
```

The following graph displays **Margin of static replication**:

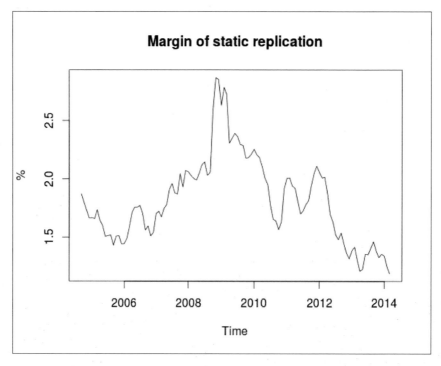

As you can see, due to the replication with this static strategy, a bank was able to earn more profit around 2010, when the term spread between the short- and long-term interest rates was unusually high.

Summary

In this chapter, we demonstrated how R can support the process of asset and liability management in a commercial bank. There is a wide range of tasks from data preparation to reporting, where the R programming language can help or solve repeating problems. However, we only gave a brief introduction about how to solve problems of interest rate and liquidity measurement. We also provided some examples about the statistical estimation of the interest rate sensitivity of non-maturity deposits. You can find practical knowledge about the following:

- Generating cash-flow from bank portfolios and market data
- Measuring and reporting tools for basic interest rate risk management
- Measuring and reporting tools for basic liquidity risk management
- Modeling the behavior of non-maturity deposits

We think that this chapter is an organic part of the bank management topics in this book. Asset and liability management brings a particular problem set of the bank management, and R, as an open-source language with a versatile package library, can effectively add valuable tools for practitioners.

References

- **Bessis, Joel (2011)**: Risk management in banking, *John Wiley & Sons*.
- **Choudhry, Moorad (2011)**: Bank asset and liability management: strategy, trading, analysis, *John Wiley & Sons*.
- **Matz, Leonard and Neu, Peter (2006)**: Liquidity risk measurement and management: A practitioner's guide to global best practices, *John Wiley & Sons*.

12
Capital Adequacy

As we learned in the previous chapter, banking is a specifically risky industry and the safety of the clients' money is a top priority. In order to ensure that banks meet this primary objective, the industry is under strict regulation. It has always been a very important task for supervisors to build rules to avoid the collapsing of banks and to protect clients' wealth. Capital adequacy or capital requirement is one of, if not, the most, important regulatory tool to serve this goal. Given the high leverage in the financial sector, banks and other financial institutions are not allowed to freely use all their assets. These firms need to hold enough capital to ensure safe operation and solvency even if things turn bad.

Different countries have different banking supervisory bodies (financial watchdog, central bank, and so on) and regulation standards. However, as the banking system became more and more globalized, a common worldwide standard became necessary. In 1974, the **Basel Committee on Banking Supervision (BCBS)** was set up by the G-10 central banks to provide banking regulatory standards that can be applied to different countries around the globe.

This area of economics has developed quite fast since then, and more and more complex mathematical methods are used in risk management and capital adequacy calculation. R is such a powerful tool that it is perfectly capable of solving these complex mathematical and analytical problems. Therefore, it is not surprising that many banks use this as an important tool for risk management.

Principles of the Basel Accords

In 1988, the BCBS published a regulatory framework in Basel, Switzerland, to set the minimum capital that a bank needs to hold to minimize the risk of insolvency. The so-called First Basel Accord, which is now referred to as Basel I, was enforced by the law in all of the G-10 countries by 1992. By 2009, 27 jurisdictions were involved in the Basel Regulatory Framework (the history of the Basel Committee can be read at http://www.bis.org/bcbs/history.htm).

Basel I

The first Basel Accord mainly focuses on credit risk, and formalizes the appropriate risk weighting considering different asset classes. Based on the Accord, the assets of banks should be classified into categories regarding credit risk, and the exposure of each category should be weighted with the defined measures (0 percent, 20 percent, 50 percent, and 100 percent). The resulted value of **risk-weighted assets (RWA)** is used for the determination of capital adequacy. According to the Basel I legislation, banks that are present on international markets are required to hold capital of at least 8 percent of their RWA. This is called the minimum capital ratio (refer to *Basel Committee on Banking Supervision (Charter)* http://www.bis.org/bcbs/charter.htm).

The so-called off-balance sheet items such as derivatives, unused commitments, and credit letters are included in RWA, and should be reported as well.

The Accord was intended to amend and refine over time in order to address risks other than credit risk as well. Furthermore, it was revised to give more appropriate definitions to certain asset classes included in the capital adequacy calculation and to recognize subsequently identified effects.

Basel I defines other capital ratios as well, in order to quantify the banks' capital adequacy. The capital ratios are considered as certain so-called tier-capital elements relative to all RWA. Tier-capital elements include types of capital grouped based on the definition of Basel I. However, each country's banking regulator might revise the classification of the financial instruments considered in capital calculation due to the different legal frameworks of the countries.

The tier 1 capital includes core capital, which is composed of common stock, retained earnings, and certain preferred stocks, which meet the defined requirements. Tier 2 is considered supplementary capital, which involves supplementary debts, undisclosed reserves, revaluation reserves, general loan-loss reserves, and hybrid capital instruments, while tier 3 is deemed as the short-term additional capital. (*Committee on Banking Regulations and Supervisory Practices (1987): Proposals for international convergence of capital measurement and capital standards, Consultative paper, December 1987,* http://www.bis.org/publ/bcbs03a.pdf.)

Basel II

Basel II was issued in 1999 as a new capital adequacy framework proposed to succeed Basel I, and was published in 2004 in order to ensure resolutions to certain issues, which was slightly regulated by the former Basel Accord.

The main objectives of Basel II were to:

- Provide more risk-sensitive capital allocation
- Implement appropriate calculation methods for not only credit risk but market risk and operational risk as well
- Improve the disclosure requirement in order to make capital adequacy more perceptible for market participants
- Avoid regulatory arbitrage

The framework of Basel II is based on the three following pillars:

- The minimum capital requirements by which the Committee intended to develop and expand the standardized capital adequacy calculations
- A supervisory review of a financial institute's capital adequacy and internal assessment process
- Effective disclosure to enhance market discipline

Minimum capital requirements

The required capital on credit risk can be calculated according to the standardized approach. Based on this method, credit exposures should be weighted by measures considering primarily the related ratings by **External Credit Assessment Institutions (ECAI)**. Claims on sovereigns, corporates, and banks or securities companies can be weighted by 0 percent, 20 percent, 50 percent, 100 percent, or 150 percent according to their ratings; however, based on the claims by international associations such as IMF, BIS, or EC, the risk weight should consistently be 0 percent.

Regarding secured claims, cash, and other assets, there are constant weights defined by the Committee and implemented by local regulators who are considering risk mitigation techniques. Eligibility can be considered on different levels regarding the different asset classes, and is regulated in local acts and decrees of the countries. Furthermore, real estate is not deemed as cover but as exposure according to the standard approach; therefore, it is included in the regulation on asset classes as well.

Minimum capital requirement is defined as 8 percent of the RWA, considering conversion factors in case of off-balance sheet items. Capital requirement determined by this method should be appropriate to cover credit risk, market risk, and operational risk as well.

Other methods for the calculation of credit risk are the so-called **Internal Ratings-Based (IRB)** approaches, including Foundation IRB and Advanced IRB. IRB approaches are allowed to use only the approved banks by their local regulator.

IRB approaches apply a capital function to determine the required capital. There are key parameters that influence the capital function, such as **probability of default (PD)**, **loss given default (LGD)**, **exposure at default (EAD)**, and **maturity (M)**.

Probability of default is considered the likelihood that the client will not (entirely) meet its debt obligation over a particular time horizon. By IRB methods, the bank is allowed to estimate the PD of its clients based on either own developed models or by applying the ratings of ECAI.

Loss given default is the percentage of a relating asset when the client defaults. LGD is related tightly to EAD. Exposure at default is the value of the outstanding liability towards the client at the time of the event of its default. Applying Foundation IRB, the calculation method of EAD is determined by the local regulator; however, by Advanced IRB, the banks are allowed to develop their own methodology.

Maturity is a duration type parameter, which indicates the average remaining part of the credit period.

Advanced IRB enables another classification of exposures and assets, which may reflect more on the characteristics of the bank's portfolio. Furthermore, the range of the possibly applied credit risk mitigation actions expands as well.

Although RWA can be determined by various methods by applying either Foundation IRB or Advanced IRB, according to Basel II, the minimum capital requirement is the 8 percent of RWA in both cases.

Determination of the operational risk can be executed by different methods. The simplest way of the calculation is the so-called **Basic Indicator Approach (BIA)**. Based on this approach, the capital requirement is defined as the average of **gross incomes (GI)** of the previous 3 years of the bank multiplied by a given measure, Alpha, which is determined as 15 percent by the legislation.

The **Standardized Approach (STA)** is a little bit more complex. This approach adopts certain methods of BIA; however, using STA, it is required to determine the gross income regarding the **lines of business (LoB)**. The GI of each LoB should be multiplied by a fixed measure, Beta (12 percent, 15 percent, or 18 percent, depending on the LoB). The capital requirement is the sum of the products of GIs and betas that refer to the LoBs.

The aim of the **Alternative Standard Approach (ASTA)** is to avoid double imposition due to credit risk. ASTA adopts the methodology of STA; however, in the case of two LoBs (Retail and Commercial banking), the calculation differs from the standardized approach. Regarding these LoBs, GI is replaced by the product of the value of loans and advances (LA) and a fixed factor (m is equal to 0,035).

The most complex methodology of the determination of operational risk is the **Advanced Measurement Approach (AMA)**. This approach has both quantitative and qualitative requirements, which should be met. The internal model developed for the estimation of the operational risk has to correspond to the standards of safe operation, such as risk measurement on 99.9 percent possibility regarding the period of 1 year. Furthermore, banks that apply the AMA have to provide data of the past 5 years in relation to their losses.

Risk-mitigation techniques can be applied for up to 20 percent of the capital requirement only by banks that use the advanced measurement approach. The banks also have to meet certain strict requirements to be allowed to adopt the risk-mitigation effects.

Regarding the calculation of capital requirement for market risk, the standardized approach is based on the measures and techniques defined by regulators. For more advanced approaches, determination of **Value at Risk (VaR)** is considered the preferred methodology.

Supervisory review

Basel II defines the supervisory and interventional responsibilities of local regulators. It enables them to prescribe a higher capital requirement than what is determined in Pillar I. Furthermore, it allows regulating and managing the remaining risks that are not described in Pillar I, such as liquidity, concentration, strategic, and systemic risks.

The **International Capital Adequacy Assessment Process (ICAAP)** is meant to ensure that the bank operates an appropriately sophisticated risk management system, which measures, quantifies, summarizes, and monitors all the potentially occurring risks. Furthermore, it should oversee whether the banks have enough capital determined, based on internal methods, to cover all the mentioned risks.

The **Supervisory Review Evaluation Process (SREP)** is defined as the procedure for the examination of risk and capital adequacy of the institutes executed by the local regulator. Moreover, considering Pillar II, the regulator has to regularly monitor the capital adequacy according to Pillar I, and intervene in order to ensure the sustainable level of capital.

Transparency

Pillar III of Basel II focuses on the disclosure requirements of banks. It refers mainly to the listed institutes, which are required to share information regarding the scope of application of Pillar I-II, risk assessment processes, risk exposure, and capital adequacy. (*Basel Committee on Banking Supervisions (1999): A New Capital Adequacy Framework; Consultative paper; June 1999*; http://www.bis.org/publ/bcbs50.pdf.)

Basel III

Even before the financial crisis, the need for review and the fundamental strengthening of Basel II framework became evident. During the crisis, it was apparent that the banks had inadequate liquidity position and too much leverage. Risk management should have been more significant, while credit and liquidity risks have usually been mispriced.

The third installment of Basel Accords was developed in 2010 with the aim of providing a more stable and safe operation framework for the financial sector. Basel III and the relating Capital Requirements Directive (CRD IV) are supposed to be implemented into the local legislation by 2019.

Although the implementation will be executed in several steps, the financial institutions are required to commence the preparation for the application of new capital standards even years before the deadline.

The areas concerned in the regulation of Basel III are the following:

- The elements of the required capital — implementing a capital conservation buffer and a counter-cyclical buffer
- Introduction of leverage ratio
- Implementation of liquidity indicators
- Measurement of the counterparty risk
- Capital requirement of credit institutions and investment companies
- Implementation of global prudential standards

In order to improve the quality of capital, Basel III regulates the composite of required capital. Core Tier 1 is defined within Tier 1 capital, and a so-called capital conservation buffer is implemented with the constant measure of 2.5 percent. A discretionary counter-cyclical buffer is introduced as well, which is considered an additional 2.5 percent of capital during periods of high-credit growth.

A leverage ratio was also defined by Basel III, as a minimum amount of loss-absorbing capital compared to all assets and off-balance sheet items regardless of risk weighting.

The most significant provision of Basel III is the introduction of two liquidity indicators. The first one, considered on a short-term horizon, is the **liquidity coverage ratio** (**LCR**), which should be implemented in 2015. LCR is the value of liquid assets relative to the cumulated net cash flow within a 30-day period. At the beginning, the minimum value of LCR should be 60 percent; however, it is intended to be raised to 100 percent by 2019. The formula for the LCR is as follows:

$$LCR = \frac{Liquidassets}{Totalnetcash\text{-}flowwithin30days}$$

The **Net stable funding ratio** (**NSFR**) is going to be implemented in 2018. The aim of this indicator is to avoid maturity gaps between the assets and liabilities of financial institutions. The objective is to provide financing of long-term assets that concern the stability of liabilities. Consequently, NSFR is defined as the stable liabilities on stable assets to be financed. The measure of NSFR should be a minimum 100 percent in 2019 as well.

$$NSFR = \frac{Stablefunding}{Long\text{-}termassets}$$

To avoid systemic risks, capital requirement is implemented also with regard to counterparty risk. Expectations regarding the capital adequacy and liquidity position of counterparties are framed according to the Basel III regulation. Regarding the capital adequacy, institutes that mainly apply internal calculation methods are involved in the new regulation, since the regulation takes into consideration the more detailed examination of potential risks that occur and the exposures towards Systematically Important Financial Institutions (SIFI). Based on the third installment of Basel Accords, the institutions should identify the SIFI based on an indicator than apply the requirements determined by the regulator regarding them (refer to *History of the Basel Committee*).

The main measures and phase-in arrangements of Basel III are included in the following table:

Phases		2013	2014	2015	2016	2017	2018	**2019**
	Leverage Ratio	Parallel run 1 Jan 2013 - 1 Jan 2017 Disclosure starts 1 Jan 2015					Migration to Pillar 1	
Capital	Minimum Common Equity Capital Ratio	3.5%	4.0%	4.5%				**4.5%**
	Capital Conservation Buffer				0.625%	1.25%	1.875%	**2.5%**
	Minimum common equity plus capital conservation buffer	3.5%	4.0%	4.5%	5.125%	5.75%	6.375%	**7.0%**
	Phase-in of deductions from CET1		20%	40%	60%	80%	100%	**100%**
	Minimum Tier 1 Capital	4.5%	5.5%	6.0%				**6.0%**
	Minimum Total Capital			8.0%				**8.0%**
	Minimum Total Capital plus conservation buffer	8.0%			8.625%	9.25%	9.875%	**10.5%**
	Capital that no longer qualify as a non-core Tier 1 or 2 capital	Phased out over 10-year horizon beginning 2013						
Liquidity	Liquidity coverage ratio - minimum requirement			60%	70%	80%	90%	**100%**
	Net stable funding ratio						Introduce minimum standard	

Risk measures

Financial risk is a tangible and quantifiable concept, a value that you can lose on a certain financial investment. Note that here, we strictly differentiate between uncertainty and risk, where the latter is measurable with mathematical-statistical methods with exact probabilities of the different outcomes. However, there are various kinds of measures for financial risks. The most common risk measure is the standard deviation of the returns of a certain financial instrument. Although it is very widespread and easy to use, it has some major disadvantages. One of the most important problems of the standard deviation as a risk measurement is that it treats upside potential the same way as downside risk. In other words, it also punishes a financial instrument that might bring huge positive returns and little negative ones than a less volatile asset.

Consider the following extreme example. Let's assume that we have two stocks on the stock market and we can exactly measure the stocks' yields in three different macroeconomic events. Next year for stock A, a share of a mature corporation brings 5 percent yield if the economy grows, 0 percent if there is stagnation, and loses 5 percent if there's a recession. Stock B is a share of a promising start-up firm; it skyrockets (+ 50 percent) when there's a good economic environment, brings 30 percent if there's stagnation, and has a 20 percent annual yield even if the economy contracts. The statistical standard deviations of stock A and B's returns are 4.1 percent and 12.5 percent respectively. Therefore, it is riskier to pick stock A than stock B if we make our choice based on the standard deviation. However, using our common sense, it is obvious that stock B is better in every case than stock A as it gives a better yield in all different macroeconomic situations.

Our short example perfectly showed the biggest problem with standard deviation as a risk measure. The standard deviation does not meet the most simple condition of a coherent risk measure, the monotonicity. We call the σ risk measure coherent if it is normalized and meets the following criteria. See the work of Artzner and Delbaen for further information on coherent risk measures:

- **Monotonicity**: If portfolio X_1 has no lower values than portfolio X_2 under all scenarios, then the risk of X_1 should be lower than X_2. In other words, if an instrument pays more than another one in every case, it should have a lower risk.

$$If\ X_1 \geq X_2\ then\ \sigma(X_1) \leq (X_2), X_1, X_2 \in R^n$$

- **Sub-additivity**: The risk of two portfolios together should be less than the sum of the risks of the two portfolios separately. This criterion represents the principle of diversification.

$$\sigma(X_1 + X_2) \leq \sigma(X_1) + \sigma(X_2), X_1, X_2 \in R^n$$

- **Positive homogeneity**: Multiplying the portfolio values by a constant multiplies the risk by the same extent.

$$\sigma(\lambda X) = \lambda \sigma(X), X \in R^n, \lambda \in R$$

- **Translation invariance**: Adding a constant value to the portfolio decreases the risk by the same amount. See the following formula:

$$\sigma(X + \varepsilon) = \sigma(X) - \varepsilon, X \in R^n, \varepsilon \in R$$

If the standard deviation is not a reliable risk measure, then what can we use? This question popped up at J.P. Morgan by CEO Dennis Weatherstone in the early 1990s. He called the firm's departments for the famous 4:15 report, in which they aggregated the so-called values at risk 15 minutes before the market closed. The CEO wanted an aggregated measure that showed what amount the firm might lose in the next trading day. As this cannot be calculated with full certainty, especially in the light of the 1987 Black Monday, the analysts added a probability of 95 percent.

The figure that shows what a position might lose in a specified time period with a specified probability (significance level) is called the Value at Risk (VaR). Although it is quite new, it is widely used both by risk departments and financial regulators. There are several ways to calculate value at risk, which can be categorized into three different methods. Under the analytical VaR calculation, we assume that we know the probability distribution of the underlying asset or return. If we do not want to make such assumptions, we can use the historical VaR calculation using the returns or asset values realized in the past. In this case, the implicit assumption is that the past development of the given instrument is a good estimator for the future distribution. If we would like to use a more complex distribution function that is hard to tackle by analytics, a Monte-Carlo simulation could be the best choice to calculate VaR. This can be used by either assuming an analytical distribution of the instrument or by using past values. The latter is called historic simulation.

Analytical VaR

When calculating Value at Risk (VaR) in an analytical approach, we need to assume that the return of a financial instrument follows a certain mathematical probability distribution. The normal distribution is used most commonly; that is why we usually call it the delta-normal method for VaR calculation. Mathematically, $X \sim N(\mu, \sigma)$, where μ and σ are the mean and the standard deviation parameters of the distribution. To calculate the value at risk, we need to find a threshold (T) that has the ability that the probability of all data bigger than this is α (α is the level of significance that can be 95 percent, 99 percent, 99.9 percent, and so on). Using the standard normal cumulative distribution for function F:

$$P\left(X \leq \frac{T - \mu}{\sigma}\right) = F(T) = 1 - \alpha$$

This indicates that we need to apply the inverse cumulative distribution function to *1- α*:

$$\frac{T-\mu}{\sigma} = F^{-1}(1-\alpha) \rightarrow T = \mu + \sigma \cdot F^{-1}(1-\alpha)$$

Although we do not know the closed mathematical formula of neither the cumulative function of normal distribution nor its inverse, we can solve this by using a computer.

We use R to calculate the 95 percent, 1 day VaR of the Apple stocks using the delta normal method, based on a two-year dataset. The estimated mean and standard deviation of Apple returns are 0.13 percent and 1.36 percent.

The following code calculates that VaR for Apple stocks:

```
Apple <- read.table("Apple.csv", header = T, sep = ";")

r <- log(head(Apple$Price,-1)/tail(Apple$Price,-1))

m <- mean(r)

s <- sd(r)

VaR1 <- -qnorm(0.05, m, s)

print(VaR1)
[1] 0.02110003
```

The threshold, which is equal to the VaR if we apply it to the returns, can be seen in the following formula. Note that we always take the absolute value of the result, as VaR is interpreted as a positive number:

$$VaR = T = |0.14 + 1.36 \cdot (-1.645)| = 2.11$$

The VaR (95 percent, 1 day) is 2.11 percent. This means that it has 95 percent probability that Apple shares will not lose more than 2.11 percent in one day. We can also interpret this with an opposite approach. An Apple share will only lose more than 2.11 percent in one day with 5 percent probability.

The chart shown in the following figure depicts the actual distribution of Apple returns with the historic value at risk on it:

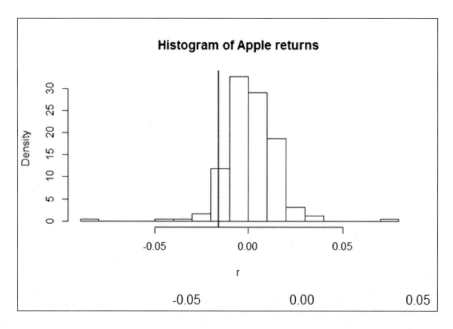

Historical VaR

The simplest way of calculating the value at risk is by using the historical approach. Here, we assume that the past distribution of the financial instrument's return represents the future too. Therefore, we need to find the threshold above which the *a* portion of the values can be found. In statistics, this is called the percentile. If we use a VaR with a 95- percent level of significance, for instance, then it will imply the lower fifth percentile of the dataset. The following code shows how to calculate the percentile in R:

```
VaR2 <- -quantile(r, 0.05)
print(VaR2)
        5%
0.01574694
```

Applying this to the Apple shares, we get a lower fifth percentile of 1.57 percent. The value at risk is the absolute value of this percentile. Therefore, we can either say that it has only 5 percent probability that Apple shares lose more than 1.57 percent in a day, or the stock will lose less than 1.57 percent with 95 percent likelihood.

Monte-Carlo simulation

The most sophisticated approach to calculate the value at risk is the Monte-Carlo simulation. However, it is only worth using if other methods cannot be used. These reasons can be the complexity of the problem or the assumption of a difficult probability distribution. Nevertheless, this is the best method to show the powerful capabilities of R that can support risk management.

A Monte-Carlo simulation can be used in many different fields of finance and other sciences as well. The basic approach is to set up a model and to assume an analytic distribution of the exogenous variable The next step is to randomly generate the input data to the model in accordance with the assumed distribution. Then, the outcomes are collected and used to gather the result and draw the conclusion. When the simulated output data is ready, we can follow the same procedure as we would do if we used the historical approach.

Using a 10,000 step Monte-Carlo simulation to calculate the value at risk of Apple shares may seem to be an overkill, but it serves for the demonstration. The related R code is shown here:

```
sim_norm_return <- rnorm(10000, m, s)
VaR3 <- -quantile(sim_norm_return, 0.05)
print(VaR3)
        5%
0.02128257
```

We get a result of 2.06 percent for the value at risk as a lower fifth percentile of the simulated returns. This is very close to the 2.11 percent estimated with the delta-normal method, which is not a coincidence. The basic assumption that the yield follows a normal distribution is the same; thus, the minor difference is only a result of the randomness of the simulation. The more steps the simulation takes, the closer the result is to the delta-normal estimation.

A modification of the Monte-Carlo method is the historical simulation when the assumed distribution is based on the past data of the financial instrument. The generation of the data here is not based on an analytical mathematical function but the historical values are selected randomly, preferably via an independent identical distribution method.

We also use a 10,000 element simulation for the Apple stock returns. In order to select the values from the past randomly, we assign numbers to them. The next step is to simulate a random integer between 1 and 251 (the number of historic data) and then use a function to find the associated yield. The R code can be seen here:

```
sim_return <- r[ceiling(runif(10000)*251)]
VaR4 <- -quantile(sim_return, 0.05)
print(VaR4)
         5%
0.01578806
```

The result for the VaR is 1.58 percent, which is not surprisingly close to the value derived from the original historic method.

Nowadays, value at risk is a common measure for risk in many fields of finance. However, in general, it still does not fulfill the criteria of a coherent risk measure as it fails to meet sub-additivity. In other words, it might discourage diversification in certain cases. However, if we assume an elliptically distributed function for the returns, the VaR proves to be a coherent risk measure. This essentially means that the normal distribution suits the estimation of VaR perfectly. The only problem is that the stock returns in real life are rather leptokurtic (heavy-tailed) compared to the Gaussian curve as it is experienced as a stylized fact of finance.

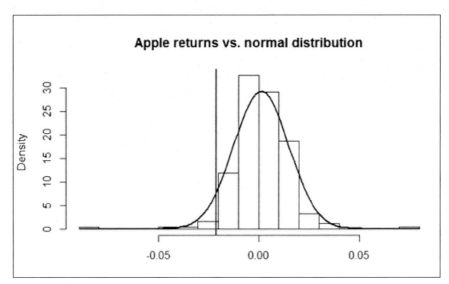

In other words, the stocks in real life tend to show more extreme losses and profits than it would be explained by the normal distribution. Therefore, a developed analysis of risk assumes more complex distributions to cope with the heavy-tailed stock returns, the heteroskedasticity, and other imperfections of the real-life yields.

The use of **Expected Shortfall (ES)** is also included in the developed analysis of risk, which is, in fact, a coherent risk measure, no matter what distribution we assume. The expected shortfall concentrates on the tail of the distribution. It measures the expected value of the distribution beyond the value at risk. In other words, the expected shortfall at α significance level is the expected value of the worst a percent of the cases. Mathematically, $ES_\alpha = \dfrac{1}{\alpha} \int_0^\alpha VaR_\gamma (X) d\gamma,$.

Here, $VaR\gamma$ is the value at risk of the distribution of returns.

Sometimes, an expected shortfall is called **conditional value at risk (CVaR)**. However, the two terminologies do not exactly mean the same thing; they can be used as synonyms if continuous distribution functions are used for the risk analysis. Although R is capable of dealing with such complex issues as the expected shortfall, it goes beyond the goals of this book. For further information on this topic, see the work of *Acerbi, C.; Tasche, D. (2002)*.

Risk categories

Banks face various kinds of risks, for example, client default, changes in the market environment, troubles in refinancing, and fraud. These risks are categorized into credit risk, market risk, and operational risk.

Market risk

Losses realized from the movements of the market prices are covered by the market risk. It may include the losses on the trading book positions of a bank or financial institution, but the losses realized on interest rate or currency that may be in connection with the core business of a bank also belong to market risk. Market risk can include several subcategories such as equity risk, interest rate risk, currency risk, and commodity risk. Liquidity risk is also covered in this topic. Based on the advanced approach of the Basel II directive, the capital needed to cover these risks is mostly based on value at risk calculations.

Currency risk refers to the possible loss on the movements of the foreign exchange rates (for example, EUR/USD) or on its derivative products, while commodity risk covers the losses on the movements of commodity prices (for example, gold, crude oil, wheat, copper, and so on). Currency risk can also affect the core business of a bank if there is a mismatch between the FX exposure in funding and lending. FX mismatch can lead to a serious risk in a bank; thus, regulators usually have strict limitations on the maximum amount of the so-called open FX positions. This results in a mismatch of the FX exposure between the liability and the asset side of the bank. This can be tackled by certain hedging deals (such as cross-currency swaps, currency futures, forwards, FX options, and so on).

Equity risk is the possible loss on stocks, stock indices, or derivative products with equity underlying. We saw examples on how to measure the equity risk using either the standard deviation or the value at risk. Now, we will show examples on how the risk of the equity derivative portfolio can be measured using the already mentioned techniques. First, we look at a single call option's value at risk, and we then analyze how a portfolio of a call and a put option can be dealt by this method.

First, let's assume that all the conditions of the Black-Scholes model consist of the market. For more information on the Black-Scholes model and its condition, refer to the book of *John. C. Hull [9]*. A stock is currently traded at S = USD 100, which pays no dividend and follows a geometric Brownian motion with μ equal to 20 percent (drift) and σ equal to 30 percent (volatility) parameters.

An ATM (at-the-money) call option on this stock matures in two years from now, and we would like to determine the 95 percent one year value at risk of this option. We know that the stock price follows a lognormal distribution, while the logarithmic rate of return follows a normal distribution with the following m and s parameters:

$$If\ dS = \mu S dt + \sigma S dW(t)$$

$$then\ ln(S) \sim N(m, s)$$

$$where\ m = \mu - \frac{\sigma^2}{2} = 15.5\ and\ s = \sigma = 30.$$

Now, let's calculate the current price of the derivative given that the Black-Scholes conditions exist. Using the Black-Scholes formula, the two-year option is trading at USD 25.98:

$$c = S_0 \cdot N(d_1) - PV(X) \cdot N(d_2) = 25.98$$

Note that the price of the call option is a monotone-growing function of the spot price of the underlying.

This characteristic helps us a lot in solving this problem. What we need is a threshold of the option price below which it goes with only a 5-percent probability. However, because it is a monotone growing function of S, we only need to know where this threshold is for the stock price. Given the m and s parameters, we can easily find this value using the following formula:

$$T = S_0 \cdot e^{\mu + \sigma \cdot F^{-1}(1-\alpha)} = 100 \cdot e^{0.155 + 0.3 \cdot (-1.645)} = 71.29$$

Therefore, we now know that there is only a 5 percent chance that the stock price goes below USD 71.29 in one year (the time period for m and s parameters is one year). If we apply the Black-Scholes formula on this price and with a one year less maturity of the option, we get the threshold for the call option price.

$$c = S_T \cdot N(d_1) - PV(X) \cdot N(d_2) = 2.90$$

Now, we know that there is a 95 percent likelihood that the option price goes above USD 2.90 in one year. So the value that we lose at most with 95 percent probability is the difference between the actual option price and the threshold. So the call option's 95 percent VaR for one year is as follows:

$$VaR = 25.98 - 2.90 = 23.08$$

$$VaR = \frac{25.98 - 2.90}{25.98} = 88.82\%$$

Therefore, the call option on the given stock may only lose more than USD 23.08 or 88.82 percent with 5 percent probability in one year.

The calculations can be seen below in the following R codes. Note that before running the code, we need to install the fOptions library using this command:

```
install.packages("fOptions")
library(fOptions)


X <- 100
Time <- 2
r <- 0.1
sigma <- 0.3
mu <- 0.2
S <- seq(1,200, length = 1000)
call_price <- sapply(S, function(S) GBSOption("c", S, X, Time, r, r,
   sigma)@price)
plot(S, call_price, type = "l", ylab = "", main = "Call option price
   in function of stock prompt price")
```

The following screenshot is the result of the preceding command:

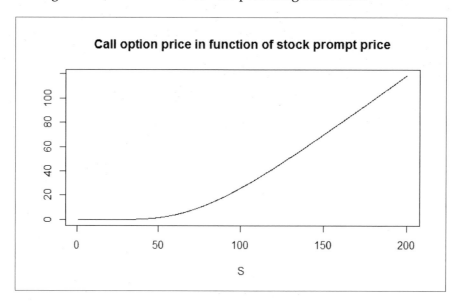

The situation is not that simple if we would like to find the value at risk of a certain portfolio of call and put options. Let's use the previous example with the stock trading at USD 100. Now, we add an ATM put option to the portfolio besides the ATM call option to form a complex position known as straddle in finance. From our point of view, the problem with this portfolio is the non-monotonicity of the function of the stock price. As seen in the chart shown in the next image, the value of this portfolio as a function of the stock price is a parabola or is similar to a V if the option is just before its maturity.

Therefore, the previous logic of finding the appropriate stock price threshold to calculate the option price threshold does not work here. However, we can call the Monte-Carlo simulation method to derive the desired value.

First, let's use the so-called put-call parity to gather the put option's value using the call price that has been calculated previously. The put-call parity is calculated as follows:

$$c - p = S - PV(X) \rightarrow$$

$$\rightarrow p = c - S + PV(X) = 7.85$$

Here, c and p is the call and put option prices, both with a strike price of X, and S is the actual stock price *Hull (2002)*. The value of the full portfolio is USD 33.82 as a consequence.

Now, we use the simulation to gather 10,000 realizations of a possible portfolio value derived from a randomly generated set of input data. We ensure that the stock follows a geometric Brownian motion and that the logarithmic rate of return follows a normal distribution with the m and s parameters (15.5 percent and 30 percent). Applying the generated logarithmic return on the original stock price (USD 100), we will reach a simulated stock price for 1 year from now. This can be used to recalculate the value of both the call and put options using the Black-Scholes formula. Note that here, we replace the original stock price with the simulated one, while we also use a one year less maturity for the calculations. As the last step, we create 10,000 realizations of the simulated portfolio value (c + p), and then find the lower fifth percentile. This will be the threshold below which the option portfolio value goes only in 5 percent of the cases. The steps can be seen in the following code:

```
X <- 100
Time <- 2
r <- 0.1
sigma <- 0.3
```

```
mu <- 0.2
S <- seq(1,200, length = 1000)
call_price <- sapply(S, function(S) GBSOption("c", S, X, Time, r, r,
    sigma)@price)
put_price <- sapply(S, function(S) GBSOption("p", S, X, Time, r, r,
    sigma)@price)
portfolio_price <- call_price + put_price
windows()
plot(S, portfolio_price, type = "l", ylab = "", main = "Portfolio
    price in function of stock prompt price")
# portfolio VaR simulation
p0 <- GBSOption("c", 100, X, Time, r, r, sigma)@price +
    GBSOption("p", 100, X, Time, r, r, sigma)@price
print(paste("price of portfolio:",p0))
[1] "price of portfolio: 33.8240537586255"
S1 <- 100*exp(rnorm(10000, mu - sigma^2 / 2 , sigma))
P1 <- sapply(S1, function(S) GxBSOption("c", S, X, 1, r, r,
    sigma)@price + GBSOption("p", S, X, 1, r, r, sigma)@price )
VaR <- quantile(P1, 0.05)
print(paste("95% VaR of portfolio: ", p0 - VaR))
```

The preceding command yields the following output:

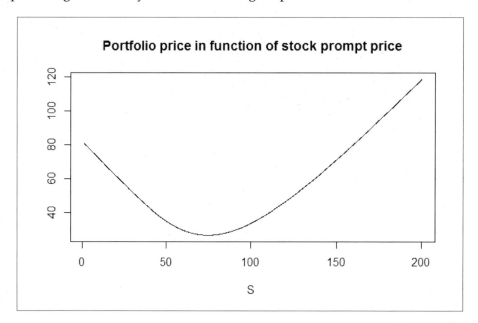

The desired threshold came out at USD 21.45; thus, the value at risk of the portfolio is 33.82 - 21.45 = USD 12.37. Therefore, the probability that the portfolio loses more than 12.37 in one year is only 5 percent.

Interest rate risk arises from the core business, that is, the lending and refinancing activity of a bank. However, it also includes the possible losses on bonds or fixed income derivatives due to unfavorable changes in interest rates. The interest rate risk is the most important market risk for a bank, given the fact that it mostly uses short-term funding (client deposits, interbank loans, and so on) to refinance long-term assets (such as mortgage loans, government bonds, and so on).

Calculating the value at risk of a position or the whole portfolio can be a useful tool to measure the market risk of a bank or financial institution. However, several other tools are also available to measure and to cope with the interest rate risk for example. Such a tool can be the analysis of the mismatch of the interest-sensitivity gap between assets and liabilities. This method was among the first techniques in asset liability management to measure and tackle interest-rate risk, but it is much less accurate than the modern risk measurement methods. In the interest-sensitivity gap analysis, asset and liability elements are classified by the average maturity or the timing of interest-rate reset in case the asset or liability is a floater. Then, the asset and liability elements are compared in each time period class to give a detailed view on the interest-rate sensitivity mismatch.

The VaR-based approach is a much more developed and accurate measure for the interest rate risk of a bank or financial institution. This method is also based on the interest rate sensitivity and is represented by the duration (and convexity) of a fixed income portfolio rather than the maturity mismatch of asset and liability elements.

Credit risk

The primary risk that a bank faces is the possible default of the borrower, where the required payment is failed to be made. Here, the risk is that the lender loses the principal, the interest, and all related payments. The loss can be partial or complete depending on the collateral and other mitigating factors. The default can be a consequence of a number of different circumstances such as payment failure from a retail borrower on mortgage, a credit card, or a personal loan; the insolvency of a company, bank, or insurance firm; a failed payment on an invoice due; the failure of payment by the issuer on debt securities, and so on.

The expected loss from credit risk can be represented as a multiple of three different factors: the PD, LGD, and EAD:

$$Expected loss = PD \cdot LGD \cdot EAD$$

Probability of default (PD) is the likelihood that the event of failed payment happens. This is the key factor of all credit risk models, and there are several types of approaches to estimate this value. The loss given default (LGD) is the proportion that is lost in percentage of the claimed par value. The **recovery rate (RR)** is the inverse of LGD and shows the amount that can be collected (recovered) even if the borrower defaults. This is affected by the collaterals and other mitigating factors used in lending. The exposure at the default (EAD) is the claimed value that is exposed to the certain credit risk.

Banks and financial institutions use different methods to measure and handle credit risk. In order to reduce it, all the three factors of the multiple can be in focus. To keep the exposure under control, banks may use limits and restrictions in lending towards certain groups of clients (consumers, companies, and sovereigns). Loss given default can be lowered by using collaterals such as mortgage rights on properties, securities, and guarantees. Collaterals provide security to the lenders and ensure that they get back at least some of their money. Other tools are also available to reduce loss given default, such as credit derivatives and credit insurance.

A **credit default swap (CDS)** is a financial swap agreement that works as insurance against the default of a third party. The issuer or seller of the CDS agrees to compensate the buyer in an event that the debt holder defaults. The buyer pays a periodical fee for the seller set in percentage of the par value of the bond or other debt security. The seller pays the par value to the buyer and receives the bond in the case of a credit event. If there is no default by the debtor, the CDS deal terminates at maturity without any payment from the seller.

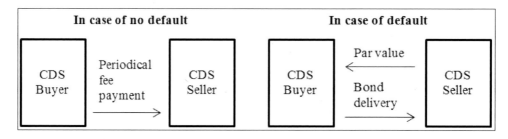

The probability of default can be mitigated by due diligence of the business partners and the borrowers, using covenants and strict policies. Banks use a broad variety of due diligence, ranging from the standardized scoring processes to more complex in-depth research on clients. By applying these methods, banks can screen out those clients who have too high probability of default and would therefore hit the capital position. Credit risk can also be mitigated by risk-based pricing. Higher probability of default leads to a higher expected loss on credit risk that has to be covered by the interest rate spread applied to the specific client. Banks need to tackle this in their normal course of business and only need to form capital to the unexpected loss. Therefore, the expected loss on credit risk should be a basic part of product pricing.

Estimating the probability of default is a very important issue for all banks and financial institutions. There are several approaches, of which we examine three different ones:

- An implicit probability is derived from the market pricing of risky bonds or credit default swaps (for example, the Hull-White method)
- Structural models (for example, the KMV model)
- Current and historic movements of credit ratings (for example, CreditMetrics)

The first approach assumes that there are traded products on the market related to the instruments as an underlying that have credit risk. It is also assumed that the risk is perfectly shown in the market pricing of such instruments. For example, if a bond of a risky company is traded on the market, the price of the bond will be lower than the price of a risk-free security. If a credit default swap is traded on the market on a certain bond, then, it also reflects the market's evaluation of the risk on that security. If there is enough liquidity on the market, the expected credit risk loss should be equal to the observed price of the risk. If we know this price, we can determine the implicit probability of the default price.

Let's take a look at a short example. Let's assume that a 1 year maturity zero-coupon bond with a par value of USD 1,000 issued by a BBB-rated corporation trades at a YTM (yield-to-maturity) of 5 percent. An AAA-rated government T-Bill with similar characteristics but without credit risk trades at 3 percent. We know that if the corporate bond defaults, 30 percent of the par value will be recovered. What is the probability of the bond defaulting if the market prices properly?

First, we need to calculate the current market price of both the corporate and the

government bond. The corporate bond should trade at $P_c = \dfrac{CF}{(1+r)^t} = \dfrac{1,000}{(1+0.05)^1} = USD\,952.4$.

Similarly, the government bond should trade at $P_g = \dfrac{1,000}{(1+0.03)^1} = USD\,970.9$.

The price difference between the two bonds is USD 18.5. The expected credit loss is PD·LGD·EAD in one year. If we wanted to take a hedge against the credit loss through insurance or CDS, the present value of this amount would be the maximum that we would pay. As a consequence, the price difference of the two bonds should equal to the present value of the expected credit loss. The LGD is 70 percent as 30 percent of the par value is recovered in the case of a default.

Therefore, $PV\left(PD \cdot LGD \cdot EAD\right) = \dfrac{PD \cdot 0.7 \cdot 1,000}{1.03} = 18.5$ or $PD = \dfrac{1.03 \cdot 18.5}{0.7 \cdot 1,000} = 2.72\%$.

So the implicit probability of default is 2.72 percent during the next year, if the market prices are proper. This method can also be used if there is a credit derivative traded on the market related to the specific bond.

Structural methods create a mathematical model based on the characteristics of the financial instrument that is exposed to the credit risk. A common example is the KMV model created by the joint company founded by three mathematicians, Stephen Kealhofer, John McQuown, and Oldřich Vašíček. Currently, this company runs under the name of Moody's Analytics after having been acquired by Moody's rating agency in 2002.

The KMV model is based on Merton's credit model (1974), which regards both the debt and equity securities of a corporation with credit risk as derivatives similar to options. The basic idea is that if a company is solvent, then the market value of its assets (or enterprise value) should exceed the par value of the debts it holds. Therefore, just before the maturity of the corporate bonds, they estimate their par value and the value of the equity (market capitalization of a public company). However, if the value of assets misses the par value of debt at maturity, the owners might decide to raise the capital or go bankrupt. If the latter is the case, the market value of corporate bonds will equal the asset value, and the equity holders will get nothing during liquidation.

The choice between the bankruptcy and capital raising is called the bankruptcy option, which has the characteristics of a put option. This exists because the equity holders have no more responsibility on the company than the value they invested (the share price cannot go to negative). More specifically, the value of the corporate bond is the combination of a bond without credit risk and a bankruptcy option, which is a short put option from the point of view of the bondholder (long bond + short put).

The equity of the company can be treated as a call option (long call). The asset value of the company is the sum of all the equations, as shown in this formula: $V = PV(D) - p + c$, where D is the par value of the corporate debt, V is the asset value, c is the market value of the equity (the call option in this regard), and p is the value of the bankruptcy option.

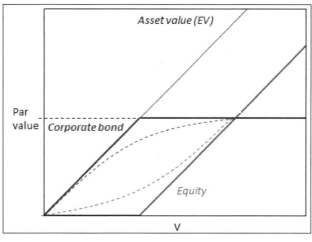

The KMV model

In practice, the volatility of both the asset value and the equity is necessary to calculate the actual value of the risky corporate bond. A public company's equity volatility can easily be estimated from stock price movements, but the asset volatility is not available as real economy goods are usually not traded publicly. The market value of assets is also a tricky one due to the same reason. Therefore, the KMV has two equations and two unknown variables. The two equations are the conditions of the Black-Scholes theory $E = V \cdot N(d_1) - PV(D) \cdot N(d_2)$, which is based on the Black-Scholes equation, and $\sigma_E \cdot E = \frac{\partial E}{\partial V} \cdot \sigma_V \cdot V$, which is based on Itō's lemma, where E and V are the market values of equity and assets, D is the par value of the bond, σ_E and σ_V are the volatilities of the equity and the assets. The $\frac{\partial E}{\partial V}$ is the derivative of E with respect to V, and it equals to $N(d_1)$, based on the Black-Scholes theory. The two unknown variables are V and σ_V.

Now, let's take a look at an example where the market value of a company's equity (market capitalization) is USD 3 billion with 80 percent volatility. The company has a single series of zero-coupon bonds with a par value of USD 10 billion, which matures exactly in one year. The risk-free logarithmic rate of return is 5 percent for one year.

The solution of the preceding equation in R can be seen as follows:

```
install.packages("fOptions")
library(fOptions)
kmv_error <- function(V_and_vol_V, E=3,Time=1,D=10,vol_E=0.8,r=0.05){
  V <- V_and_vol_V[1]
  vol_V <- V_and_vol_V[2]
  E_ <- GBSOption("c", V, D, Time, r, r, vol_V)@price
  tmp <- vol_V*sqrt(Time)
  d1 <- log(V/(D*exp(-r*Time)))/tmp + tmp/2
  Nd1 <- pnorm(d1)
  vol_E_ <- Nd1*V/E*vol_V
  err <- c(E_ - E, vol_E_ - vol_E)
  err[1]^2+err[2]^2
}
a <- optim(c(1,1), fn = kmv_error)
print(a)
```

The value of the aggregate of the corporate bonds is USD 9.40 billion with a logarithmic of yield to maturity at 6.44 percent, and the value of the assets are USD 12.40 billion with 21.2 percent volatility.

The third way of estimating the probability of default is the rating-based approach. This method of estimation starts from the credit rating of different financial instruments or economic entities (companies, sovereigns, and institutions). CreditMetrics analytics was originally developed by JP Morgan's risk management division in 1997. Since then, it has evolved further, and now, it is widely used among other risk management tools. The basic idea of CreditMetrics is to estimate probabilities on how the credit rating of an entity can change over time and what effect it can have on the value of the securities issued by the same entity. It starts with the analysis of the rating history and then creates a so-called transition matrix that contains the probabilities of how the credit rating might develop. For further information on CreditMetrics, see the technical book published by MSCI (*Committee on Banking Regulations and Supervisory Practices (1987)*).

Operational risk

The third major risk category is the operational risk. This refers to all the possible losses that can arise during the operation of a bank, financial institution, or another company. It includes losses from natural disasters, internal or external fraud (for example, bank robbery), system faults or failures, and inadequate working processes. These risks can be categorized into four different groups seen below:

- **Low impact with low probability**: If the risk as well as its potential impact on the operation is low, then it is not worth the effort to handle it.

- **Low impact with high probability**: If a risk event happens too often, it means that some processes of the company should be restructured, or it should be included in the pricing of a certain operation.

- **High impact with low probability**: If the probability of a high-impact event is low, the most suitable method to mitigate the risk is to take insurance on such events.

- **High impact with high probability**: If both the impact and the probability of such a risk are high, then it's better to shut down that operation. Here, neither the restructuring nor the insurance works.

This part of the risk management belongs rather to the actuarial sciences than financial analysis. However, the tools provided by R are also capable of handling such problems as well. Let's take an example of the possible operational losses on the failures of an IT system. The number of failures follow a Poisson distribution with λ = 20 parameter, while the magnitude of each loss follows a lognormal distribution with m equal to 5 and s equal to 2 parameters. The average number of failures in a year is 20 based on the Poisson distribution, while the expected value of the

magnitude of a loss is: $e^{\left(m+\frac{s^2}{2}\right)} = 1097$.

However, we need to determine the joint distribution, the expected value, and the quantile of 99.9 percent of the aggregate annual loss. The latter will be used to determine the necessary capital set by the advanced measurement approach (AMA) of Basel II. We use a 10,000 element Monte-Carlo simulation. The first step is to generate a discrete random variable that follows a Poisson distribution. Then, we generate independent variables with lognormal distribution in the number of the previously generated integers, and we aggregate them. We can create the distribution of the aggregated losses by repeating this process 10,000 times. The expected value of the aggregate losses is USD 21,694, and the quantile of 99.9 percent is USD 382,247.

Therefore, we will only lose more than USD 382 thousand in a year by the failure of the IT system in 0.1 percent of the cases. The calculations can be seen in R here:

```
op <- function(){
n <- rpois(1, 20)
z <- rlnorm(n,5,2)
sum(z)
}
Loss <- replicate(10000, op())
hist(Loss[Loss<50000], main = "", breaks = 20, xlab = "", ylab = "")
print(paste("Expected loss = ", mean(Loss)))
print(paste("99.9% quantile of loss = ", quantile(Loss, 0.999)))
```

The following is the screenshot of the preceding command:

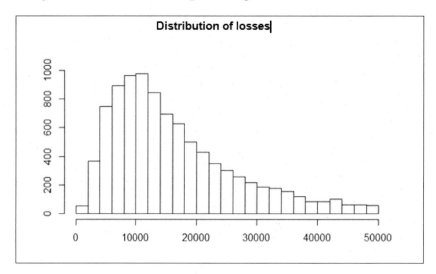

We see the distribution of the aggregated losses in the chart shown in the preceding figure, which is similar to a lognormal distribution but is not necessarily lognormal.

Summary

In this chapter, we learned the basic principles of the Basel Accords, the capital adequacy requirements in banking regulation, the risk measures and different risk types, and most importantly, the powerful tools of R used in risk management.

We saw that the Basel Accords are a world wide harmonized banking regulatory framework, and we learned the ongoing development and more sophisticated approaches of the financial regulations. Furthermore, we provided insights on risk measures, starting from the most simple standard deviation of returns to the more sophisticated ones, most importantly, Value at Risk (VaR). However, we saw that VaR is not necessarily a coherent risk measure, but it is still one of the most widely used figures in both regulation and risk management.

We went through the main risk types a bank or financial institution faces, that is, the credit risk, the market risk, and the operational risk. You can see how the different risk management approaches can be used to calculate the possible losses of the different risk types and the related capital adequacy. Finally, we presented several examples to show how R can be used to easily solve complex problems in risk management.

References

[1] History of the Basel Committee

[2] Basel Committee on Banking Supervision (Charter)

[3] Committee on Banking Regulations and Supervisory Practices (1987): Proposals for international convergence of capital measurement and capital standards; Consultative paper; December 1987

[4] Basel Committee on Banking Supervisions (1999): A New Capital Adequacy Framework; Consultative paper; June 1999

[5] Artzner, P.; Delbaen, F.; Eber, J. M.; Heath, D. (1999). *Coherent Measures of Risk*. Mathematical Finance, 9 (3 ed.): p. 203

[6] Wilmott, P. (2006). *Quantitative Finance 1* (2 ed.): p. 342

[7] Acerbi, C.; Tasche, D. (2002). *Expected Shortfall: a natural coherent alternative to Value at Risk*. Economic Notes 31: p. 379–388

[8] Basel II Comprehensive Version

[9] Hull, J. C. (2002). *Options, Futures and Other Derivatives* (5th ed.)

[10] *Principles for the Management of Credit Risk - final document.* Basel Committee on Banking Supervision. BIS. (2000)

[11] Crosbie, P., Bohn, J. (2003): *Modeling default risk. Technical Report, Moody's KMV*

[12] Crouhy, M., Galai, D., Mark, R. (2000): *A comparative analysis of current credit risk models.* Journal of Banking & Finance, 24:59–117

[13] MSCI CreditMetrics Technical Book

13
Systemic Risks

One of the main lessons of the current crisis is that some institutions bear an outstanding risk for the financial system due to their size or special role. During a crisis, these institutions usually get state aid to prevent the whole system from collapsing, which would mean higher costs for the state and the real economy as well. One of the best examples is the AIG. Due to its activity on the CDS market, the Federal Reserve helped the insurer company to avoid defaulting since nobody knew the possible effects of the collapse of the institution.

These lessons motivated central banks and other regulators to put more emphasis on the examination and the regulation of **systemically important financial institutions (SIFI)**. To do this, sophisticated identification of SIFIs is getting more and more important in financial literature. Expanding the former simple techniques, central banks and supervisory authorities tend to use more complicated methodologies based on network theory approaches using transaction data of financial markets. This information is important for investors as well because it helps to diversify their exposure towards the financial sector.

This chapter aims to introduce two techniques based on network theory, which can be used in the identification of SIFIs beyond the commonly used centrality measures.

Systemic risk in a nutshell

The global financial crisis highlighted that the size of some financial institutions was too big compared to the real economy, or they had too many connections with important counterparties. Because of this, any problems that affect these institutions can have fatal results on the whole financial system and the real economy. For this reason, governments spared no effort in saving these institutions. There are several global examples where governments or central banks give guarantees, inject capital, lend funding, or support the acquisition of their most important financial institutions (for example, Northern Rock, AIG, or Bear Stearns).

Without these steps, the chance for a collapse seemed to be too high, which would have been accompanied with extreme high costs because of bailouts. All in all, identification of systemically important financial institutions again became a hot topic. One of the main lessons of the crisis was that the biggest and most interconnected institutions have to be handled differently even during normal times. According to the new Basel framework, systemically important institutions have to be more strictly regulated than their less important partners. Due to their central role and their interconnectedness, the failure of these institutions can send shock waves through the financial system, which, in turn, can harm the real economy. The rational choices of individual institutions, which target the maximum possible profit, may be suboptimal on a system-wide level because they do not take into account their possible negative effects during stress periods.

Before the crisis, the systemic role of individual financial institutions was mainly assessed during the decision about the lender-of-last-resort support. Central banks took into account a bank's systemic role in their decision on lending to this bank in case of serious problems. A survey about analysis techniques used in different countries found that in many cases, authorities applied a similar methodology in the assessment of systemic importance. A wide variety of methods exist in practice, from traditional techniques (for example, indicator-based approaches that focus on market shares) and complex quantitative models to qualitative criteria, which include market intelligence (*FSB (2009)*). Several different types of ratios might be included in indicator-based methods (*BIS (2011)*). Usually, financial markets, financial infrastructure, and financial intermediation are in the focus of the examination, but the actual set of indicators can vary from country to country, depending on the special characteristics of the investigated banking system.

Indicator-based methods mainly focus on each bank's market share in different parts of banking (from assets to liabilities and from notional values of OTC derivatives to payments cleared and settled, it may cover several fields, *BIS (2011)*). These indicator-based methodologies sometimes don't contain information about the interconnectedness of the institution on financial markets. *Daróczi et al. (2013)* provided some suggestions on how to include this information in the identification of systemically important banks. Simple measures of networks applied for each bank can expand the traditional indicator-based methods. In the financial literature, many different measures are used to evaluate the stability of the network or assess the role of individual institutions. *Iazetta and Manna (2009)* used the so-called geodesic frequency (also known as "betweenness") and degree to assess the resilience of the network.

They found that the use of these ratios helps in the identification of the big players in the system. *Berlinger et al. (2011)* also used network measures for the examination of individual institutions' systemic role.

In this chapter, we won't include these methods since *Daróczi et al. (2013)* showed the theory and its application in R. Our focus will be on two different methodologies of network theory, which are relevant in the identification of systemic importance and can be easily applied. First, we will show the core-periphery decomposition of financial markets. Second, we will show a simulation method that helps us to see the contagious effects in case any individual institution defaults.

The dataset used in our examples

In this chapter, we will use a fictional banking system and its interbank deposit market. We use this market as it usually has the biggest potential loss because these transactions are not collateralized.

For this analysis, we need a connected network, so we constructed one. This network should contain information on the exposure of banks against each other. Usually, we have data on the transaction, like in *Table 13.1*. Since the average maturity of transactions is very low on the interbank market, it is also possible to use this data. For example, we can construct the network by using the average monthly transaction size between every pair of banks. For this type of analysis, only the partners of each transaction and the contract sizes matter.

Lender	Borrower	Start of the transaction	End of the transaction	Size	Interest (%)
1	2	02-Jul-07	03-Jul-07	5,00	7,70
2	28	02-Jul-07	03-Jul-07	2,00	7,75
7	28	02-Jul-07	03-Jul-07	4,90	7,75
11	24	02-Jul-07	03-Jul-07	2,00	7,90
13	7	02-Jul-07	03-Jul-07	1,00	7,70
21	23	02-Jul-07	03-Jul-07	4,00	7,75
39	11	02-Jul-07	03-Jul-07	1,20	7,70
39	20	02-Jul-07	03-Jul-07	1,20	7,60

Table 13.1: The data set of the transaction

With all this information, we can put together the matrix of a financial market (which can be visualized as a network).

1	2	3	4	5	6	7 ....
	11,1	1		11,6		5,5
						8,4
				7		23,4
		1		87		12,3
		9,9			3	26
	11,3	7,1		9		21,5
	1,5	8,4			1,5	
				2,5	2	6,5

The matrix used

The first step will be the core-periphery decomposition of the matrix. In this case, we will only need the so-called adjacency matrix A where $A_{i,j} = \begin{cases} 1, & i\,bank\,lends\,to\,j \\ 0, & otherwise \end{cases}$.

The simulation method will be a bit more complicated since we will need some more information, both about the banks and the transactions. Instead of using the adjacency matrix, we will need a weighted matrix W, where the weights are the transaction sizes:

$$W_{i,j} = \begin{cases} w, & sum\,i\,lends\,to\,j \\ 0, & otherwise \end{cases}$$

Figure 13.2 shows the weighted network of the examined market in the sample period:

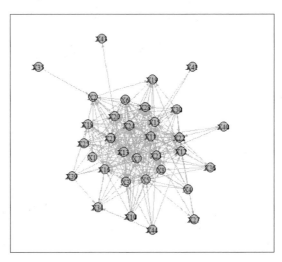

Figure 13.2: The network of the interbank deposit market

We will also need some bank-specific information. Vector C will contain the information about the bank's capital position. C_i shows the capital buffer of bank i over the regulatory minimum in the given currency. Of course, it is a matter of decision whether the capital buffer or the whole regulatory capital is considered during these exercises. In our view, it is better to use capital buffer since if a bank loses the entire buffer, the supervisory institution will make some steps. Vector S will contain the size of each bank. S_i will then be the balance sheet total of bank i.

	Balance sheet total	Capital buffer over regulatory minimum
1	693	9
2	2 018	17
3	2 189	29
4	149	47
5	1 921	25
6	641	32
7	1 313	7
.	.	.
.	.	.
.	.	.
.	.	.

Figure 13.3: Vectors of capital position and size

Core-periphery decomposition

Interbank markets are tiered and operate in a hierarchical fashion. It is a well-known characteristic of these markets that many banks are dealing with only a small number of big institutions, while these big institutions are acting like intermediaries or money-center banks. These big institutions are considered to be the core of the network, and the others are the periphery.

Many papers focused on this characteristic of real-world networks. For example, *Borgatti and Everett (1999)* examined this phenomenon on a network made of citation data, and found three journals to be the members of the core. Craig and von Peter (2010) used this core/periphery structure for the German interbank market. Their findings suggest that bank-specific features help to explain how banks position themselves in the interbank market. There is a strong correlation between the size and position in the network. As tiering is not random but behavioral, there are economic reasons (for example, fixed costs) why the banking system organizes itself around a core of money-center banks. This finding also implies that coreness can be a good measure of systemic importance.

A perfect core-periphery structure of a network can be presented easily by the matrix in *Figure 13.3*. Core banks are in the upper-left corner of the matrix. All of these banks are connected to each other. They can be considered as intermediaries. They are responsible for the stability of the market, and other banks are connected to each other through these core institutions. In the lower-right corner, there are periphery banks. They have no connection with other periphery institutions. They are only connected to the core as shown in the following screenshot:

Bank codes	1	14	3	4	38	32	6	33	36	26	24	15
1	0	1	1	1	1	0	0	0	0	0	0	0
14	1	0	1	1	0	0	0	0	1	0	0	0
3	1	1	0	1	0	0	1	0	0	0	0	0
4	1	1	1	0	0	0	0	0	0	0	0	1
38	0	0	0	0	0	0	0	0	0	0	0	0
32	1	0	0	0	0	0	0	0	0	0	0	0
6	0	1	0	0	0	0	0	0	0	0	0	0
33	0	0	0	1	0	0	0	0	0	0	0	0
36	0	0	0	0	0	0	0	0	0	0	0	0
26	0	0	1	0	0	0	0	0	0	0	0	0
24	0	0	0	0	0	0	0	0	0	0	0	0
15	0	0	0	0	0	0	0	0	0	0	0	0

Figure 13.4: The adjacency matrix in a core periphery structure

Craig and von Peter (2010) also suggest that not only the core-core or the periphery-periphery part of the matrix is important but the core-periphery part is important as well (the upper-right and the lower-left part). They emphasize that all of the core banks should have at least one connection with a periphery institution. This characteristic means that this periphery bank has no other possibility to be on this market but through a core bank. Although it is an important issue, we think that due to possible contagious effects, being a core bank in itself can result in systemic importance.

In many cases, it is impossible to get pure core/periphery decomposition in the case of real-world networks. This is true especially when we also have requirements for the core-periphery part of the matrix. For this reason, in the first step, we will try to solve the maximum clique problem (for example, by using the Bron-Kerbosch algorithm, *Bron and Kerbosch 1973*), and then, in the second step, we will choose the result with the lowest average degree in the periphery-periphery part. There are many other different methods to make a core-periphery decomposition. Due to its simplicity, we have chosen this one.

Implementation in R

In this subsection, we show how to program the core-periphery decomposition. We will cover all the relevant information, from downloading essential R packages to loading the data set, and from the decomposition itself to the visualization of the results. We will show the code in small parts, and will give a detailed explanation on each of them.

We set the library that we will use during the simulation. The code will look for the input data files in this library. We download an R package `igraph`, which is an important tool in the visualization of financial networks. Of course, after the first run of this code, this row might be deleted since the installation process should not be repeated again. Finally, after the installation, the package should also be loaded first to the current R session.

```
install.packages("igraph")

library(igraph)
```

As the second step, we load the dataset, which is only the matrix in this case. The imported data is a data frame that has to be converted in a matrix form. As we have shown before (*Figure 13.1*), the matrix doesn't contain data when there are no transactions between two banks. The third row fills those cells with a 0. Then, since we only need the adjacency matrix, we change all the non-zero cells to 1. Finally, we create a graph as an object from the adjacency matrix.

```
adj_mtx <-  read.table("mtx.csv", header = T, sep = ";")

adj_mtx <- as.matrix(adj_mtx)

adj_mtx[is.na(adj_mtx)] <- 0

adj_mtx[adj_mtx != 0] <- 1

G <- graph.adjacency(adj_mtx, mode = "undirected")
```

The `igraph` package has a function called `largest.clique`, which results in a list of the solutions of the largest clique problem. CORE will contain all the sets of the largest cliques. The command is as follows:

```
CORE <- largest.cliques(G)
```

The largest clique will be the core of the graph and its complement will be the periphery. We create this periphery for every resulted largest clique. Then, we set different colors for the core nodes and for the periphery. This helps to distinguish them on the chart.

```
for (i in 1:length(CORE)){
core <- CORE[[i]]
periphery <- setdiff(1:33, core)
V(G)$color[periphery] <- rgb(0,1,0)
V(G)$color[core] <- rgb(1,0,0)
print(i)
print(core)
print(periphery)
```

Then, we count the average degree of the periphery-periphery matrix. For the identification of systemically important financial institutions, the best solution is when this average degree is the lowest.

```
H <- induced.subgraph(G, periphery)
d <- mean(degree(H))
```

Finally, we plot the graph in a new window. The chart will also contain the average degree of the periphery matrix.

```
windows()
plot(G, vertex.color = V(G)$color, main = paste("Avg periphery
  degree:", round(d,2) ) )}
```

Results

By running the code, we get the charts of all the solutions for core-periphery decomposition. In every case, the average periphery degree will be presented on these charts. We have chosen the solution with the smallest average periphery degree. This means that in this solution, the periphery banks have very limited connection with each other. A problem in the core might make them unable to access the market. On the other side, as the core is completely connected, the contagion process might be fast and can reach every bank. All in all, the default of any core banks jeopardizes the access of periphery banks to the market and may be the source of a contagious process. *Figure 13.5* presents the best solution of core-periphery decomposition with this simple method.

According to the results, 12 banks can be considered as systemically important institutions, namely 5, 7, 8, 11, 13, 20, 21, 22, 23, 24, 28, and 30.

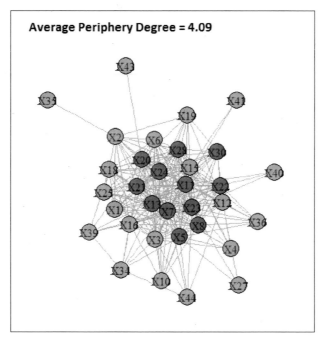

Figure 13.5: Core-periphery decomposition with the smallest periphery degree

The simulation method

The best way to understand the role of a bank from a systemic point of view is to simulate the effects of its default. We can get this way the most precise results on a bank's systemic importance. Usually, the main problem with these methods is its data need. The main characteristics of individual institutions (for example, capital buffers or size) are not enough for this kind of exercise. We also have to precisely know its exposures to other banks through financial markets since the most important contagious channels are financial markets.

In this section, we will show a simple method to identify systemic importance of a financial institution. To make it as simple as possible, we have to make some assumptions:

- We will investigate the effect of idiosyncratic defaults. After the default, all the contagious effects go through the network abruptly.

- Since all the effects go through abruptly, there won't be any adjustment procedure by banks.

- LGD is constant for all the banks. There are models that take into account the fact that the LGD can change from bank to bank (for example, *Eisenberg and Noe, 2001*), but this would make our model too complicated.

- We don't take into account the length of the legal procedure after the default. In practice, it should be considered in the LGD.

As we mentioned in the data section, we will need three datasets. First, we need the matrix that contains the exposures of the banks to each other on the interbank deposit market. Since these transactions are not collateralized, the potential losses are the biggest on this market. Second, we need the size of the capital buffers for each bank. The possibility of contagious effects can be significantly mitigated by a high capital buffer. For this reason, it is always important to check what can be considered as a capital buffer. Our opinion is that only the capital that exceeds the regulatory minimum should be taken into account in this exercise to be as prudent as possible. Third, we need the size of each bank. To evaluate the effect of one bank's default, we need the size of infected banks. In our example, we use the balance sheet total, but other measures can be used as well. The chosen measure has to proxy the effects on the real economy (for example, it can be the size of the corporate loan portfolio or the stock of deposits and so on).

The simulation

As a first step, we randomly choose a bank (any of them, since we will do this for every bank), and we assume that it is defaulted after an idiosyncratic shock. The matrix contains all the information about the banks that were lending to this one. W_{ij} is the size of the loan that was borrowed by bank j from bank i. L is the LGD, that is, the size of the loss proportional to the exposure. When the following inequality stays, that is, the loss of bank i from the default of bank j exceeds the capital buffer of bank i, bank i has to be considered as defaulted.

$$E_{ij}L > C_i$$

As a result, we get all those partner banks of bank *j*, which defaulted after the collapse of bank *j*. We make the first step in case of the partner banks of all the newly defaulted banks. We continue this simulation until we reach an equilibrium situation where there are no new defaults.

We make this simulation for every bank, that is, we try to find out which banks will default after their collapse due to contagious effects. Finally, we aggregate the balance sheet total of the defaulted banks in each case. Our final result will then be a list that contains the potential effect of the default of each bank based on the market share of the affected banks.

Implementation in R

In this section, we will show how to implement this simulation technique in R. We will present the whole code as before. Some parts of the code were also used in the core-periphery distinction as well, so we won't give a detailed explanation for them.

In the first few rows, we set some basic information. There are two rows where explanation is needed. First, we set the value of the LGD. As we will see later, it is important to make our examinations by using different LGDs since our simulation is sensitive on the level of the LGD. The value can be anything from 0 to 1. Second, those algorithms that plot the network use a random number generator. The Set.seed command sets the initial value of the random number generator to ensure that we get graphs with the same outlook.

```
LGD = 0.65

set.seed(3052343)

library(igraph)
```

In the next part of the code, we load the data, which will be used in the model, namely the matrix of the network (mtx.csv), the vector of the capital buffer (puf.csv), and the vector of the bank's size (sizes.csv).

```
adj_mtx <-  read.table("mtx.csv", header = T, sep = ";")

node_w <-  read.table("puf.csv", header = T, sep = ";")

node_s <- read.table("sizes.csv", header = T, sep = ";")

adj_mtx <- as.matrix(adj_mtx)

adj_mtx[is.na(adj_mtx)] <- 0
```

During the simulation, the adjacency matrix is not enough, contrary to the core-periphery distinction. We need the weighted matrix **G**.

```
G <- graph.adjacency((adj_mtx ), weighted = TRUE)
```

The next step is technical rather than essential, but it helps to avoid any mistakes later. *V* is the set of the graph's nodes. We put together all the relevant information about each node, that is, in which step it has defaulted (non-defaulted banks get 0), the capital buffer, and the size.

```
V(G)$default <- 0
V(G)$capital <- as.numeric(as.character(node_w[,2]))
V(G)$size <- as.numeric(as.character(node_s[,2]))
```

Then, we can easily plot the network. We have used this command to create *Figure 13.2*. Of course, it is not essential for the simulation.

```
plot(G, layout = layout.kamada.kawai(G), edge.arrow.size=0.3,
  vertex.size = 10, vertex.label.cex = .75)
```

As we mentioned, our goal is to get a list of banks and the effect of their collapse on the banking system. However, it is also worth seeing the process of the contagion in every case. For this reason, we use a function that can generate a chart about it. The sim function has four attributes: *G* is the weighted graph, the starting node that is the first defaulted bank, the LGD, and finally a variable to switch the plotting of the graph on or off. The last two attributes have a default value, but of course, we can give them a different value during each run. We also set different colors for each node depending on in which step it has defaulted.

```
sim <- function(G, starting_node, l = 0.85, drawimage = TRUE){
node_color <- function(n,m) c(rgb(0,0.7,0),rainbow(m))[n+1]
```

We create a variable that helps us know whether the contagion has stopped or not. We also create a list that contains the defaulted banks. The *j*th component of the list contains all the banks collapsed in the *j*th step.

```
stop_ <- FALSE
j <- 1
default <- list(starting_node)
```

The next part is the essence of the whole code. We start a while loop and check whether the contagion goes on or not. Initially, it goes on for sure. We set the default attribute to *j* for those banks that collapse in the *j*th step.

Then, in a `for` loop, we take all the banks that have connections with bank *i*, and deduct *exposure*LGD* from their capital. The banks that default after this will be on the default list. Then, we start again with the exposure to the newly defaulted banks and continue with it until there won't be any new defaults.

```
while(!stop_){
V(G)$default[default[[j]]] <- j
j <- j + 1; stop_ <- TRUE
for( i in default[[j-1]]){V(G)$capital <- V(G)$capital - 1*G[,i]}
default[[j]] = setdiff((1:33)[V(G)$capital < 0], unlist(default));
if( length( default[[j]] ) > 0) stop_ <- FALSE
}
```

When `drawimage` is equal to T in the `sim` function, the code will plot the network. The color of each node depends on the time of default, as we mentioned before. Banks that defaulted later get a lighter color, and those that have not defaulted get a green color.

```
if(drawimage) plot(G, layout = layout.kamada.kawai(G),
  edge.arrow.size=0.3, vertex.size = 12.5,
    vertex.color = node_color(V(G)$default, 4*length(default)),
      vertex.label.cex = .75)
```

Then, we count the proportion of the collapsed banks that are contained in the default list.

```
sum(V(G)$size[unlist(default)])/sum(V(G)$size)}
```

Using the function `sapply`, we can run the same function for every component of a vector and collect the results in a list.

```
result <- sapply(1:33, function(j) sim(G,j,LGD, FALSE))
```

Finally, we make a barplot that contains the result of every bank in the system. This chart makes it possible to decide about systemic importance.

```
dev.new(width=15,height=10)
v <- barplot(result, names.arg = V(G)$name, cex.names = 0.5,
  ylim = c(0,1.1))
text(v, result, labels = paste(100*round(result, 2), "%", sep = ""),
  pos = 3, cex = 0.65)
```

Results

Our main question during this exercise was: which banks were the systemically important financial institutions. After running the code we have shown in the last subchapter we get an exact answer on our question. The chart pops up after the run summarizes the main results of the simulation. The horizontal axis has the codes of the banks, while the vertical axis has the proportion of the banking system affected by the idiosyncratic shock. For example, in figure 13.6., 76 percent at X3 means that if bank number 3 defaults due to an idiosyncratic shock, 76 percent of the whole banking system will default as a result of contagion. It is a matter of decision to set a level above which a bank has to be considered as systemically important. In this example, it is easy to distinguish between institutions that have to be taken as SIFIs and those that have minor relevance for the system. According to *Figure 13.6.*, 10 banks (with codes 3, 7, 12, 13, 15, 18, 19, 21, 24, and 28) can be considered as systemically important.

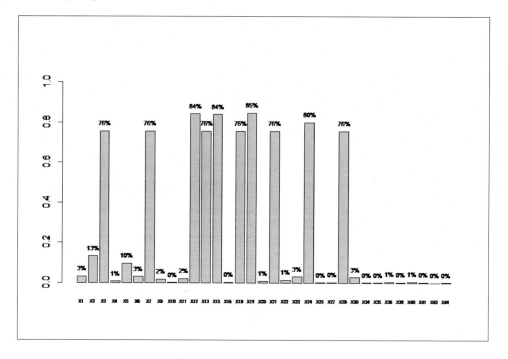

Figure 13.6: Proportion of the banking system based on the balance sheet total affected by the idiosyncratic shock LGD = 0.65

It is important to mention that the result is dependent on the LGD parameter, which has to be set in the code. In this first run, the LGD was set to 65 percent, but it can differ significantly in different cases. For example, if the LGD is 90 percent, the result will be much worse. Five more banks (their codes are 2, 8, 11, 16, and 20) will also have a significantly negative effect on the banking system in the case of an idiosyncratic shock. However, with a much lower LGD, the result will also be milder. For example, if the LGD level is set to 30 percent bank number 13 will have the biggest effect on the banking system. However, by comparing this to the former examples, this effect will be very limited. 36 percent of the banking system will default in this case. Using the 30 percent LGD level, only 4 banks will have more than 10 percent effect on the system (*Figure 13.7*).

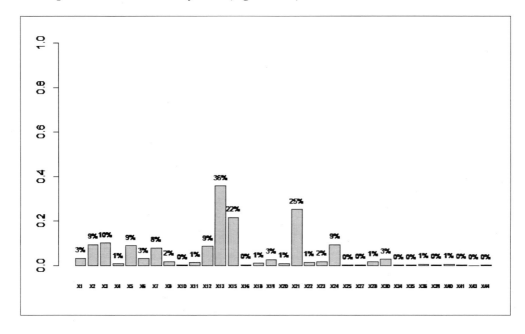

Figure 13.7.: Proportion of the banking system based on balance sheet total affected by the idiosyncratic shock LGD = 0.3

This R code is also able to show us the process of contagion. By running the `sim` function, it is possible to find out which banks are affected directly by the default of an examined bank and which banks are affected in the second or third or later step of the simulation. For example, if we want to know what happens when bank 15 defaults, we write in the R console the following command: `sim(G, 13, 0.65)`, where *G* is the matrix, 13 is the ordinal number of bank number 15, and 65 percent is the LGD. As a result, we get figure 13.8. We sign the bank that launches the contagion with a red color. Orange is the color of those institutions that are affected directly by the idiosyncratic shock of bank number 15. Then, when the color is lighter, the bank is affected later. Finally, banks with green nodes are the survivors. LGD was set at 65 percent in this example. It can be seen that the collapse of bank number 15 will result directly the default of five other banks (with codes 8, 18, 20, 21, and 36). Then, with the default of these banks, many more will also lose their capital. At the end, more than 80 percent of the banking system will be in default.

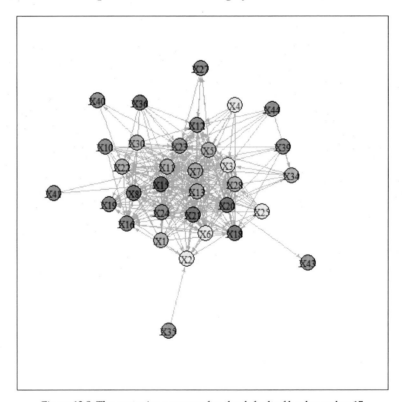

Figure 13.8: The contagion process after the default of bank number 15

It has to be emphasized that with this simulation method, not only were the interbank exposures taken into account but also the size of the main partners and the capital buffer of them. In this case, systemic importance can be a result of undercapitalized partners. Or on the contrary, it is possible that a bank with many partners and borrowed money won't have any negative effect on the market since its direct partners have a high enough capital buffer. Bank number 20 is a good example of this. In the core-periphery decomposition, it is definitely in the core. However, when we run the `sim` function with a 65 percent LGD, the result will be very different. *Figure 13.9* presents that none of the other banks will default after its idiosyncratic shock.

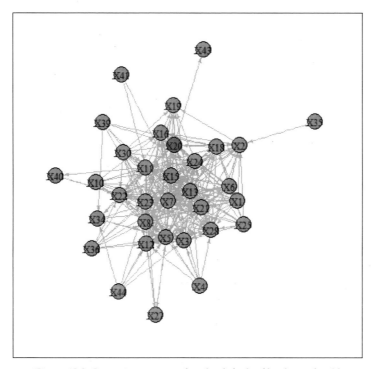

Figure 13.9: Contagion process after the default of bank number 20

Possible interpretations and suggestions

The main difficulty of the examination of systemic importance is always its huge data need. From this point of view, core-periphery decomposition is an easier method because we only need the exposure of the banks on the interbank market. Although in many cases this may also result in some difficulty since direct linkages between banks are often unknown. However, in the literature, we can find some good solutions to fill these gaps, for example, the minimum density approach by *Anand et al. (2014)*. Alternatively, there are some other suggestions on how to create a network from market data (for example, *Billio et al., 2013*).

Due to the differences between the two methods, the results can be confusing. We will give you some ideas on how to interpret the results. The core-periphery decomposition focuses only on one market. It implies that being in the core means that the bank is important on this market. The importance for the whole banking system then depends on the importance of this market. Without this information, we might only say that the core banks are important for the operation of the market.

On the contrary, the simulation method strictly focuses on the banking system's stability. As a result, we get those banks that may trigger a severe crisis. However, it doesn't mean that other banks won't have a crucial effect on the operation of the interbank market. A bank that has well-capitalized partners may freeze the market without jeopardizing the stability of the whole banking system. On the longer horizon, the lack of a well-functioning market will result in ineffective liquidity management.

Summary

Systemic importance of financial institutions is a crucial information for supervisory authorities and central banks since maintaining the stability of the financial system is their responsibility. However, this information is important for investors as well because it helps to diversify their exposure towards the financial sector.

In this chapter, we have shown two of the several different methods that can help in the identification of systemically important financial institutions. These two methods are based on the tools of network theory. The first was focusing only on the position of each institution in a financial network. So it doesn't take into account the structure of the balance sheet at each institutions. The second was a simulation method that took into account some important data on the bank's capital position as well. The results of these two methods should be taken into account subsequently to get a clear picture.

References

- **Anand, Kartik, Ben Craig and Goetz von Peter (2014)**: Filling in the blanks: network structure and interbank contagion, Discussion Paper Deutsche Bundesbank, No. 02/2014

- **Berlinger, E., M. Michaletzky and M. Szenes (2011)**: A fedezetlen bankközi forintpiac hálózati dinamikájának vizsgálata a likviditási válság előtt és után (Network dynamics of unsecured interbank HUF markets before and after the liquidity crisis). Közgazdasági Szemle, Vol LVIII. No. 3

- **Billio, Monica, Mila Getmansky, Dale Gray, Andrew W. Lo, Robert C. Merton and Loriana Pelizzon**: Sovereign, Bank, and Insurance Credit Spreads: Connectedness and System Networks, Mimeo, 2013

- **BIS (2011)**: Global systemically important banks: assessment methodology and the additional loss absorbency requirement, Rules text November 2011

- **Borgatti, Stephen, and Martin Everett (1999)**: Models of core/periphery structures, Social Networks 21

- **Bron, Coen and Kerbosch, Joep (1973)**: Algorithm 457: finding all cliques of an undirected graph, Communications of the ACM volume 16 (9): 575–577

- **Craig, Ben and Goetz von Peter (2010)**: Interbank tiering and money center banks – BIS Working Papers No 322, October 2010

- **Daróczi, Gergely, Michael Puhle, Edina Berlinger, Péter Csóka, Daniel Havran, Márton Michaletzky, Zsolt Tulassay, Kata Váradi, Agnes Vidovics-Dancs (2013)**: Introduction to R for Quantitative Finance, Packt Publishing (November 22, 2013)

- **Eisenberg, L., Noe, T.H. (2001)**: Systemic risk in financial systems. Management Science 47 (2), 236–249

- **FSB, IMF, BIS (2009)**: Guidance to Assess Systemic Importance of Financial Institutions, Markets, and Instrument: Initial Considerations – Background Paper, Report to the G-20 Finance Ministers and Central Bank Governors, October 2009

- **Furfine, C.H. (2003)**: Interbank exposures: quantifying the risk of contagion. Journal of Money, Credit, and Banking 35 (1), 111–128

- **Iazzetta, I. and M. Manna, (2009)**: The topology of the interbank market: developments in Italy since 1990, Banca d'Italia Working Papers No. 711, May 2009

Index

candle patterns, key reversal 237-239
cap
  pricing, with Black model 119-121
capital asset pricing model (CAPM) 39
cash-flow
  generator functions 262-265
  preparing 265, 266
charts, bitcoin
  plotting 230-233
  URL 231
classification rules
  setting 215, 216
cointegration 8-12
connections
  revealing 207
contingency risk 258
core-periphery decomposition
  about 319, 320
  implementation, in R 321, 322
  results 322
Cox-Ingersoll-Ross model 128-131
credit default swap (CDS) 306
credit risk 305-310
currency options 96-99

D

data
  about 64, 65
  collecting 203-206
  loading 66, 67
  obtaining, from open sources 78-82
data preparation
  about 258, 259
  cash-flow, generator functions 262-265
  cash-flow, preparing 265, 266
  data source, calling 260-262
data selection 43-45
dataset
  using 317-319
data source
  calling 260-262
data warehouse (DWH) 259
delta hedge performance
  comparing 185-189

derivatives
  delta hedge performance,
    comparing 185-189
  dynamic delta hedge 179-184
  hedging 177, 178
  market risk 178
  static delta hedge 179
double-knock-in (DKI) 140
double-knock-out (DKO) 140
double-no-touch option
  defining 161-168
  pricing 148-159
  pricing, alternate way 160
double-one-touch (DOT) 168
dynamic delta hedge 179-184
dynamic hedging 138

E

EGARCH model 31, 32
EMA 234
Enterprise Risk Management (ERM) 257
exchange options
  about 99
  application, in R 106-109
  Margrabe formula 102-105
  two-dimensional Wiener processes 100-102
exotic options
  about 137-145
  embedded, in structured products 168-173
Expected Shortfall (ES) 299
Exponential GARCH model. *See* EGARCH
    model
exposure at default (EAD) 288
External Credit Assessment Institutions
    (ECAI) 287
extract, transform, and load (ETL) 259

F

Fama-French model
  estimating 48-54
Fama-French three-factor model 42
Federal Reserve Economic Data (FRED) 80
feed-forward neural networks (FFNN) 244
fundamental analysis 201-203

M

Margrabe formula **102-105**
market efficiency **228**
market risk **299-305**
market risk, of derivatives **178**
market value of equity (MVoE) **257**
maturity (M) **288**
minimum capital requirements **287-289**
modeling, in R
  about **43**
  APT, estimating with principal
     component analysis **46-48**
  data selection **43-45**
  Fama-French model, estimating **48-54**
model, of deposit interest rate
     development **273-278**
money management **241, 242**
Monte-Carlo simulation **297-299**
multiple variables
  including **208, 209**
multivariate time series analysis
  about **8**
  cointegration **8-12**
  VAR **12-14**
  VAR and VECM, cointegrated **19-22**

N

net interest income (NII) **257**
net stable funding ratio (NSFR) **291**
neural networks (NN) **243-245**
non-maturity deposits (NMD)
  modeling **273**
  model, of deposit interest rate
     development **273-278**
  static replication, of non-maturity
     deposits **278-282**

O

open sources
  data, obtaining from **78-82**
operational risk
  about **311, 312**
  high impact with high probability **311**

high impact with low probability **311**
low impact with high probability **311**
low impact with low probability **311**

P

pair trading **11**
parameter
  estimating, of interest rate models **132, 133**
position, TA
  managing **240, 241**
pricing formula
  for call quanto **110-112**
principal component analysis
  APT, estimating with **46-48**

Q

quanto options
  about **109**
  call quanto, pricing in R **113**
  pricing formula, for call quanto **110-112**

R

recovery rate (RR) **306**
relative strength indicator (RSI) **234**
relative transaction costs
  optimal hedging **196, 197**
results
  interpreting **72, 73, 332**
risk categories
  about **299**
  credit risk **305-310**
  market risk **299-305**
  operational risk **311, 312**
risk measures
  about **292-294**
  analytical VaR **294, 295**
  historical VaR **296**
  monotonicity **293**
  Monte-Carlo simulation **297, 298**
  positive homogeneity **293**
  sub-additivity **293**
  translation invariance **294**
risk-weighted assets (RWA) **286**
RSI **234, 235**

Thank you for buying
Mastering R for Quantitative Finance

About Packt Publishing

Packt, pronounced 'packed', published its first book, *Mastering phpMyAdmin for Effective MySQL Management*, in April 2004, and subsequently continued to specialize in publishing highly focused books on specific technologies and solutions.

Our books and publications share the experiences of your fellow IT professionals in adapting and customizing today's systems, applications, and frameworks. Our solution-based books give you the knowledge and power to customize the software and technologies you're using to get the job done. Packt books are more specific and less general than the IT books you have seen in the past. Our unique business model allows us to bring you more focused information, giving you more of what you need to know, and less of what you don't.

Packt is a modern yet unique publishing company that focuses on producing quality, cutting-edge books for communities of developers, administrators, and newbies alike. For more information, please visit our website at www.packtpub.com.

Writing for Packt

We welcome all inquiries from people who are interested in authoring. Book proposals should be sent to author@packtpub.com. If your book idea is still at an early stage and you would like to discuss it first before writing a formal book proposal, then please contact us; one of our commissioning editors will get in touch with you.

We're not just looking for published authors; if you have strong technical skills but no writing experience, our experienced editors can help you develop a writing career, or simply get some additional reward for your expertise.

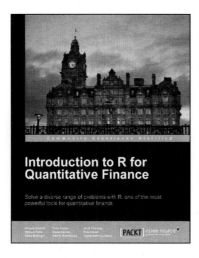

Introduction to R for Quantitative Finance

ISBN: 978-1-78328-093-3   Paperback: 164 pages

Solve a diverse range of problems with R, one of the most powerful tools for quantitative finance

1. Use time series analysis to model and forecast house prices.

2. Estimate the term structure of interest rates using prices of government bonds.

3. Detect systemically important financial institutions by employing financial network analysis.

R Object-oriented Programming

ISBN: 978-1-78398-668-2   Paperback: 190 pages

A practical guide to help you learn and understand the programming techniques necessary to exploit the full power of R

1. Learn and understand the programming techniques necessary to solve specific problems and speed up development processes for statistical models and applications.

2. Explore the fundamentals of building objects and how they program individual aspects of larger data designs.

3. Step-by-step guide to understand how OOP can be applied to application and data models within R.

Please check **www.PacktPub.com** for information on our titles

Learning Data Mining with R

ISBN: 978-1-78398-210-3   Paperback: 314 pages

Develop key skills and techniques within R to confidently create and customize data mining algorithms

1. Develop a sound strategy for solving predictive modeling problems using the most popular data mining algorithms.

2. Gain understanding of the major methods of predictive modeling.

3. Packed with practical advice and tips to help you get to grips with data mining.

Advanced Quantitative Finance with C++

ISBN: 978-1-78216-722-8   Paperback: 124 pages

Create and implement mathematical models in C++ using Quatitative Finance

1. Describes the key mathematical models used for price equity, currency, interest rates, and credit derivatives.

2. The complex models are explained step-by-step along with a flow chart of every implementation.

3. Illustrates each asset class with fully solved C++ examples, both basic and advanced, that support and complement the text.

Please check **www.PacktPub.com** for information on our titles